"Steven Félix-Jäger takes us on a journey back into the music of our growing up, reminding us that 'upon this rock' we built our lives. This is a work of Christian theology, but don't let that turn you off, because it's good fun. It stands out as being generous to the message of both secular and Christian rock, reflecting on the ways in which different genres—folk, heavy metal, punk, grunge, and more—transformed our thinking about God and the world we live in. It's a book for anyone looking for new ways to explore theology in conversation with pop culture."

—**Shane Clifton**, Alphacrucis College

"For many people, the conjunction of religion and rock is an unpropitious or embarrassing alliance that can only lead to bad art and a weakening of faith. And yet, as Steven Félix-Jäger's lucid and informative study shows, rock is 'an agitator of the status quo,' whose countercultural postures have a transformative potential that may serve religious as well as secular purposes."

—**Gavin Hopps**, University of St. Andrews

"With God on Our Side offers readers a convincing case study in theology and popular culture that will both inform and provoke. The book's aim is to show how rock music can help Christians engage life theologically and existentially. Rock is an agitator against our culture's status quo, and as such often invites theological and spiritual probings. Readers will be surprised as themes found in the music of various genres of rock (southern, punk, folk, grunge, and so on) are put into theological dialogue with the likes of Barth, Moltmann, Tillich, Gutierrez, Hauerwas, and Brueggemann. Here is a book that will stretch theologians and rock enthusiasts alike."

—**Robert K. Johnston**, Fuller Theological Seminary

With God on Our Side

With God on Our Side

Towards a Transformational Theology
of Rock and Roll

Steven Félix-Jäger

WIPF & STOCK · Eugene, Oregon

WITH GOD ON OUR SIDE
Towards a Transformational Theology of Rock and Roll

Wipf & Stock
An Imprint of Wipf and Stock Publishers
199 W. 8th Ave., Suite 3
Eugene, OR 97401

www.wipfandstock.com

PAPERBACK ISBN: 978-1-4982-3179-4
HARDCOVER ISBN: 978-1-4982-3181-7
EBOOK ISBN: 978-1-4982-3180-0

Manufactured in the U.S.A.   JANUARY 12, 2017

Contents

Acknowledgments

I have been thinking about rock and theology for a long time. I've had countless of great conversations with friends driving to and from shows, and have had my faith come to a head with the music scene many times. I remember one instance when I was in a Christian metal band and we were playing a big festival with a bunch of other touring and local bands. There was a band playing before us that consisted of nominal Satanists who spread some vitriol against Christ from their "pulpit." When we played our set, one of the "devil band's" fans ran through our crowd with hand-drawn signs of upside down crosses and 666s. That show made us think about something Jesus said: "If the world hates you, be aware that it hated me before it hated you (Matt. 15:18)." Our concert offered a competing narrative of the world than what the devil band was offering, and this agitated some folks. But isn't that what rock music is all about? Isn't rock music a countercultural force for today's dominant society? We were right where we needed to be, and maybe our music somehow helped to transform our surroundings for the kingdom of God. Since then I've played in other bands ranging from indie rock to CCM, and have many more stories from the road like this. What my experiences and conversations got me thinking about was how rock music can help shape our thoughts and lives theologically and existentially. It was this concern that prompted me to write this book.

I owe a lot of gratitude to various people. I would like to thank Matthew Wimer and the folks at Wipf & Stock and Robert Johnston at Fuller for putting me on track to publish this book. I would also like to thank all of those involved in proofing, editing, and offering insight to the book, especially Bryan Ellrod, Jimmy Paton, Jessica Felix, Chase Dixon, Georgia McMillen, and Kari Seeley the copy editor. Any mistakes that are found throughout this book are mine and shouldn't reflect on them. I want to thank some of my more influential theology teachers, namely, Peter Althouse, William K. Kay, and Waite Willis Jr. I also want to thank my comrades-of-rock that performed, wrote music, and traveled with me through the years: Stephen Snyder, Will Werly, Bryan Soto, Zack Hoskinson, Mikel Larrinaga, Branden Keim, Mikey Gibson, Ben Arnold, Andy Wingate, Dusten Gann, Tim Serdynski and many more. I also met my wife Connie Felix at a concert I was performing at, and we've been making music (literally and figuratively) ever since. I want to thank my dad Wilfredo Felix and the Parkers for all their support throughout the years as well. Lastly I'd like to thank the two most important ladies in my life, Connie my wife, and Mila my daughter.

INTRODUCTION

Setting the Stage

I was twenty and a first-time youth pastor at a tiny church in Central Florida. I just finished my internship at a mega-church up the road and landed this new gig six months later. As you might expect, a twenty year old is going to make some stupid mistakes. Every week I found myself listening intently to a mild rebuke in the pastor's office. One particular rebuke, however, baffled me.

The pastor began, "Steven, some of the council people were upset about the shirt you wore to youth last Sunday night."

"Shirt?" I asked.

"Yes the black shirt with the demonic red lettering all over the front," the pastor clarified. It was my Guns N' Roses shirt. *Yes!* Guns N' Roses, the slightly cheesy 1980s hard rock band that sang about pretty girls and how cool Axl Rose was. Sure, the band occasionally littered their lyrics with sexual innuendo, but demonic? I don't think so.

I do think my Guns N' Roses fiasco uncovers an underlying problem in Christian approaches to culture. Namely, that rock music is somehow evil or incompatible with God. For some Christians, rock is the devil's music, but I've played in rock bands since I was eighteen years old, and I do not think this is true. I have defended, in numerous conversations, the position that a metal band can also be Christian. I've seen the activity of God in the world of rock and roll and cannot simply dismiss it as "the devil's music."

God made all things and declared them good. God made all humans and endowed us with the awesome ability to be creative. Because of this, we engage the world, reflect on it, and influence culture. Rock music is the work of *our* hands that mirrors the divine creativity innate within us (Gen 1). In this way, it is a cultural expression that portrays our concerns in the world today. I wrote this book because I believe that we can learn a lot from cultural engagement, and when we truly dig in and see what is going on beneath the surface, we will find that people are concerned with deep theological issues. Rock music is an open forum for theological and existential contemplation. While the same can be said about any cultural phenomenon, rock answers life's big questions in its own unique way. Rock music creates a space for these questions, but it is a contextual space. That is to say, rock uses a particular vantage point to address issues that only affect people in similar situations. Since contextual theologies from any vantage point are possible, I have chosen to approach theology from the context of rock music.[1] Rock music has profoundly shaped my life, and I have come to know God and myself better because of it. I believe that a *transformational theology of rock* will be beneficial to those who, like me, have been changed by rock; therefore, I would like to propose that *rock music is an artistic outlet that allows devotees the freedom to express religious and spiritual concerns about God in relation to humans and the world.*

Engaging Culture and Thinking about God

Before proceeding, some definitions are in order. For our purposes, let us say that theology is thinking and talking about God in a structured way. As Christians in the past two millennia tried to make sense of God's greater narrative in light of Scripture, history, and their revelatory experiences, they began to compartmentalize groups of teachings into "doctrines." Systematic theology is a collection of doctrines that deal with God's nature, work, plan, and purposes. Systematic theologies usually begin with a prolegomena or method, and then move from the doctrine of the Bible (bibliology) all the way through the doctrine of the last things (eschatology). This book, however, will not approach theology systematically. Instead, we will employ a contextualized approach to theology, which reflects on cultural engagement alongside the doctrinal tenets of the faith. In other words, we will look at a cultural phenomenon, in our case rock music, in order to tease out

---

1. Some earlier theological precedents of similar character include: Cone, *The Spiritual and the Blues*; Pinn, *Noise and Spirit*; Fillingim, *Redneck Liberation*; and Watkins, *Hip Hop Redemption*.

and engage the theological and existential questions that begin to surface. This approach allows us to avoid getting bogged down by fringe theological issues that do not speak to our present situation. It also allows our theology to remain fresh and not stuffy. So while many systematic theologies are wonderfully complex, paradigm-shifting triumphs, our approach will be more modest, but more accessible.

In their book, *A Matrix of Meaning*, Craig Detweiler and Barry Taylor say questions of ultimate existence and reality emerge in the midst of "messy" culture where they are posed in honest and unembellished ways, " . . . devoid of the religious language of etiquette and propriety."[2] Theology happens, for Detweiler and Taylor, in the marketplace instead of the lofty rises of the theological ivory tower. Thus, cultural theologies are a more appropriate way to talk and think about God because they allow God to become real in the lives of their adherents. Contextual theologies remind us that God is not a far off commodity, or a detached deistic force. Instead, God is here with us now, and God wants to speak to us in our present situation—in the present moment. Detweiler and Taylor write, "We must get back to that street-level discussion, where our faith was forged. People of faith need to become conversant with the new canon, the new literacy, and join the new conversation. Only in this way can we hear Jesus afresh. Only in this way can the Spirit quicken our spirits. Only in this way can we allow God to be fully God."[3] Christians should understand the world around them and speak into it by expressing a Christian worldview in meaningful and imaginative ways. Moreover, we should not be afraid of the world that we're called to engage. I sense that many Christian rock bands stand at the vanguard of such cultural engagement. My hope is that this book can aid the missional person to think of cultural engagement in contextualized theological ways.

Limitations and Overview

This book is by no means intended to give an exhaustive account of rock music. There are already many excellent books and documentaries that trace the origins and history of rock music and evaluate its particular genres. My goal for this book is to offer a foray into rock music culture in order to show how rock can help us engage life theologically and existentially. This book

2. Detweiler and Taylor, *A Matrix of Meanings*, 27.
3. Ibid., 23.

attempts to offer a sample that will provoke our interest in how rock music affects our spiritual formation and theological insight. Our reflections form what I have termed a *transformational theology of rock* that not only informs us on an important cultural reality, but also expands our theological imagination. At times the chapters will provide helpful analogies and illustrations for theological claims, but my hope is that you will begin to notice our reflections on rock actually extending, challenging, and adding to the insights of the theological traditions evaluated. For instance, though I liken folk rock to wisdom literature and alternative rock to apophatic theology, I also argue that punk rock can become the song of the oppressed, which is sadly missing in many accounts of liberation theology. I challenge the cultural Christianity that is expressed in southern rock, and advocate for appropriate ministerial engagement in metal and grunge rock. Though this book offers no paradigm-shifts in theological inquiry, my hope is that it becomes more than merely a primer on rock music and an introduction to theological thought. I hope that this book will challenge and encourage you to engage the world theologically in new and creative ways. I hope that this *transformational* theology of rock will lead to a transformation of your thoughts and desires, even if only in part.

Because of space, we cannot evaluate every genre of rock music. While the first two chapters focus on the historical and cultural presence of rock, I have chosen to emphasize folk rock, heavy metal, southern rock, punk rock, grunge rock, and alternative rock. While these are not the only genres in rock, these six were certainly major players in their respective eras. I've grouped the chapters chronologically. For instance, folk rock formed in the early 1960s, heavy metal began in the late 1960s, southern rock emerged in the early 1970s, punk rock took off in the mid-1970s, grunge rock dominated the airwaves in the 1980s, and, though alternative rock has technically been around since the 1960s, I put particular emphasis on mid-1990s alternative rock and the post-punk revival rock of the 2000s. Thematically some couplets begin to emerge. For instance, southern and punk rock offer two contrasting views on political theology, whereas grunge and alternative rock both deal with identity and existential issues in different ways. Throughout the chapters you will begin to notice commonalities and cross-references between the genres and subgenres.

There are many genres of rock that deserve to be talked about that are not (like psychedelic, electronic, and pop rock), many genres that were spoken about but did not command entire chapters (like college, indie, hardcore, and variations of punk and metal), and also some genres that defy categorizations. For instance, so-called "art-rock" and "progressive rock" genres exhibit more aesthetic tendencies that cross several subgenres, rather than a single stylistic category.[4] In this book, I define a genre as a category of musical composition that is characterized by similar form, style, and content, whereas a subgenre is a subdivision of a genre. While subgenres hold all the characteristics of their respective genre, there is enough variance between styles of music that further distinction is necessary. For instance, metal and punk are genres within the umbrella term "rock," whereas death, thrash, and grind core are all subgenres of metal. Similarly, hardcore, pop punk, and ska are all subgenres of punk.

I am also taking for granted that rock is a legitimate art form that carries cultural significance. I do not argue for the cultural significance of art; rather, I assume that art *is* significant. If you pick up a book about rock and theology, chances are I do not have to convince you about rock's cultural significance anyway! Rock music, among the general public, has not always garnered the level of respect that you or I would give it. In fact, many cultural theorists see rock as, "inferior and 'non artistic.'"[5] Well, I don't care much for labels or hierarchies. An overly hierarchical view of art can lead to a rational aesthetics that supposes proofs can be provided to show that an object is beautiful or worthy. Instead, I listen subjectively to what I like, allowing the music and lyrics to speak to me. Often, I find that what rock is telling me speaks to my spiritual yearnings. Sometimes I find myself thinking about my existence, the world, and God, all because of the music that is playing. This is why I think rock has a lot to say. All we need to do is sit back and enjoy the music.

4. Mazullo, "The Man Whom the World Sold," 727–728.
5. Regev, "Producing Artistic Value," 98.

1

Rock and the Kingdom of God

I see a big black stage fully equipped with stage monitors, a front of house PA system, a drum rise, and lighting. This equipment amplifies a five-piece band consisting of two guitarists, a bassist, a keyboardist, and a drummer. The guitarists and the keyboardist are mic'd up leading the crowd in an arena rock style anthem. What have I described? A rock concert, right? Wrong. This is a common Sunday morning sight in churches across the US and around the world. The song service–often referred to as "worship"–is thought to provide a direct connection with God. One need only recognize the language of closeness and encounter in evangelical worship songs to see that this is true.

In a similar way, it is not uncommon to leave a rock concert and hear fans talking about how a song changed their lives, or how they felt connected to a deeper reality during the performance. With these two images, one can clearly see common ground between rock music and religious sensibilities. Both create space for people to address their deepest spiritual concerns, and both affect people aesthetically and offer life-changing experiences. Considering this, both seem to be on a similar wavelength when it comes to cultural engagement. The main thesis of this book is that *rock music is an artistic outlet that allows devotees the freedom to express religious and spiritual concerns about God in relation to humans and the world.*

But why rock music? What is unique about rock music as a prospective language for expressing religious concerns? What about, say, classical, country, or jazz music?[1] What does theology gain from an engagement with rock and roll? These are questions that will be discussed in this chapter and throughout the book. Simply put, rock is unique because it is a critical force against other forms of music, leveling a critique against the cultural forces that dictate what is normal. Rock music is an agitator of the status quo–one that offers people alternative ways to experience the world. The issues that we will explore in this book are how theological and existential concerns are approached by rock music, and how this dialogue can benefit us spiritually today. I am not, however, claiming that rock music is orthodoxly Christian, or that Christians need not be concerned with the anti-religious sentiments found in rock music. Instead, I am claiming that the language of theology can benefit from dialogue with rock music because, as will be demonstrated, both rock and theology approach identity formation in often analogous ways.

In the contemporary culture of the West, rock music has emerged as a powerful image-making force. As Howard and Streck point out, "At times the moves may seem illusory and gestural, but by offering a rejection of dominant cultural values (or at least a particular subset of those values), rock and roll provides its audiences with the opportunity to create identities through difference."[2] So rock music, at its best, is an identity forming phenomenon that allows young people to stand against some of the oppressive dominant values of culture, while affirming others. In fact, youth culture's self-expression is so tied to popular music that young people are said to "live inside music . . . " tethering together their musical and spiritual lives.[3]

This chapter will attempt to ascertain some of the critiques and affirmations that rock music has put forward since its inception. Chapter two will trace the origins and influence of Christian rock, and the rest of the book will reflect on how individual genres of rock music engage the world theologically and existentially. Exploring the different genres of rock is important in that each genre uniquely engages the world from different points of emphasis. As Simon Frith writes, "It is through genres that we experience music and musical relations, that we bring together the aesthetic and the

---

1. I believe that any viable cultural form can be a source for theological engagement. So, a theology of country or jazz is not only possible, but would be interesting and beneficial to inquisitive fans of the music and culture.

2. Howard and Streck, *Apostles of Rock,* 4–5.

3. Beaudoin, "Theology of Popular Music as Theological Exercise," ix.

ethical."[4] In other words, the different rock genres will give us a clue as to how and by what terms one can engage the world. Thus, this chapter will begin our journey of teasing out how the musical and spiritual lives of Western people are tied together in rock music. While this chapter will offer us a brief history of rock music, it is not intended to rehash the many "history of rock" books out there. Rather, the goal of this chapter is only to place the rest of the book in a historical and cultural context. We will begin this journey by looking at how rock and roll answers life's big questions, which will lead us to describe the character of rock music. Next, we will see rock music's role in expanding the kingdom of God on earth, which will lead us to articulate the basis for a transformational theology of rock. Consequently, this chapter and the next will serve as a ground floor, or historical/cultural and methodological foundation for the rest of the book.

Rock and Roll's Answers to Life's Big Questions

In his book *The Secret History of Rock 'N' Roll*, Christopher Knowles contends that rock music was not created in a vacuum but is rather the modern expression of some very old forces. Knowles is not, however, referring to the well-documented roots of rock and roll found in blues, jazz, and gospel music. Instead, he traces the *spirit* of rock and roll to ancient mystery religions. According to Knowles, the ancient mystery religions of the eastern Mediterranean that began at the end of the Neolithic Age are predecessors of rock and roll, " . . . which had evolved and adapted to suit the needs and customs of postwar American secular culture."[5] The mystery cults often promoted a substance-induced feeling of transcendence similar to what can be found at a rock concert.[6] Some of the rites and rituals of the mystery traditions were mild and subdued while others, like the Bacchanalia, were wild and raucous.[7] Knowles sees several new incarnations of the mystery cults, which are reminiscent of the style and character of various gods and goddesses found throughout the Mediterranean. Though Knowles categorizes many bands with labels such as the "New Eleusinians,"

---

4. Frith, *Performing Rites*, 95.

5. Knowles, *The Secret History of Rock 'N' Roll*, 6.

6. Ibid., 7.

7. Ibid., 84.

the "New Plutonians," or "Hermetic Rock," the two strongest mystery forces found at the genesis of rock music are the Apollonian and Dionysian spirit.[8]

The Apollonian spirit is what brought rock into the mainstream of popular culture. Knowles sees Apollo as the "original rock god" whose heroic and populist persona makes him the archetype of other gods.[9] The rockers who gained early notoriety and set precedents for rock music had some significant traits that evince the Apollonian spirit. Rock and roll's early manifestations were up-tempo, modally Ionian, and boisterous. Rock superstars filled arenas by their charisma, uniting the people in song. Knowles writes, "The Apollonian archetype often trades in political and religious moralism, serving up its sing-along anthems with social conscience."[10] Accordingly, the Apollonian rock star is among those who are formative for rock. They may not be the originators of rock and roll as a genre (a distinction often given to the likes of Bill Haley or Chuck Berry), but they are the figureheads who propelled rock into the mainstream. The clearest example of the Apollonian rock star is Elvis Presley. Presley's fame has been recounted numerous times, and is now etched into the walls of rock history. His persona and life have been canonized and mythologized, and Presley has since "embodied an archetype all his own."[11] But there are others like Bob Dylan, Bruce Springsteen, The Beatles, The Beach Boys, The Eagles, Journey, and U2 who also embody this Apollonian spirit. The Apollonian's focus is on order, and the Apollonian rock star performs songs that feel "simultaneously dangerous . . . and safe."[12] The spirit is one of power, triumph, and valor—one that unites disparate people in song for a greater cause. The cause can be spiritual, moralistic, political, or merely cultural, but in every case, one is granted meaning and significance when s/he follows the Apollonian rock god.

The Dionysian archetype, on the other hand, embodies the maxim "sex, drugs, and rock and roll." This archetype displays the anti-authoritarian hedonism that is commonly associated with rock music. Knowles identifies bands of this archetype as, " . . . the sex-crazed madmen of rock 'n' roll, the bands that caused thousands of parents to lock up their daughters

---

8. Ibid., 95.

9. Ibid.

10. Ibid.

11. Ibid., 96.

12. Leibovitz, *A Broken Hallelujah*, 153.

(and sometimes their sons) when they rolled into town."[13] In other words, it is the Dionysian spirit of rock music that produced the carefree and often careless lifestyle that rock stars often adopt.

According to Greek mythology, Dionysus is the son of Zeus. He is the god of wine and the harvest and worshipped for his resurrection, which gave his followers hope for eternal life. His most devout followers were called the Maenads, a group of women who would consume wine and, " . . . perform sexual, or violent, or sometimes violently sexual rituals to the thrashing of drums and flutes . . . " during the Bacchanalia.[14] Knowles does not see the Dionysian archetype as strictly synonymous to hedonism, however. The Bacchanalia had an anti-authoritarian and political dimension that gave power to women and disrupted the usual societal norms.[15] The Dionysian spirit is one of libertine nonconformity for the purpose of public critique and societal deprecation, rather than the pursuit of pleasure. Knowles sees the partying, world-touring, rock bands of the 1960s and 1970s as fitting examples of the Dionysian spirit.[16] Bands such as The Rolling Stones, The Doors, Led Zeppelin, and Van Halen set the precedent for rock culture consisting of virtuosic music and wild, party-filled debauchery (usually in that order).

The Dionysian spirit can be traced throughout Rock history and appears even today. Together the Dionysian and Apollonian dynamisms form the basis of the rock ethos–one that has been around as Knowles claims for thousands of years–and will continue to carry on beyond our contemporary times. But are these dispositions the most ancient forces that rock music is tapping into, or are these merely two common responses to a more primal human yearning? In his first book, *The Birth of Tragedy*, Friedrich Nietzsche also juxtaposes the dichotomy of the Apollonian and Dionysian to understand the nature and effect of the tragic form. The Apollonian presents an ordered causality of ideas, whereas the Dionysian is disordered and united with the pain and contradictions found in the "truly existent" or "primal unity" of universal will rolling underneath all appearances.[17] For Nietzsche, these two forces always battle for primacy in human existence.[18]

13. Knowles, *The Secret History of Rock 'N' Roll*, 121.

14. Ibid., 22.

15. Ibid., 24.

16. Ibid., 121.

17. Nietzsche, *The Birth of Tragedy*, 29.

18. Ibid., 27.

The Apollonian view of the world was well represented initially by the idealism of ancient Greece. Then, the Dionysian element sought to displace Apollonian idealism with wild parties and festivals. These two forces coexisted and gave birth to tragedy, which represents both Apollonian and Dionysian qualities.[19] This is why tragedy, for Nietzsche, is such a high art form, and why he so admired the "total works of art" by the prolific composer Richard Wagner.[20]

These primal forces do not exist as ends in themselves, but rather appear to be responses to even deeper yearnings. Even Nietzsche admits that his "primal unity" is a metaphysical assumption that lies beneath the Apollonian and Dionysian.[21] Thus, the Apollonian and Dionysian dispositions are, I would argue, first and foremost responses to questions concerning existential significance and identity. From Gilgamesh to Genesis, ancient writers were concerned with how the world came into existence, and what role humans play in this grand narrative. Ancient Sumerian and Semitic people found their own identity in their myths, which were used to explain natural phenomena. These questions are existential and theological by nature in that they deal with the nature of reality in order to explain why and for what reason they occur. Therefore, I would suggest that the Apollonian and Dionysian dispositions are reactionary and follow the deeper existential and theological yearnings that humans portend. Rock and roll, in this light, is not a "Neo-Dionysian" or "Neo-Apollonian" phenomenon but exhibits similar responses to the ageless questions of meaning and existence. While the Apollonian and Dionysian dispositions are not ends in themselves, they may actually describe the conditions out of which such questions of meaning and identity arise in the first place. The so called "secret history of rock and roll" is actually a contextual response to the primal questions of meaning and identity.

What then were the historical conditions that brought about rock music? Rock and roll emerged from the post-war context of the West.[22] The effects of the two world wars, the Cold War and McCarthyism, and the proliferation of mass media were such that young people were, " . . . not only bored . . . and afraid, but lonely and isolated from each other and the adult

19. Ibid., 27–28.
20. Ibid., 13.
21. Ibid., 25.
22. Regev, "Producing Artistic Value," 91.

11

world as well."[23] The world saw the bloodiest war in human history in World War II and was then plunged into fear and paranoia with the Cold War. The Enlightenment optimism of human progression was called into question and the paradigms of the American dream were shattered, to say the least.[24] Children struggled with their identity in a rapidly changing world with no way to envisage a teleological end, which forced young adults to come face to face with their own existence apart from any predicted results. Lawrence Grossberg writes, "There is in fact no sense of progress which can provide meaning or depth and a sense of inheritance. Both the future and the past appear increasingly irrelevant; history has collapsed into the present."[25] Grossberg solemnly adds, "As history becomes mere change—discontinuous, directionless and meaningless—it is replaced by a sense of fragmentation and rupture, of oppressive materiality, of powerlessness and relativism."[26]

Rock emerged as a self-critical, identity-forming phenomenon in a world that desperately needed a vision of what it means to be human; however, rock culture does not elicit a particular cultural or even countercultural identity in the midst of a dominant culture. Rather, rock promotes the struggle against these identities. It revels in the transience of culture and, " . . . transforms the despair of its context into an embracing of its possibilities as pleasure."[27] In other words, rock is intentionally contrarian to dominant culture, but often adopts its precepts. It is identity forming only because it helps one form his or her identity in a pluralistic world. It is countercultural only because it resists following dominant norms for the sake of convention. Rock does not induct its fans into a monolithic ideology. Nor does rock answer life's big questions of meaning and identity in a singular fashion. Instead, rock and roll has splintered off into many genres, each taking a different approach to answering these questions. One of my goals in this book is to explore the ways in which different genres of rock answer life's big questions and to see what theological and existential solutions materialize in each.

Since rock music attempts to answer life's big questions in, albeit, varied ways, one can construct a theology of rock from the implicit and explicit

---

23. Grossberg, "Another Boring Day in Paradise," 229.

24. Kramer, *The Republic of Rock*, 11.

25. Grossberg, "Another Boring Day in Paradise," 229.

26. Ibid., 230.

27. Ibid., 235.

theological commitments that these answers purport. While rock music, at times, only poses questions without actually offering substantive answers, there are occasions in which rock's focus moves beyond "possibility" and "changing-ness" toward resolution or finality. Throughout this book we will look at several approaches rock takes to answering life's big questions, stringing them together to form a theology of rock. This approach to theology is worthwhile because it can illuminate nuances about God and humanity that would otherwise be overlooked in a traditional systematic theology.[28] As Jeffrey Keuss writes, " . . . academic and ecclesial theology will be deficient without the correlational counterpoint of other voices. The voice of popular culture speaking a distinctly different language is a critical and necessary voice that needs to be taken seriously in order for theology to fulfill its mandate."[29] Rock music creates, therefore, an excellent perspective for theology. Rock provides thought-provoking retorts to questions that were asked at the beginning of recorded history and offers answers that can help people navigate through even some of their lives' most difficult times. Before diving into this discussion, it would be beneficial to analyze the character of rock and roll.

The Character of Rock and Roll

Rock culture is, in many ways, paradoxical. It critiques *and* affirms dominant culture, it is rebellious *and* patriotic, and it is both enriching *and* at times debasing. Some of this can be accounted for by the many different genres of rock and their diverse approaches to life, but the rock ethos is such that these apparent contradictions can coexist in a network of commonality. While each genre may define these root characteristics of rock differently, there are, so it seems, four common features uniting rock music: it is countercultural, identity forming, communal, and transformative.

Rock is Countercultural

As alluded to earlier, it would be reductionistic to see rock music only as a contrarian force prevailing at the fringes of society. It is not enough to say that rock music is merely countercultural because its association with

28. Keuss, "Tom Waits, Nick Cave, and Martin Heidegger," 152.

29. Ibid.

dominant culture is multifarious. Grossberg sees three ways that rock differentiates itself from dominant culture. There is "oppositional rock," which confronts and critiques dominant culture directly. He says that a mantra for this type of rock is, " . . . we want the world and we want it now."[30] This sort of character is seen, but not exclusively so, in various forms of punk, hardcore, and metal. It is this type of rock that is truly countercultural and wishes to stand up against the oppressions of dominant culture. "Alternative rock," not to be confused with the genre of the same name, fronts an implicit attack on dominant culture. A mantra for this type of rock might be, " . . . we want the world but on our terms."[31] While this type of rock may be standing against many factions of dominant culture, it does so in an ambiguous and thought-provoking way. Folk and alternative rock bands often function in this way. Finally, there is "independent rock," which does not challenge dominant culture either implicitly or explicitly. Rather, it crafts its own world apart from the dominant culture as an escape. A mantra for this type of rock is, " . . . we want our world."[32] This type of rock shows up in every genre since it creates its own identity despite what the dominant or countercultures are demanding. Independent rock provides an escape from both the dominant and the counterculture.

What is consistent in each of these modes of counterculture is that rock music never exists as a proxy of dominant culture. While rock utilizes elements of the dominant culture (such as sounds and symbols), it does so in a way that transforms them to serve its own countercultural purposes. Grossberg writes,

> . . . the power of rock and roll lies in its practice of 'excorporation', operating at and reproducing the boundary between youth culture and the dominant culture. Rock and roll reverses the hegemonic practices of incorporation—by which practices claiming a certain externality are relocated within the context of hegemonic relations. Rock and roll removes signs, objects, sounds, styles, etc. from their apparently meaningful existence within the dominant culture and relocates them within an affective alliance of differentiation and resistance.[33]

---

30. Grossberg, "Another Boring Day in Paradise," 241.

31. Ibid.

32. Ibid.

33. Ibid., 232.

Grossberg helps us see that rock is countercultural in a variety of ways, and endures in a complex relationship with dominant culture. Thus, rock music exists in a counterculture of plurality with conflicting strands running counter to dominant culture at varying speeds.

Rock is Identity Forming

Rock is also identity forming as it allows listeners to, " . . . probe the nature of human individuality, liberty, freedom, community, commitment, and coercion."[34] Just as rock is countercultural in a variety of ways, it is also freeing. It does not subscribe its listeners to a particular ideological position, but allows people the freedom to mediate, " . . . uncertain questions of citizenship . . . "[35] in a pluralistic world. Rock is more a structure of enablement than an institute of indoctrination.

To illustrate rock and roll's countercultural foundations, let us return briefly to the historical conditions that brought rock music about. Doubt was cast upon the national ethos of the American Dream. After the devastations of the world wars, rock music came along with the message that it is okay to be different. Rock reminded society that there is no stability in the status quo and that change is actually bearable. Altschuler shows that rock helped to foster an "intergenerational identity" for post-war youth of the 1950s.[36] It helped to develop the first Western "youth culture" with its own mores and institutions.[37] But it was the youth of the 1960s, the baby boomers, who really helped to give rock its distinctiveness as a countercultural phenomenon. Altschuler writes, " . . . through the music and other stimulants to the soul, young people sought to bring together, 'right now,' a nation divided by race and class, and by regional and local values."[38] In the 1960s, therefore, rock found its identity as an identity forming and countercultural force.

---

34. Kramer, *The Republic of Rock*, 11.
35. Ibid.
36. Altschuler, *All Shook Up*, 185.
37. Ibid.
38. Ibid., 185.

Rock is Communal

Rock is the music of the natives and arises from the reality of everyday life.[39] While rock promotes the freedom for one to find his or her own identity, it does so in the context of a community. Woodstock is perhaps the best-recognized example of rock's communal ethos. In the summer of 1969, Bethel, New York saw more than 300,000 young people converge for a massive clannish gathering focused on music and the arts.[40] Woodstock, which boasted a superstar lineup including Jimmy Hendrix, The Who, Janis Joplin, and Jefferson Airplane, had bands play every hour for three straight days. Although a strong Dionysian spirit surrounded the festival, one cannot ignore the incredible sense of community that was created around rock music and culture. This community, however, was not built on structure and proselytization but on freedom, ambiguity, and irony. Bernice Martin points out that rock uses a symbolism of disorder and ambiguity in order to paradoxically reinforce group integration.[41] Symbols are supposed to be "instruments of order" that exist to help people make sense of the world; however, symbols are imprecise and context-bound, which inevitably makes them "instruments of ambiguity," that often raise as many questions as they answer.[42] Martin writes, "Symbols are thus inherently treacherous: they have a foot in both camps—order and disorder."[43] Humans navigate through a grey world. The symbols they create in order to communicate their worldview reflect this same ambiguity. Rock music uses symbols of disorder, which it places prominently in the foreground, to bring in a new diverse order. This enables the community that forms to be one of acceptance and plurality. Martin claims that rock, " . . . embodies the contrary principle of group solidarity . . . not just age-group solidarity but racial, sexual, class and local solidarity."[44] So rock helps to blur fragmenting sociological lines and in so doing inducts members into a new pluralistic and diverse community of rock.

39. Regev, "Producing Artistic Value," 91.

40. Altshuler, *All Shook Up,* 186.

41. Martin, "The Sacralization of Disorder," 89.

42. Ibid., 90.

43. Ibid.

44. Ibid.

Rock is Transformational

Once one concedes that rock is countercultural, image forming, and communal, it does not take much to recognize that it is consequently transformational. Rock is a vehicle for transformation, both in society and in individuals. Its critique of dominant culture is concrete, and not merely ideological. It critiques what is outmoded in culture so as to bring real change to the world. Grossberg writes, "Rock and roll, at its best, transforms old dreams into new realities. It rejects that which is outside of its self-encapsulation not on political grounds but because their organisations [*sic*] of affect are no longer appropriate in the post-modern world."[45] Rock, in this way, takes culture to task as a prophetic voice in the present age.

Rock is also transformational for the individual because of its image forming quality. As rock helps people to find their place in the world, it transforms them into contributing members of society. Fans of rock then join in the societal critique that takes place, making them part of rock's solution for culture's problems. Rock not only transforms a person's outlook of the world, but also affects what s/he believes to be true about the world. This takes place as the individual joins the freethinking community of rock. Rock does not simply tease dominant culture to raise awareness. Rather, it creates an alternative lifestyle for its adherents.

If what I have argued is true, that rock is in its very nature countercultural, image making, communal, and transformational, then one can tease out the theological implications that follow. Self-discovery presupposes questions about a Creator, and cultural criticism presupposes an ethical authority beyond the values of the dominant culture. Community and transformation are cardinal aspirations of the Church. So what has become evident is that rock as a cultural phenomenon shares many talking points with Christian theology. But what role does rock play in God's world?

Rock and the Kingdom of God

The Bible speaks of two opposing kingdoms: the kingdom of God, and the kingdom of "the world," or of Satan. Embedded in these two concepts is a discussion about the relationship between God's people and mission in the world. Simply put, how can God's kingdom be established culturally and politically in a corrupt world? This has been a longstanding exchange

45. Grossberg, "Another Boring Day in Paradise," 236.

within Christian theology and is pertinent to our discussion because rock music is a cultural phenomenon that has the power to work for or against the kingdom of God. The question is invariably asked: to which kingdom does rock music bear allegiance? I would submit that this inquiry is too reductionistic because the relationship between the kingdom of God and the kingdom of the world is multifaceted and complex. Nevertheless, we can come to *some* sense of rock music's place in the exchange surrounding the two kingdoms. Before embarking on this issue, however, let us take a (very) brief look at the theology surrounding the kingdom of God.

Reformed theologian Donald Bloesch writes, "Scripture postulates two kingdoms—light and darkness. God is ruler over both, but he is Savior only in the former. This present world is a battleground between light and darkness, Christ and Satan."[46] Bloesch is not suggesting a metaphysical dualism, as in Zoroastrianism, but a moral dualism that shows the kingdom of evil as the antithesis of the good.[47] There are two opposing forces, and there can be no compromise. To begin with, consider the first chapter of Genesis where God separates light from darkness. This may be an image of the kingdoms of light and darkness. Although not explicitly stated, some medieval theologians interpreted these verses as depicting the war in heaven, which culminated in the separation of the angels.[48] Furthermore, the tempting serpent later in Genesis 3 typifies the anti-god force in the Garden.[49] Satan and his angels are already present on earth as a result of being cast down from heaven after the war in heaven. The demonic influence on earth offers an antithesis to God, producing the possibility of choice for humanity, and thus opens the occasion to sin.

In ancient Hebraic tradition, the sources of evil were illustrated as both the watery chaos of Genesis 1 and the personification of this chaos in the dragon called Leviathan in Job 41. There is earlier Babylonian precedent for these images as *Tehom* (the deep) is the philological equivalent to *Tiamat*, the chaos monster in the Babylonian creation myth *Enuma Elish*.[50] While it is difficult to know exactly when Satan was equivocated with the Leviathan, it is certain that the book of Revelation uses the images of the dragon, the serpent, the devil, and Satan interchangeably. As the kingdom of God is

---

46. Bloesch, *The Last Things,* 52.

47. Ibid.

48. Ibid., 51.

49. Ibid.

50. Davies and Rogerson, *The Old Testament World,* 112.

concerned, Israel is biblically depicted as the elect kingdom of priests in a holy nation, and the adversary is the kingdom of the world led by Satan.[51] Slowly but surely, the prophets realized that God's kingdom is spiritual. The narrative in Revelation shows that the evil city of the world will ultimately be overthrown, and the beloved city of God will reign forever.[52]

One of the earliest and most influential theologies of the two kingdoms came from Augustine of Hippo.[53] In *City of God*, Augustine articulated the two kingdoms in systematic fashion. In a sense, *City of God* served as an apologetic of the Christian church as Romans increasingly blamed Christianity for the decline of the Roman Empire.[54] In light of this, Augustine posited that the city of God is a regenerated remnant reflecting, but not identical to, the church, and the city of the world is under the dominion and powers of darkness.[55] His views were metaphysically, dualistic in that the community of faith has been predestined to eternal life, whereas the members of the earthly city have been predestined to eternal damnation. As a mission, the kingdom of God is to expand into the kingdom of the world. In this way, Christianity did not supplant the Roman Empire, but rather the kingdom of God was an outworking of God's sovereign plan for the world.[56]

Over a millennium later, Martin Luther and John Calvin, the two most instrumental Reformers, established two important yet divergent theologies of the two kingdoms. Luther sustained Augustine's dualism by envisioning the kingdom of God as the kingdom of grace and mercy, and the kingdom of the world as the kingdom of wrath and judgment. The kingdom of the devil was always in rebellion against the kingdom of God, so God established the law after the fall as humans were internally divided between the two kingdoms. God established the law to govern human affairs through reason, and the state became the earthly power that would "uphold the law by force."[57] The gospel was therefore assigned to the "spiritual regiment" but would be available to guide the secular regiment morally.[58] As theologian Jesse Couenhoven writes,

51. Bloesch, *The Last Things*, 55.

52. Ibid., 58.

53. Ibid., 95.

54. Augustine, *City of God*, 45.

55. Ibid., 829.

56. Ibid., 196.

57. Couenhoven, "Law and Gospel, or the Law of the Gospel," 183.

58. Luther, *A Commentary on St. Paul's Epistle to the Galatians*, 139.

> Luther intends the two regiments, each under its own proper form of God's word, to limit and complement one another, and to challenge the kingdom of the devil. This leads him to stress the separation of and difference between church and state, which has the positive effect of limiting, or, at least, putting in question, the self-legitimating use of religion by the state, and the self-aggrandizing use of the state by religion.[59]

In Luther's theology, God is still in control and uses the kingdom of the world to display God's wrath. Thus, Satan is not lord of the earth but is only a pawn of God.

Calvin also sees two distinct governments under Christ's rule. While Luther said the *renunciation* of the kingdom of the world is the hallmark of the kingdom of God, Calvin believed that the power of the state is *part* of the kingdom of God.[60] Couenhoven writes, "Both thinkers (Calvin and Luther) agree that there is one God over the two governments, but since Calvin tends to see Christ as the *telos* of the law, where Luther simply sees Christ as the law's limit, Calvin also pictures Jesus Christ as the lord of the secular kingdom."[61] In other words, the kingdom of God is the area that God established God's reign in Christ, but the kingdom of God could be advanced by power via the secular kingdom.[62] Calvin saw the church and the state as complimentary and thought that a theocracy was possible as both the church and state abide under the revealed law. Thus Calvin is not a dualist in Luther's sense, avoiding a complete split between church and state. Calvin is a dualist like Augustine since he thinks Satan is trying to steal away the worldly government and claim it for himself.

The post-Enlightenment tendency was to overthrow any such dualistic notion of the two kingdoms in favor of a monistic understanding of the kingdom of God. This modern trajectory saw the whole world as the family of God and, with technical precision, called the supernatural into question.[63] Beginning with Friedrich Schleiermacher, angelology was demoted to a non-essential belief that, if held, must not affect a Christian's ethics.[64] Later, biblical scholars like Rudolf Bultmann pushed the trend even further

---

59. Ibid., 183–184.

60. Calvin, *Institutes of the Christian Religion*, 184.

61. Couenhoven, "Law and Gospel, or the Law of the Gospel," 185.

62. Bloesch, *The Last Things*, 71.

63. Ibid., 57.

64. Schleiermacher, *The Christian Faith*, 159.

by demythologizing Satan as an adverse consciousness roote
norance and disregard of divine law.[65] This means that there i:
between God and the devil, heaven and hell, holiness and sin,
nature and freedom, or flesh and spirit. Reinhold Niebuhr saw the king-
of God as a transcendental ideal.[66] In other words, the kingdom of God is
a heavenly, ideal world. The world, on the other hand, is the actual world,
which strives to be like the ideal.[67] Niebuhr allows for the reality of the demonic but sees the demonic as a symbol of possession of something that is
less than God. Niebuhr's view is thus still moderately demythologized. Karl
Barth also adopted the modern, monistic understanding of the kingdom of
God, but instead of looking at the kingdom of God in only modern terms,
Barth's position harkened back to Augustine and the Reformers' theology.

Barth, who is arguably the most prominent modern theologian, also
posited an influential theology of the two kingdoms. Like Augustine, Barth
saw evil as nothingness, a negative, non-created reality. Therefore, the kingdom of Christ signifies the whole world not just the community of faith. For
Barth, the kingdom of Satan is defeated by Christ and is slowly crumbling
away. This is akin to the process of sanctification in the believer. Barth resists the word "Church" as God's elect, opting to use the term "community."
Barth sees the community as the " . . . commonwealth gathered, founded,
and ordered by the Word of God, the 'communion of the saints.'"[68] As such,
the community is the society of people who are called to, " . . . believe in,
and simultaneously to testify to, the Word in the world."[69] This elect community of the called is thus the "inner circle" of the kingdom of God, while
the rest of the world is the "outer circle" of the kingdom.[70] Barth, drawing
on his revision of reformed theology, sees Christ in control of everything,
including the structures and institutions of the secular world. Christ thus
mediates his power through the elected community, which exercises influence over the secular world in order to bring about God's kingdom. This
gives the state a positive role in the kingdom of God. Barth comes to this
conclusion because of his Christocentric theology, which subsumes every
theological matter into a Trinitarian Christological framework. Couen-

65. Bultmann, *Jesus Christ and Mythology*, 14–18.

66. Rasmussen, *Reinhold Niebuhr*, 175.

67. Bloesch, *The Last Things*, 30.

68. Barth, *Evangelical Theology*, 37.

69. Ibid.

70. Barth, *Church Dogmatics*, II.2, 197.

hoven writes, "He [Barth] maintains, further, that there is only one Word of God, the saving and gracious word spoken in Jesus Christ. The relationship of gospel and law is established in Christ, in whom the law is fulfilled and made clear."[71] Both the inner and outer circles are dependent on each other to establish God's sovereign plan on earth. As Barth writes,

> The inner circle is nothing apart from the relation to the outer circle of the election which has taken place (and takes place in Jesus Christ).
>
> But this outer circle, too, is in its turn nothing without the inner one; all the election that has taken place (and takes place in Jesus Christ is mediated, conditioned and bounded by the election of the community. It mirrors in its mediate and mediating character the existence of the one Mediator, Jesus Christ, Himself. In its particularity over against the world it reflects the freedom of the electing God, just as in its service to the world (that is, in the provisional nature of its particularity) it reflects His love.[72]

Thus, the community of the elect is not wholly apart and separate from the world but consists of the called out ones who are to bring transformation to a broken reality. The community is to carry out Christ's great commission and, in so doing, will help to bring the kingdom of God to its end state of glory.

Although Barth's theology of the kingdom is compelling, it is not without criticism. Livingston and Schüssler Fiorenza point out that Barth's dialectical understanding of the relationship between God and the world does not adequately account for the evils brought about by humans.[73] If every institution is part of the kingdom of God, as Barth postulates, even when the state acts in demonic ways; it still somehow serves God.[74] Couenhoven believes Barth means that, " . . . every state upholds order in some way, even those that are mainly evil,"[75] and since, " . . . no state ever becomes totally demonic—it fulfills its calling to some degree, even against its will."[76] Barth sees the inner circle encroaching onto the outer circle until the eschaton when the kingdom of God is fully realized. Barth distinguishes between the kingdom of grace and kingdom of glory to his theology of the kingdom

71. Couenhoven, "Law and Gospel, or the Law of the Gospel," 188.

72. Barth, *Church Dogmatics*, II.2, 197.

73. Livingston and Schüssler Fiorenza, *Modern Christian Thought*, 111.

74. Couenhoven, "Law and Gospel, or the Law of the Gospel," 193.

75. Ibid.

76. Ibid., 194.

of God, thereby adding an eschatological dimension and the opportunity for tension or progress. Grace indicates the restoring and renewal of the world through Christ whereas glory indicates the fulfillment and revelation of grace. Grace is here now, and glory is to come. As such, the kingdom of God is already here in the inner and outer circles but only as a foretaste of its fulfillment when the kingdom of God will be fully realized in glory. As Couenhoven explains,

> By emphasizing, on the one hand the 'already' in the not yet, Barth is able to see the unity of gospel and law that shows that the Kingdom of God is the end goal of the civil community. He is therefore, as he hoped, able to find a stronger theological basis for making political claims than either of the Reformers. By emphasizing, on the other hand, the continuing importance of seeking God's Kingdom in the 'not yet,' Barth also makes a compelling theological case for avoiding the quietism that haunts Luther's work—because the state is still on the way—and the clerical guardianship that followed Calvin's—because the church, too, is on the way.[77]

So Barth's theology of the kingdom of God denies the idea that anything in the world, whether cultural or political, can be completely evil. There is no black and white, but rather shades of grey. The task of the elected community is to overcome the darker shades of grey until the negation of white is fully abolished.

For our purposes, we now turn to the work of theologian Christian Scharen who picks up these themes in his excellent book *Broken Hallelujahs*. Scharen approaches rock and pop music in general in order to discover a robust imagination that can deal with the difficult concerns of today's world.[78] To this end, Scharen realizes that there is no completely secular cultural arena that Christians must be separate from.[79] If one truly believes that God is Lord over heaven and earth, then one must adopt a kingdom theology like Barth's, which renders all of creation as potentially good yet in need of redemption. Rock music, for Scharen, has the unique ability to approach life's major issues head on and without a filter.[80] Rock, in this way, offers a refreshing point of engagement with a world that is broken and grey. Christians exist in a broken world and are not capable of offering an

---

77. Couenhoven, "Law and Gospel, or the Law of the Gospel," 202.

78. Scharen, *Broken Hallelujahs*, 17.

79. Ibid., 21.

80. Ibid., 74.

unfettered response to God.[81] Scharen writes, "In this life, all we are capable of is a broken hallelujah. And the fact that we're able to raise even a broken hallelujah results from what God has done for us."[82] Rock music, when it is truly transformational, holds issues such as earth and heaven, spirituality and sexuality, and faith and doubt in tension, allowing a person to negotiate his or her place in the world.[83]

Putting a cultural phenomenon in strict opposition to its counterpart neglects the important task of spiritual discernment in life. Instead, we must trust that God is present in the midst of each conversation and tease out the transformative reality that often sits at the heart of the world's cries of brokenness.[84] Rock music is an expression of the grey existing between the white and black, which reflects a kind of eschatological longing. As such, rock music is a source for discernment through which one can sense God's action in the world. Disregarding such an approach will invariably lead to a "constricted imagination": a checklist theology that reduces everything to simple matters of good or bad.[85] This is, however, tremendously dangerous and often creates legalistic judgmentalism coupled with cultural narrow-mindedness. Scharen writes, "God gets terribly small when we follow the trail of constricted imagination: God's here (with me), God's not there (with you). No, I say!"[86] As Scharen suggests, entering the conversation of rock and theology with openness and grace will suit us best. Let us hear the cries of the broken in the world today and be keen to hear God's vision of transformation that lies within these cries. This is the way that we can approach a transformational theology of rock.

Conclusion

In his book *Transforming Christian Theology*, Philip Clayton argues that Christianity in the West today is radically different from the mid-twentieth

---

81. Ibid., 93.

82. Ibid., 46. Scharen is here referencing Leonard Cohen's masterful song "Hallelujah," where Cohen explores issues of love that has grown stale in romantic and religious contexts.

83. Ibid., 22.

84. Ibid., 141.

85. Ibid., 142.

86. Ibid., 142.

century Christianity in the US and Europe.[87] The 1950s were the "Golden Age" of Judaism and Christianity in the US. Church membership grew twice as fast as the American population, and 95% of the American population identified as Catholic, Protestant, or Jewish.[88] Today, however, the Western population is stepping away from the institution of the church and synagogue altogether, for a myriad of reasons. In the US, only 51 percent of the population identifies as Protestant, and of this 51 percent, only 18 percent belong to a mainline denomination.[89] Part of the reason for this decline, according to Clayton, is the reductionistic conservative/liberal dichotomy in Western theology and culture.[90] These labels are divisive and unhelpful in our contemporary cultural climate. As the world grows to be more pluralistic and global, it becomes more and more evident that most of us do not fit neatly into such dichotomous camps. Though the world has experienced cultural and sociological change in recent times, the biggest catalyst for the change in ideological perspective is technology and globalism.[91] Today we can see what is going on around the world at any time, and the mysterious lands beyond our oceans have been demystified. At the same time, this broader perspective gives us Westerners better insight into the cultural and religious differences around the world. These changes have made our society more pluralistic and culturally relative.

This is the cultural climate in which we find ourselves doing theology. Rock music, like art in general, offers us the ability to cut through cultural differences and engage the deep issues of the day honestly and robustly. There is a lot of grey in the world, but artists and rock musicians can help instill hope in a broken world.

This first chapter traced how rock music answers life's big questions and considered the nature and character of rock music. It then entered into a discussion about the kingdom of God in order to show that rock music fits into that narrative as a cultural force. We approached the topic of what a transformational theology of rock would entail, but in the next chapter, after a discussion about the origins and nature of Christian rock, we will trace out the prolegomena of a transformational theology of rock.

---

87. Clayton, *Transforming Christian Theology*, 11.

88. Ibid., 12.

89. Ibid., 14.

90. Ibid., 118.

91. Ibid., 15.

2

Upon This (Christian) Rock

The idea of *Christian* rock is a bit nebulous. What is it anyways? Is Christian rock simply music performed by Christians? Should the lyrics be explicitly evangelistic? Is it only for Christian listeners, or for everyone? Is it really a *genre* of rock? These are the questions one might ask when first encountering Christian rock. Jon Foreman, frontman of the band Switchfoot, suggests that using the word "Christian" as an adjective describing music is somewhat puzzling. In an interview, Foreman answered the question, "If Switchfoot a Christian band?" by stating:

> Many songs are worthy of being written. . . . Some of these songs are about redemption, others about the sunrise, others about nothing in particular: written for the simple joy of music. None of these songs has been born again, and to that end there is no such thing as Christian music. No. Christ didn't come and die for my songs, he came for me. Yes. My songs are a part of my life. But judging from scripture I can only conclude that our God is much more interested in how I treat the poor and the broken and the hungry than the personal pronouns I use when I sing. I am a believer. Many of these songs talk about this belief. An obligation to say this or do that does not sound like the glorious freedom that Christ died to afford me. I do have an obligation, however, a debt that cannot be settled by my lyrical decisions. My life will be judged by my obedience, not my ability to confine my lyrics to this box or that.[1]

1. Foreman in Challies, "Another Switchfoot Concert."

Foreman's statement has been quoted again and again by blogs and ministry websites for over a decade now.[2] He seems to have articulately voiced an idea that is on the minds of many Christians who are seeking a more profound discourse with culture. His quote elevates the intrinsic difficulties that surround the identity of Christian cultural engagement. How can Christians make music that both engages culture as part of culture and also speak to the world about matters of faith? In this chapter, I will briefly discuss the history and character of Christian rock in order to shed some light on these issues. This survey will also create a context from which we will develop the prolegomena of a transformational theology of rock. This chapter thus supports my main thesis that *rock music is an artistic outlet that allows devotees the freedom to express religious and spiritual concerns about God in relation to humans and the world* by tracing the ways that the industry of Christian rock has previously engaged culture. This chapter forms a critical basis for the subsequent chapters that deal with individual genres of rock. While there are a myriad of cultural channels that engage in theological dialogue, rock music has done so from its inception and thus sports a rich history of theological interchange.

Three Waves of Christian Rock

While the terminology may be limiting, there is a general consensus that music is deemed Christian if it portrays Christian lyrics or is created from a backdrop of Christian faith. [3] David Nantais observes that often times the only difference between secular and Christian rock is the words; in other words, its lyrical content. Christian Contemporary Music (CCM) has posited, in general, that the style of music can sound like any genre, but for music to be considered Christian (as in part of the CCM label), it must portray religious lyrics. Nantais maintains, however, that CCM tends to overlook the importance of intention in music. He argues that if the musician or band has intentions that are in line with the gospel, then the music, whether it has overtly religious lyrics or not, does communicate a message about God.[4] This would elicit a more intrinsic, rather than apparent, Christian message. All things considered, adequately defining Christian rock is a tall order.

2. For example see Eshelman, "Is Switchfoot a Christian Band?" and, "Why Switchfoot Won't Sing Christian Songs."

3. Thompson, *Raised by Wolves,* 11.

4. Nantais, *Rock-A My Soul,* 9.

Not only is the term Christian rock problematic in what it sets out to describe, it is also reductionistic in that it lumps every style of rock music into a single category. Bands can be punk, metal, folk, indie, alternative, pop, hardcore, etc., and all be subjected to the blanket label of Christian rock once the artists are identified as followers of Christ.[5] Even more troubling is the continual labeling of all Christian music as "gospel" regardless of genre or disposition. Because gospel literally means "good news," it could be applied to all Christian music as "good news music." But the term "gospel" is typically used synonymously to describe the "urban contemporary gospel" or "black gospel" music that derived from the African American religious experience. Nevertheless, Christian rock is invariably known as rock music made by Christians.

One of the purposes of this book is to tease out how the different genres of rock approach theological and existential ideas about life and humanity. In subsequent chapters, I refer to "Christian rock bands" as bands of the genre that are consciously constructing their music from a Christian worldview. While I hate using the term "Christian rock" because of the problems mentioned above, I will do so (reluctantly) for the sake of simplicity. There is, after all, a whole market of "Christian rock" that is both influential and profitable. It must be noted that I am fully aware of these difficulties and appreciate Foreman's sentiments about the issue. Christian rock bands often have their own philosophies about how music can engage God and the world. In this way, Christian artists are working to bridge the gap between the secular and the sacred, allowing their own spiritual commitments to manifest in their music and performances. Christian rock is in the business of engaging culture, and each genre of rock does so in unique ways. Before diving into how Christian rock can engage culture, however, it would be helpful to contextualize our conversation by tracing the major movements that comprise Christian rock's history.

In his book *Raised by Wolves*, writer and critic John Thompson claims we can best understand the history of Christian rock as existing in three waves.[6] The first wave, according to Thompson, began with the Jesus movement and spans throughout the 1970s, the second wave comprises the 1980s, and the third wave spans the 1990s.[7] Thompson described what

---

5. Thompson, *Raised by Wolves*, 11.

6. Ibid., 37.

7. Ibid., 37–38.

would happen in the 2000s as "Beyond the Third Wave."[8] Though his book was published nearly 20 years ago in 2000, his principle of categorizing the first three formative decades of Christian rock in waves is still useful. Christian rock evolved greatly in the 1970s, 1980s, and 1990s but has found stability as a market since the 2000s. While rock genres constantly come in and out of vogue, there is today a general sense of plurality, which allows the different genres (in rock and Christian rock alike) to coexist amiably.

The first wave of Christian rock began in the late 1960s in conjunction with the Jesus Movement. The Jesus Movement was a movement in American Christianity beginning in the late 1960s and fizzling out by the 1980s. The movement began in California as a group began to evangelize the San Francisco Bay area hippies. One of the central locations of the hippie movement, Haight-Ashbury, was quickly devolving towards despondency. Historian Larry Eskridge writes,

> For all its colorful eccentricity and idealistic hopes, the hippie reality of the Summer of Love in Haight-Ashbury had devolved into a mixture of overcrowding, hunger, filth, bad drug trips, crime, and predatory personal behavior. The streets of San Francisco's do-your-own-thing hippie ethos often turned into an every man for himself struggle for existence.[9]

This dejection caused the hippies to question their idealism and seek something more spiritual. It also exposed many unmet needs within the hippy community. Christians started missions where they could share the gospel and supply food to the needy young people.[10] With mixed press reviews, the movement spread all over California causing the growth of many prominent church and ministry groups such as Calvary Chapel and the Shiloh Youth Revival Centers of Costa Mesa, and His Place of Hollywood, which gained a lot of success ministering to those in the hippie culture.[11] Churches began to utilize an informal "come as you are" worship style with folk music instead of hymns, and hippies would sit barefoot in the isles of churches.[12] Christian hippie communes began as places of refuge and quasi-halfway homes for ex-drug addicts. Eventually, these ex-hippies would become known as "Jesus People" or "Jesus Freaks."

8. Ibid., 237.
9. Eskridge, *God's Forever Family,* 29–30.
10. Ibid., 31.
11. Ibid., 98.
12. Ibid., 70–72.

The movement rapidly spread throughout the Northwest, Midwest, and all over the United States.[13] Although the movement began in California, many of the centers and communes began indigenously without influence from California, as local church groups set out to minister to their own youth. In the early 1970s, however, the Jesus Movement moved into the mainstream with Explo '72. In 1972, Billy Graham and Campus Crusade for Christ organized a massive gathering in Dallas, Texas that emulated the culture and promotional style of the Jesus Movement. Explo '72 attracted tens of thousands of both "Jesus People" and mainline youth known as "Jesus Kids." Even though the Jesus Movement began as a countercultural outreach, the media fare of the early 1970s, and Explo '72 shifted the focus of the movement to the Christian, baby-boomer, youth culture in general.[14] In terms of the broader cultural context, the Jesus Movement allowed Christians to reimagine Christ and the church in their day. As Davis writes,

> By the early 1970s, a new Jesus had hit the American mind—communal, earthy, spontaneous, anti-establishment. And this Jesus continued to transform American worship long after the patchouli wore off, inspiring a more informal and contemporary style of communion and celebration that, while holding true to core principles, unbuckled the Bible Belt from American Christian life.[15]

The Jesus People looked and dressed like the "peace freaks" and other hippies from the late 1960s[16] but expressed Christ in a way that was fresh and relevant to the culture of the late 1960s and early 1970s.

The Jesus Movement was the catalyst for great change in the way American church was done. The timing of the Jesus Movement was also fortuitous for its music, because rock music was beginning to dig deeper spiritually in the late 1960s. Eskridge writes, "As the emergence of the Jesus People reflected religious undertones within the counterculture, so, too, the world of popular music began to evidence a new spirituality during the late 1960s, part of the serious undertaking that rock music had become for both musicians and their listeners."[17] Essentially, "Jesus Music" was well received in popular culture, as the culture was ripe for spiritual engagement.

---

13. Ibid., 94.

14. Ibid., 178.

15. Davis, "I'd Like to Dedicate This Next Song to Jesus."

16. Thompson, *Raised by Wolves*, 29.

17. Eskridge, *God's Forever Family*, 125.

The First Wave

The face—and some would say father—of the first wave of Christian rock was Larry Norman. Based in the Bay Area of San Francisco, Norman gained early success with his band People! People! eventually signed with Capitol Records and released two albums. The second album, *I Love You* (1968), was very successful; its title track making it to number 14 on the pop charts.[18] The album was supposed to be titled *We Need a Whole Lot More of Jesus and a Lot Less of Rock and Roll*, and the cover sported a picture of the band "jamming with Jesus."[19] However, before the album was released, Capitol Records vetoed these plans, titled the album *I Love You*, and used a simple picture of the band on the cover. This allegedly caused Norman to quit the band.[20] Nevertheless, Capitol signed Norman back to the label as a solo Christian artist. Norman's first album *Upon This Rock* (1969) is considered the first full-blown Christian rock album although the first "Christian" album that made an impact on a national level was *I Love You*.[21]

A couple of Norman's songs have become archetypal for early Christian rock and the Jesus movement. The song "I Wish We'd All Been Ready" from the album *Upon This Rock* expresses the popular premillennial eschatology supported by the Jesus Movement and, in some ways, has become the theme song of rapture theology. The song recounts the gloomy aftereffects of the rapture for both nominal Christians and the unsaved. This song has been covered by several recording artists such as dc Talk and Jordin Sparks and has become the title track to two iterations of the *Left Behind* movie franchise. The song "Why Should the Devil Have All the Good Music?" from the album *Only Visiting This Planet* (1972), acted as an apologetic for Christian rock. The opening lines of the first verse are, "I want the people to know that he saved my soul, but I still like to listen to the radio,"[22] taking aim at the idea that rock music intrinsically opposes Christianity. The chorus rehashes this idea in a less subtle way:

---

18. Thompson, *Raised by Wolves,* 48.

19. Ibid., 48–49.

20. Ibid., 49. It should be noted that this is the story that Norman likes to tell, although his former bandmates disagree with the particulars (Stowe, *No Sympathy for the Devil,* 35.).

21. Beaujon, *Body Piercing Saved My Soul,* 21.

22. Norman, "Why Should the Devil Have All the Good Music?"

People say to me that Jesus and rock and roll can never go together
But I think they're wrong, they're wrong, they're wrong!
Listen to my song, my song, my song!
Why should the devil have all the good music?[23]

For many young Christians in America, this song became the anthem for Christian rock. With his national success, Norman became the unofficial spokesperson of the Jesus Movement and one of the progenitors of Christian contemporary music.[24] Thompson writes, "By 1970, Norman was featured in *Time* and other national media outlets. As the spokesman for the Jesus Movement, and probably its most engaging personality, he had become Christianity's first rock star."[25]

One of the more famous and influential first wave Christian rock bands was Love Song. Love Song was described as "the Christian Beatles" in the early 1970s.[26] They sounded somewhat like the Beatles but, as Powell states, " . . . were instrumental in creating a new type of music—what would eventually be called 'contemporary Christian music.'"[27] Chuck Girard, Tommy Coomes, Jay Truax, and Fred Field formed Love Song in 1970 in southern California. The four explored philosophical and religious issues together and eventually were converted to Christianity after accepting Jesus as their "personal Lord and savior."[28] They joined a Bible study at Calvary Chapel and received guidance and counsel from Pastor Chuck Smith.[29] Although the band shifted members later on, it epitomized the Jesus Movement's pietistic focus on conversion and Christ as a personal savior. Calvary Chapel would also later become a major player in Christian rock forming the record label Maranatha! Music. Maranatha! began with a concentration of Christian rock artists coming out of the Jesus Movement but later turned its focus to praise and worship.

There were many other influential Christian rock bands in the first wave of Christian rock. This era saw rock bands that were directly influenced by the Jesus Movement, such as Agape, who came to epitomize Jesus

---

23. Ibid.

24. Thompson, *Raised by Wolves,* 37.

25. Ibid., 49.

26. Powell, *Encyclopedia of Contemporary Christian Music,* 543.

27. Ibid., 543.

28. Ibid., 544.

29. Ibid.

Music. Coming from another area of the US, Resurrection Band was the musical manifestation of Jesus People U.S.A. (JPUSA), a Christian commune in Chicago. There were also folk bands such as Malcolm & Alwyn and 2nd Chapter of Acts, and new wave rock bands like the prodigious Daniel Amos. By the 1970s, there were Christian hard rock bands like Petra and Jerusalem, who would later be heralded as precursors to Christian metal. Finally, there were famous secular artists creating music from a Christian perspective like Pat Boone, Johnny Cash, and Bob Dylan (more on Dylan in Ch. 3). As the 1970s came to a close, there was an artist who perfectly embodied the passion and convictions of the first wave: Keith Green.

Green was a child prodigy singer/song writer. He signed a major-label deal with Dekka Records in 1965 at the age of twelve after having written more than forty songs.[30] Green was supposed to be a teen star and achieved some success, but his early career fizzled out. He later became a spiritual seeker, dabbling in drugs and spiritual practices ranging from Buddhism to astral projection[31] until 1975 when he and his young wife Melody converted to Christianity. They quickly became involved with the Vineyard Christian Fellowship in Southern California, which began as a more charismatic offshoot of Calvary Chapel.[32] At that point, Green began his music ministry and signed with Sparrow Records.

Green's music was prodigious and passionate. One could hear a hunger in his voice, in both his music and preaching, to reach the lost. He often preached between songs, challenging people in their faith. For instance, right before performing the song "A Billion Starving People," Green once proclaimed,

> Think about how much money you spent on concerts, music, and entertainment last year and compare it with how much you gave to the poor. . . . Becoming a Christian means giving up your desires for His. It means seeing the poor, hungry, and hurting though His eyes. It means committing your material assets to Him in any way that seems right to Him.[33]

In his day, Green was seen as a radical who wore his faith on his sleeve. Thompson writes, "Green became a sort of John the Baptist figure,

---

30. M. Green and Hazard, *No Compromise*, 20.

31. Ibid., 3.

32. Ibid., 88.

33. K. Green, *Make My Life a Prayer*, 222. Green also performed many free concerts, taking up only love offerings as payment.

vehemently calling for Christians to get serious about their faith. He railed against casual or social Christianity and declared that it wouldn't have taken him so long to see the truth of the gospel if Christians had acted like true followers of Christ."[34] Indeed, one of Green's main tasks was to move nominal Christians to a place of fervent faith. In his aptly-titled book *A Cry in the Wilderness*, Green wrote, "Someone once said, 'Everybody wants to go to heaven, but nobody wants to die.' We all want the benefits of God's promises, but we don't want to die to ourselves to get them. Then we wonder why our Christianity seems so blah."[35] Though he was unabashedly Christian, Green was respected by critics in and outside of the Christian realm because of his musical proficiency and genuine approach to faith. Beaujoin sees Green as a transitional figure; the last major Christian artist from the early days of the Jesus Movement who had both critical and popular success. Beaujoin writes, " . . . he was the last significant Christian artist for a long time to be both a critical favorite and a bestseller. After Green, music that some unkind souls call 'Christian mush' began to dominate the Christian mainstream, while a loosely organized underground of misfits began to haunt the corners of the '80s Christian experience."[36] Though Beaujoin may be judging the 1980s a bit unfairly, the second wave of CCM was very different from the first. For us, Green can be seen as a bookend to the first wave, which began with Norman. From Norman to Green there was a shift in agenda. Whereas the early first-wavers responded to secular culture, Green turned his polemical arrow at cultural Christianity.

The Second Wave

Towards the end of the 1970s, conservative evangelicals began to seriously support CCM,[37] which influenced the shape of Christian rock in the 1980s. The passion of the Jesus Movement was suppressed as CCM learned to market itself as a business, resulting in rock bands softening their sound to accommodate more conservative evangelical churches.[38] This went on throughout the 1980s, forming the newly christened "Christian pop scene." As Thompson writes, "By the mid-1980s, the Christian pop scene had be-

34. Thompson, *Raised by Wolves*, 64.

35. K. Green, *A Cry in the Wilderness*, 142.

36. Beaujon, *Body Piercing Saved My Soul*, 27.

37. Thompson, *Raised by Wolves*, 87.

38. Ibid., 87–89.

come a machine that could sell a certain amount of anything, regardless of quality."[39] The concept of what Christian rock can be was regulated in the 1980s by CCM as music that is either about Jesus or about what can be revealed by Jesus.[40] A new status quo developed within CCM, and rock bands had to follow it in order to achieve success. Howard and Streck write,

> . . . if in its earliest days the Christian music industry could perhaps have escaped these difficulties by virtue of its limited scope and scale, the stunning growth of Christian music sales during the 1980s led not only to increases in the scope and scale (as well as profit) of the Christian music industry itself but also to much closer ties between CCM and the larger machine of the mainstream recorded music industry.[41]

The radical and fresh institutions that began with the Jesus Movement, such as Calvary Chapel and Maranatha!, have now become the mainstream. While the first wave of Christian rock saw mainstream success (by Christian music standards), the second wave caused a splintering between CCM and underground Christian rock.

One of the great innovations of the second wave was the formation of the Cornerstone Festival in Illinois. JPUSA (who also formed Resurrection Band in the 1970s) had a vision to create a festival that blended rock music, communal living, and Christian faith.[42] The festival was one of the biggest ongoing annual Christian rock festivals in the world boasting a yearly attendance of 20,000 people. Unfortunately, after 29 years, in 2012, JPUSA had to shut down the festival due to financial deficiency.[43] This festival was a haven for underground and mainstream rock musicians, hosting both CCM artists and underground punk, metal, alternative, and indie acts. It also helped launch the careers of many notable artists such as P.O.D., Sixpence None the Richer, and Eisley, who all played the New Band Showcase at the festival.

Although there were other prominent Christian festivals such as Pennsylvania's Creation Festival, which is the largest Christian festival in the world, and Kentucky's Icthus Festival, which was formed in the 1970s

39. Ibid., 89.
40. Ibid., 93.
41. Howard and Streck, *Apostles of Rock,* 151.
42. Johnston, "Constructing Alternative Christian Identity," 37.
43. Nazworth, "After 29 Years, Cornerstone Festival Comes to a Close."

as a response to Woodstock;[44] Cornerstone was distinctive in important ways. Cornerstone had a more low-key presence then the other festivals and did not require a certain quota of salvations or spiritual recommitments to satisfy sponsors and stakeholders.[45] As Brian Johnston writes,

> JPUSA's event is not structured to 'target' attendees for conversion, recruitment, or recommitments of faith. While there are formalized settings for worship services and conversion testimonies, during which altar calls are part of the performance, these are clearly cited in the festival program, avoiding the bait-and-switch tactics of typical evangelical services.[46]

This made Cornerstone feel more genuine than other CCM-backed events. Johnston's ethnographical study of the Cornerstone Festival shows us how it fit into the larger scope of the American religious experience.[47] Because of its communal approach to Christian spirituality, Johnston claims that Cornerstone helped form a larger and more ethereal sense of identity and community among young Christians.[48] Johnston writes,

> Instead of recruiting or resocializing attendees into traditional, or typical, Christian membership, the festival envisions an alternative trajectory for the 'converted', one that does not fully assimilate, per se, into traditional Christian institutions but rather carves its own self-sustaining niche into the evangelical scene. Indeed, Cornerstone reflects a certain degree of sophistication about socialization as it is organized around a transcendent social phenomenon, rock music.[49]

Cornerstone, in this way, was able to retain the passion and creative spirit of the first wave while adapting to the new commercial climate of the second wave.

Another response to the commercialization and homogenization of CCM was a turn towards secular music. Some Christian artists distanced themselves from CCM, referring to it as a "gospel ghetto."[50] Though CCM initially tried to market to non-Christians as a form of evangelism, their

44. Johnston, "Constructing Alternative Christian Identity," 38.

45. Ibid., 39.

46. Ibid.

47. Ibid., 4.

48. Ibid., 7.

49. Ibid.

50. Howard and Streck, *Apostles of Rock,* 60.

audience ironically became more and more Christian, not because of successful evangelism but because of exclusivist marketing and separationist jargon.[51] Perhaps history's best example of a secular band comprised of Christians is U2. U2 formed in Dublin, Ireland in the late 1970s because three of the members (Bono, The Edge, and Larry Mullen) were part of a charismatic Bible study called the Shalom Group.[52] Bono was baptized in the Irish Sea and dove deep into Christian thought and spirituality. "The Shalom Group," writes Powell, ". . . . encouraged its members to integrate their faith into every aspect of their lives and to find ways of articulating this without being preachy."[53] The fourth member of the band Adam Clayton did not share the faith with the rest. This did not hinder the band, however, because they do not self-identify as a Christian band or as part of CCM. Powell writes,

> Though Christian music fans may have regarded U2 as one of theirs, the group had never given them permission to do so, nor had they ever been a part of any separatist Christian music subculture. All of their albums had been released on a general market label. Bono did not grant interviews to *CCM* or other Christian music magazines. . . . They did not view their music as a vehicle for promoting Christianity, but as art with intrinsic (even spiritual) value of its own.[54]

The band wrote lyrics about whatever was going on in their lives or in the world, and since most of them dealt holistically with spiritual matters, Christian themes became evident in their music.[55] In fact, their early albums *October* (1981) and *War* (1983) were marketed as Christian albums and sold in Christian bookstores.[56] U2 has since avoided CCM's gospel ghetto but has also frustrated some CCM insiders who believe the band does not live according to Christian standards. Beaujon writes, "To this day, many Christian radio stations will play covers of U2 songs by other Christian artists but not by the band itself as the Christianity of its members is considered to be in doubt. The evidence? Bono swears, smokes, and drinks. The band's music often evinces ambiguity about truth . . . and its

51. Ibid., 69.

52. Powell, *Encyclopedia of Contemporary Christian Music*, 978.

53. Ibid., 978.

54. Ibid., 980.

55. Scharen, *One Step Closer*, 179.

56. Powell, *Encyclopedia of Contemporary Christian Music*, 979.

stage shows can play with challenging imagery."[57] Today, U2 is one of the most commercially successful bands of all time.

There were also some second wave CCM artists who crossed over into the mainstream: notably pop star Amy Grant and glam-metal band Stryper. For the purposes of this book, I will only comment on Stryper. California-based heavy metal band Stryper once shared the looks of novelty glam bands with long "big" hair, heavy makeup, and tight yellow and black spandex.[58] Performing throughout the 1980s and 1990s, they were energetic and light-hearted on stage performing songs like "To Hell with the Devil" from their 1986 album of the same name (which went platinum!). They would bring boxes of New Testaments to concerts and toss them out to fans.[59] Stryper is still making music today, but they have toned down their style and lost the makeup and spandex.

Powell refers to Stryper as "the ultimate crossover metal band"[60] because of their mainstream success. According to Powell, over two-thirds of Stryper's album sales came from non-Christians. Unlike U2, however, Stryper was blatant and evangelistic about their faith from the start. Similar to Switchfoot, part of the reason Stryper went mainstream was because of the philosophical issue of calling a band a "Christian band." In an interview, Stryper guitarist/vocalist Michael Sweet said, "We are not a Christian rock band; we are a rock band comprised of Christians."[61] These are similar sentiments to those of Jon Foreman, which we recounted in the beginning of this chapter. Sweet went on to explain, "Some people misinterpret that as saying that I am ashamed of my faith or I am running from my faith. I think the exact opposite. We never ran from our faith, we have always been the most full Christian rock band that is comprised of Christians the whole time. We have never held back a punch."[62] For these artists, the issue is not with Christian-identity, but rather that the description "Christian band" is loaded with CCM pigeonholes. What's more, such a label does not make sense. How can a band be saved? All in all, the second wave of CCM saw the splintering of Christian rock into a "Christian mainstream," a "Christian underground," and a "Christian Crossover." The second wave was far more

---

57. Beaujon, *Body Piercing Saved My Soul,* 36.

58. Powell, *Encyclopedia of Contemporary Christian Music,* 892.

59. Ibid.

60. Ibid.

61. M. Sweet from "Michael Sweet of Sweet & Lynch and Stryper."

62. Ibid.

organized and profitable than the first, but some might argue that it lost the zeal of the Jesus Movement.

The Third Wave and Beyond

Since the CCM juggernaut had already taken root, the third wave was commercially similar to the second wave. However, there was a cultural shift from the 1980s to the 1990s that affected both CCM and rock music in general. The 1990s saw a rebellion against the glam and posh of the 1980s portraying a decidedly grittier aesthetic. The 1990s advanced the catchall term "Alternative Rock" to describe bands that did not fit neatly into the mainstream. Grunge rock also gained popularity as a genre, especially with bands like Nirvana, Soundgarden, and Pearl Jam. Grunge perfectly embodied the disenfranchised attitude of the 1990s slacker. This new aesthetic initially left CCM without a response. For the first time, CCM had difficulty finding a Christian expression of the fringe music that was on display. Thompson writes, " . . . when Nirvana and Nine Inch Nails became mainstream, youth pastors across the country simultaneously convulsed. Suddenly, the church's irrelevance was staring them in the face as their own youth became increasingly pierced, tattooed, and successfully wooed by the machinations of the entertainment industry."[63] The underground Christian rock scene gained popularity in the 1990s while mainstream CCM rock bands like dc Talk, Audio Adrenaline, The Newsboys, and Jars of Clay thrived. Bands like dc Talk were able to adapt to the cultural changes. For instance, dc Talk became noticeably heavier with their fourth studio album *Jesus Freak* (1995), shifting from an eclectic pop/hip hop sound, to an equally eclectic pop/rock sound. Similarly, Jars of Clay fully assumed the mid-90s alternative rock sound with their 1995 self-titled debut album. While these bands were influential, achieving both critical and commercial success, the biggest change for Christian rock in the third wave was the distribution of fringe underground bands to the general public.

Entrepreneur Brandon Ebel founded the California-based Tooth & Nail Records in 1993. Tooth & Nail gained quick notoriety signing a stylistic mixture of bands, including Focused, Joy Electric, Starflyer 59, and Sometime Sunday, but they struck gold with the Washington-based pop-punk band MxPx.[64] MxPx signed with Tooth & Nail while its members

63. Thompson, *Raised by Wolves*, 172.
64. Ibid., 176.

were still in high school and gained immediate popularity with Christian and mainstream audiences by developing a pop-punk sound similar to Green Day and Blink 182.[65] In 1997 Tooth & Nail created a subsidiary label named Solid State Records that would exclusively release hardcore and metal music. This sub-label quickly became a huge success, eventually releasing about thirty albums a year.[66] In the following decades Tooth & Nail and Solid State would produce albums for some of the world's trendiest and best-known Christian rock and hardcore bands such as Underoath, Demon Hunter, Blindside, Hawk Nelson, Copeland, August Burns Red, P.O.D., mewithoutYou, Anberlin, and Pedro the Lion. These bands were able to gain notoriety in both Christian and secular arenas. Ebel began Tooth & Nail to create a safe place for artists with similar beliefs. He did not believe that the term "Christian rock" made much sense but believed that Christian music, if one must use the term, should refer to music that comes from a shared belief system.[67] Perhaps this philosophy, coupled with cutting-edge production, allowed Tooth & Nail/Solid State bands to flourish in the secular realm. At any rate, the third wave saw a wider variety of rock bands gain popularity. As Thompson suggests, "One of the main distinctions about the third wave of Christian rock is that more rock bands sold over 200,000 units in the 1990s than adult contemporary bands did. Several factors coalesced to bring rock to the fore in the 1990s, but perhaps the most important were retail and radio."[68] Much of this can be attributed to Ebel and Tooth & Nail Records.

If the different "waves" of Christian rock were separated by decades, then the 2000s and 2010s would be the fourth and fifth waves, but there was more continuity in Christian rock and CCM after the third wave. Labels continued producing and marketing music, and bands persisted in one of the fractured streams of Christian rock. Thus, it is not useful to divide the contemporary Christian rock scene in further waves. Today, there are still polished CCM rock bands like Tenth Avenue North, Third Day, and Big Daddy Weave, underground bands like Haste the Day, Emery, and The Almost, and crossover bands like Switchfoot, Flyleaf, and Relient K. There does not seem to be any change coming concerning the splintered nature of Christian rock. An additional phenomenon in Christian rock developed

65. Ibid., 177.

66. Ibid., 176.

67. Beaujon, *Body Piercing Saved My Soul*, 70.

68. Thompson, *Raised by Wolves*, 196.

during the first wave with artists like Keith Green and has become a major contributor to Christian rock today. That phenomenon is contemporary worship music.

Since the 1990s, worship music has become a mainstay in CCM. Beaujon describes worship music as, " . . . Christian music, and it's rock music, but, confusingly, it's not quite the same thing as Christian rock. Most good-size evangelical churches have their own worship bands, which lead the congregation in a sort of amplified folk mass."[69] As Maranatha! and Vineyard Music began putting out praise and worship records throughout the 1980s, other independent and church ministry-based groups began gaining popularity as well. Australian Pentecostal worship leader Darlene Zschech of Hillsong Church became world-renowned with her hit song "Shout to the Lord" from the album *People Just Like Us* (1993). Hillsong Church also spawned Hillsong United, a band of talented worship leaders who began as the worship leaders of the church's youth group. Similar charismatic/Pentecostal ministries such as Jesus Culture and Bethel Music hail from the States, and independent worship bands such as Crowder and Unhindered write and perform many of the songs sung in contemporary church services all over the world. The new wave of Christian rock can thus be classified as a continuation of the third wave with a new emphasis on the development and marketing of high quality worship music. After looking at the history of Christian rock in corresponding waves, we can now look at how Christian rock engages our broader culture.

The Parallel Universe of Christian Rock

CCM has created a sort of parallel universe for Christians interested in pop culture. Because of the staggering amount of CCM artists, Christians can get by listening to only a few stations and still have a diverse musical experience. The Jesus music of the 1960s and 1970s began as something countercultural, offering people not only a chance to listen to music that was often dogmatic and evangelistic, but also in dialogue with the broader surrounding culture. When CCM gained steam as its own market, however, the scene morphed into a parallel universe, a succinct culture within a broader culture, rather than a counterculture critiquing the dominant culture. This notion invariably raises the question, "is Christian rock really rock?" CCM as a parallel universe does not meet the four criteria of rock

69. Beaujon, *Body Piercing Saved My Soul,* 151.

set out in chapter one. It seems that CCM's marketing and agenda created something entirely new and different from rock, and it will take a transformational Christian rock band to recover the countercultural characteristic found in rock music.

In his book *Body Piercing Saved My Life*, Andrew Beaujon, a self-avowed agnostic, offers a fair, and often humorous, account of the Christian rock subculture from an outsider's perspective. Beaujoin was fascinated by the idea that Christian rock formed as a response to popular culture. He writes, "I felt there was something so quintessentially American about the idea of religious people creating an alternate version of popular culture. If nothing else, Christian music, as has been noted by better critics than myself, exists in a parallel universe."[70] Today, one can become immersed in CCM in order to avoid general market rock. This contradicts the evangelistic notion of letting Christian rock speak to the broader rock and roll culture. Moreover, it changes the type of transformation that a theology in conversation with Christian rock would be able to bring about. Does CCM have any earthly kingdom to talk to? To whom does it tell its story and to what effect? A transformational theology of rock will need to avoid these separationist CCM trappings in order to truly engage the world in meaningful dialogue.

There are some notable differences between the broader rock and roll culture discussed in the last chapter and Christian rock culture. Unlike the general market, controversy disrupts CCM album sales. Many fans think that by buying music from a CCM artist, they are supporting a ministry. So when controversies arise, the fans feel cheated as partners in ministry. In this way, CCM fans are not just buying music but are buying into an artist's ministry. Also, as Beaujoin points out, sex does not sell in CCM. Since CCM is based on a Christian ethical system, Christian rock opposes the overt sexuality found in rock and roll culture. Beaujoin writes, "The merest hint of sexuality, so central to the mythology of rock 'n' roll, will derail an artist's career."[71] Christian rock is thus sonically akin to general market rock but does not boast a Dionysian predisposition. Rock music is countercultural and subversive, and while Christian rock follows this trend, it does not pick up the character of rock music wholesale. Christian rock rebels against different aspects of the dominant culture, sometimes alongside general market rock, and other times in the face of it. For instance, Christian

70. Ibid., 6.

71. Ibid., 175.

rock might not only speak out against wars and greedy consumerism *with* mainstream rock, but also against partying and sexual immorality *despite* mainstream rock's endorsement of such actions. Even though Christian rock speaks the language of rock, it tells a different story.

These differences represent the difficulties a Christian rock band might face figuring out what it means to be, " . . . in the world but not of the world."[72] The parallel universe of Christian rock seems to, at times, suffer from an identity crisis. CCM music wants to be conversant as a part of mainstream music, while simultaneously being set apart. Ideologically, this has caused some tension as to what Christian rock's function in culture should be. As one might expect, Christian rock bands have dealt with these issues differently, so for the remainder of this chapter, I would like to explore how those involved in Christian rock have negotiated the tensions that come with cultural engagement.

Christ & Rock Culture

In his memorable 1951 book *Christ & Culture*, theologian H. Richard Niebuhr sets out to identify the different ways Christians live in the world by constructing a typology of five different responses a Christian might have when engaging his or her culture. Niebuhr never advocates for a particular position. Instead, he presents a sociological account that highlights the differences and similarities of each position.

According to Niebuhr, there are five main types of Christian ethics that demonstrate how a Christian should behave in the world.[73] The two polls of the cultural-engagement spectrum are set by the New Law Type, which he calls "Christ Against Culture," and the Natural Law Type, which he calls "Christ of Culture."[74] The Christ Against Culture type extends the idea that Christian morality stands against that of culture. There is the law of God and the law of the world, and each forges a different path in the world. The outside culture of the world intrinsically opposes the law of God and must therefore be avoided. Niebuhr writes, "The tendency in exclusive Christianity is to confine the commandments of loyalty to Christ, of love of God and neighbor, to the fellowship of Christians."[75] Thus, when Christians

72. This phrase is a popular expression derived from John 15:19.

73. H. Niebuhr, *Christ & Culture*, xli.

74. Ibid., xliii-xlv.

75. Ibid., 71.

live in the world but not of the world, they do so by creating a community in opposition of the world. Conversely, the Christ of Culture type maintains that Christ belongs in culture as the Christ who enters into a person's world, offering infinite meaning to his or her temporal actions and obligations.[76] Adherents of this type, " . . . seek to understand the transcendent realm as continuous in time or character with the present life."[77] Just as Christ Against Culture can be critiqued for being separationalist and exclusive, Christ of Culture can be seen as consisting of honorific, yet non-affective agents in the world.[78]

Niebuhr asserts, however, that many theorists in cultural history cannot be wholly associated with either of these camps and must fall somewhere in the middle. While these "median types" vary in approach, they all share the conviction that ethical values are negotiated from two points of view, the church's values and culture's values. If this is the case, one cannot simply interpret one through the other.[79] These views all hold that, " . . . divine imperatives come through two mediators, Christ (Bible, church) and nature (reason, culture)."[80] Niebuhr refers to the Architectonic Type as "Christ Above Culture," the Oscillatory Type as "Christ and Culture in Paradox," and the Conversionist Type as "Christ Transforming Culture."[81] Christ Above Culture is a Thomistic position that asserts that culture is God's and is fundamentally good. Christian revelation, however, perfects culture and the Church because Christ reigns highest above both.[82] Thus, it is the Christian's task to use culture to his or her advantage while avoiding its negative influences.[83] Christ and Culture in Paradox basically asserts that Christians must navigate these two differing streams in conjunction with each other even as culture is often in tension with God's law.[84] This dualist position recognizes that God still sustains the world and its culture; otherwise, the world would cease to exist. As such, Christians must be cognizant of the fact that they live in a grey and broken world, and

---

76. Ibid., 93.

77. Ibid., 84.

78. Ibid., 107.

79. Ibid., xlix.

80. Ibid., xlix.

81. Ibid., li-liii.

82. Ibid., 121.

83. Ibid., 128.

84. Ibid., 155.

must, therefore, discern their ethics within culture, keeping what is good and rejecting what is evil.[85] The third and final medial position is Christ Transforming Culture. This view also sees the world as good, but fallen. Since God is bringing transformation to the world, Christians must take up this task and work alongside Christ in transforming culture for the glory of God.[86] A conversionist Christian's Christology refers to Christ as, " . . . the Redeemer more than the giver of a new law."[87] There is an eschatological function in Christ Transforming Culture because the people of God work together to usher in the eschaton, at which time culture is transformed and made new. These five views are types but not canon. They are helpful for us to understand the different ways Christians engage culture, but they are not comprehensive and do have room for modification. In fact, much cultural engagement likely falls into more than one category, making exceptions to the rules along the way. Nevertheless, Niebuhr's typology gives us a good starting point for understanding Christian engagement of culture and how it is plays out in Christian rock.

For the past fifty years since the publication of *Christ & Culture*, scholars have applied Niebuhr's typology to different cultural arenas.[88] Of particular interest to our study is Jay Howard and John Streck's book *Apostles of Rock*, where the authors appropriate Niebuhr's typology to Christian contemporary music. Howard and Streck argue that CCM has not only developed its own artworld but is also fractured.[89] As recounted earlier in this chapter, the Jesus Movement was the genesis of a new genre of music that would subsequently veer off in different directions. These divergent paths represent different ideologies on how CCM should engage the world. Howard and Streck identify three different approaches of cultural engagement by CCM: separational, integrational, and transformational.

The separational approach is likened to Niebuhr's Christ Against Culture and views CCM as an evangelistic ministry. Howard and Streck write that

85. Ibid., 156.

86. Ibid., 195.

87. Ibid., 190.

88. For example James Cone put black theology in dialogue with Niebuhr's typology in Cone, *God of the Oppressed*, and Leonard Sweet critiques and modifies Niebuhr's approach and appropriates it for postmodern church culture in L. Sweet, *The Church in Emerging Culture*. Others have tried to reevaluate Niebuhr's premises in a more contemporary climate. See Carter, *Christ and Culture*; Carson, *Christ and Culture Revisited*; and Stassen, Yeager, and Yoder, *Authentic Transformation*.

89. Howard and Streck, *Apostles of Rock*, 15–16.

separational Christians are, " . . . by virtue of their faith set off and apart from the rest of world. The emphasis is on difference and on the behaviors that mark those differences."[90] The separational approach seeks first and foremost to evangelize through music. The Jesus Movement had a dispensational[91] eschatological bent and urgently pursued conversions through creative means as they anticipated the second coming, but as Howard and Streck point out, the CCM audience of separational music grew to comprise mostly evangelical listeners.[92] Thus, the evangelism of separational music was, ironically, not evangelistic at all, as most of their efforts were spent preaching to the choir. Consequently the separational approach later turned toward praise and worship music, creating music that would aid Christian ministry and further establish a separationist culture.[93] The separational approach to rock had an important place in early Christian rock, but in our increasingly pluralistic society, this approach is no longer as affective.

Howard and Streck's next category, integrational CCM, is consistent with Niebuhr's Christ of Culture type. This approach to CCM sees recording artists defining themselves as Christians in a band rather than as a Christian band.[94] This attitude is similar to that expressed by Jon Foreman and Michael Sweet earlier in this chapter, but integrational artists also choose not to write explicitly Christian lyrics.[95] Instead, integrational artists prefer to let their Christian worldview subtly speak through their music.[96] In this way, Foreman's music might be considered integrational, but Sweet's would not because it is so kerygmatic.[97] Howard and Streck write, "Niebuhr argues that this approach is generally ineffective in converting the unbelieving to Christ. For Integrational CCM artists, however, this latter issue is somewhat beside the point. They enter the marketplace not as ministers or evangelists but as entertainers."[98] While separational CCM artists

90. Ibid., 49–50.

91. Dispensationalism is an interpretive system of the Bible that divides history into seven periods or dispensations. It typically subscribes to a premillennial eschatology, which sees Christ's millennial reign following the tribulation as the eighth dispensation.

92. Howard and Streck, *Apostles of Rock,* 60.

93. Ibid., 61.

94. Ibid., 81.

95. Ibid., 82.

96. Beaujon, *Body Piercing Saved My Soul,* 53.

97. *Kerygma* is a Greek word used in the New Testament to describe Christian proclamation.

98. Howard and Streck, *Apostles of Rock,* 83.

see themselves as ministers, integrational CCM artists see themselves as entertainers.

Howard and Streck's third category, transformational CCM, comprises Niebuhr's medial types because each of these takes a nuanced approach to Christian cultural engagement. Unlike separational and integrational CCM artists, transformational CCM artists approach their music as art.[99] These *avant garde* CCM artists (to use Jay Howard's word) often critique the world and the church as they explore what it means to be Christians in a broken world.[100] Transformational artists are not reductionistic when it comes to tough cultural issues but explore the complexities in open and honest ways. Howard and Streck write, "In attempting to present a picture of Christianity that includes the brokenness of life after the fall (if at the same time offering glimpses of hope amid the rubble), transformational artists risk being marginalized by a Christian music industry dominated by the separational view, which prefers clear-cut answers over hard questions."[101] Transformational CCM artists are not only focused on what to say in their music like separational artists, but also on how to say it and on the appropriate context in which to say it.[102] This is because transformational artists view their music as expression (making one's thoughts and feelings known) rather than communication (exchanging information or views).[103] Expression is the first-order, affective utterance of communication whereas communication itself involves the exchange of considered ideas. Instead of the judgmental didacticism of separational CCM, the expressive focus of transformational CCM allows artists to testify of their own experiences. It is this sort of ministry, and precisely because it is not intentionally perceived as one, which is effective in a post-Christendom West.

Since we have considered the history and mission of Christian rock, we can now begin to look at how the different genres of rock have engaged the world in their own way. Before doing this, however, I would like to express the basis of a transformational theology of rock. One of the main theses of this book is that different rock genres approach the world in different ways, which cause them to embrace particular theological motifs in distinctively. Thus, the following section will outline the foundation that

99. Ibid., 112.

100. Howard, "Contemporary Christian Music," 129.

101. Howard and Streck, *Apostles of Rock,* 119.

102. Ibid., 128.

103. Ibid., 134.

runs through the subsequent chapters, and these unifying theological commitments will be expressed as we go on.

Towards a Transformational Theology of Rock

Although not directly indicated, it is heavily implied by the authors above
that the most appropriate way for Christians to engage culture is through
what Howard and Streck call transformational CCM and what Neibuhr
referred to as the median types. In other words, Christians would do well
to avoid the extremes of radical enculturation and radical separation when
engaging culture. The median types not only offer an approach to cultural
engagement that is not only sensitive to the ethical ambiguity found in
today's cultural artifacts but also takes seriously the notion that healthy
dialogue comes only when the participants are gracious and open. Not everything in the world is bad, and nothing in the world is all good. Only God
as love itself is objectively good, true, and beautiful. We are all meander-
ing in the world operating from our own subjective perceptions.[104] As such,
Christians make mistakes, and since the Holy Spirit is the cosmic Spirit
drawing all people towards Christ in a prevenient grace, God's goodness
can be found everywhere, even if in limited order. The task for a transformational theology of rock, therefore, is to tease out the good and true
found in *all* rock and roll. What I call the good and true will then become
the touchstones and catalysts for dialogue. They will not only frame the
narrative but will also allow the conversation to turn towards the gospel.
Rock music does not need to be seen simply as a tool for evangelism. This
is a cheap gimmick. Everyone can sense the duplicitous nature of such bait
and switch tactics. Instead, rock music, seen through a transformational
lens, can become fertile ground for fruitful dialogue. From this soil can
spring deep theological reflection. Jesus said in Matt. 7:7–8, " . . . knock and
the door will be opened. . . . " A transformational theology of rock creates
the space for seekers to seek without judgment or proselytism.

As we saw in chapter one, the kingdom of God is already here, expanding and transforming culture as history draws nearer to the eschaton.
Niebuhr writes,

> The kingdom of God is transformed culture, because it is first
> of all the conversion of the human spirit from faithlessness and

104. Westphal, *Whose Community? Which Interpretation?*, 74.

self-service to the knowledge and service of God. This kingdom
is real, for if God did not rule nothing would exist; and if He has
not heard the prayer for the coming of the kingdom, the world of
mankind would long ago have become a den of robbers. Every
moment and period is an eschatological present, for in every moment men are dealing with God.[105]

The duty of the Christian is to take up this ministry of transformation and
work alongside the Holy Spirit to bring redemption and transformation to
the world. This will not come about through separation from the world, nor
will it come through entire enculturation. Instead, sensitive and intentional
engagement will provide space in which transformation can occur. The
common ground between rock music and theological thought stems from
rock music's characteristics discussed in the last chapter. Rock is countercultural, identity forming, communal, and transformational. While this
transformational theology of rock is a prolegomena to deeper theological
speculation, one can utilize these same characteristics as a starting point for
theological reflection. After all, theologies are themselves identity forming
and communal and often carry a prophetic countercultural and transformative attitude. No matter which genre the bands emulate, Christian rock
should always offer hope to people living in a grey world.

So far we have tracked the nature of rock and roll, with an emphasis
on Christian rock, since its genesis. We have also explored ways in which
Christians and rock bands can engage culture. We also outlined the prolegomena for a transformational theology of rock in order to craft a foundation for the rest of the book, which explores the way particular genres of
rock approach the world existentially and theologically. It is to this task that
we now turn.

---

105. H. Niebuhr, *Christ & Culture*, 229.

3

The Wisdom of Folk Rock

C onsider these two poetic utterances about the cyclical and capricious
nature of life and existence:

> *Hands wither in time*
> *But we cannot stop the branch of the vine.*
> *Days that will come*
> *And nights that have gone*
> *Are washed in the tides*
> *And cast in the brine.*[1]

> *All streams run to the sea,*
> *but the sea is not full;*
> *to the place where streams flow,*
> *there they flow again.*
> *All things are full of weariness;*
> *a man cannot utter it;*
> *the eye is not satisfied with seeing,*
> *nor the ear filled with hearing.*
> *What has been is what will be,*
> *And what has been done is what will be done,*
> *and there is nothing new under the sun.*[2]

1. Musée Mécanique, "Cast in the Brine."
2. Ecclesiastes 1:7–9. ESV.

These passages both carry similar traits. Both discuss the fickleness of time and the prospect of seasons and generations coming to an end only to begin again. Both have an air of pensiveness dealing with the issues of being and belonging. The difference, however, is that the first passage comprises lyrics from a song titled "Cast in the Brine" from the album *From Shores of Sleep* (2015) by the Oregon-based folk rock band Musée Mécanique, and the latter passage was written by Qoheleth millennia ago and is found in the book of Ecclesiastes. It appears to me that the biblical wisdom tradition approaches deep spiritual and existential issues in a way that is analogous to the genre of folk rock.

In this chapter I would like to submit that contemporary folk rock music, stemming back from its inception in the 1960s and the prevailing influence of Bob Dylan, approaches the hard spiritual issues of life in a fashion consonant to the writers of the biblical wisdom tradition. Drawing from the work of David Penchansky and William Brown, I argue that *folk rock artists, like wisdom tradition writers, revel in the wonder and dissonance of diverging truths.* Rather than force-feeding prescriptive agendas and supplying answers, folk rock artists are prone to soliciting questions. This is carried out in order to draw the listener into deeper levels of social and existential contemplation. The writers of the wisdom tradition follow a similar *modus operandi*, which is evident in the conflicting messages and anecdotes sometimes found side by side in the Hebrew texts.

I will investigate both the musical genre and the biblical tradition and then excavate the connections. I will begin the chapter by looking at the nature and character of the biblical wisdom tradition. I will then survey folk rock as a genre with a particular emphasis on Bob Dylan's music. I will also look at the contemporary landscape of indie folk to trace the subsequent lineage of the genre. Finally, I will draw out the pertinent connections of folk rock and wisdom literature to show how folk rock's propensity towards faith in the midst of struggle aids our transformational theology of rock. I will contextualize my theological reflections by displaying examples of Christian folk rock artists such as Gungor and John Mark McMillan that fit squarely within such a theological framework.

Wonder and Dissonance in Wisdom Literature

Among the most perplexing books of the Bible are those that fit into the wisdom tradition. The wisdom books of the Old Testament (namely Job,

Proverbs, and Ecclesiastes) deal with big theological and existential issues and often draw conflicting conclusions. No other biblical genre shows so much diversity of perspective. William Brown cleverly remarks, "If the wisdom corpus were a choir, melodious harmony would not be its forte. Dissonance would resound at almost every chord."[3] Wisdom is also a universal genre as the teachings found in the text can be applied timelessly and cross-culturally without having to jump through many hermeneutical loops. Although the wisdom corpus comes from a Hebrew tradition, it conspicuously avoids any mention of the events of Israel's history or the law, which the Jews so fervently abided by.[4] In fact, there is nothing uniquely Jewish or Christian about the wisdom corpus.[5] David Penchansky writes that the authors " . . . did not intend their writing for Israel only. It was meant for all people and for all time. It was not meant for Israel in particular, so the first three books scarcely give a hint of the authors' own national identity."[6] These books expound advice and reflection that draw readers from any historical or geographical position into deeper spiritual and existential contemplation.[7] Furthermore, there is enough influence from the other cultures to suggest that the sages were not concerned with syncretism the way the law books and the prophets were.[8] These features give wisdom a unique focus in the Bible.

Grant Osborne defines the four characteristics of wisdom literature as having 1) a practical orientation, 2) an emphasis on depending on God, 3) indirect authority, and 4) a creational theology.[9] Wisdom bears a practical orientation and is shared with the young in order to uphold societal mores.[10] For example, Proverbs was intended for the edification of youth so that they would direct their passions towards seeking wisdom rather than material desires (Pro 1:2–4). Job and Ecclesiastes, however, were designed for more profound intellectual engagement as they deal with deep issues like theodicy and the meaning of existence.[11] Nevertheless, the books are

---

3. Brown, *Wisdom's Wonder,* 3.

4. Ibid., 3.

5. Ibid.

6. Penchansky, *Understanding Wisdom Literature,* 12.

7. Priest, "Humanism, Skepticism, and Pessimism in Israel," 325.

8. Osborne, *The Hermeneutical Spiral,* 255.

9. Ibid., 243.

10. Ibid.

11. Brown, *Wisdom's Wonder,* 186.

written in a practical manner and deal with everyday issues. Because wisdom literature was inscribed primarily to be studied and recited, the books are composed of pithy sayings and quips.[12]

Although there is nothing distinctively Jewish about the wisdom corpus, there is a recurring theme of dependence on God. Osborne writes, "The many variables and paradoxes faced in life forced the wise person to recognize his limitations and depend on God as the true source of wisdom."[13] This seems to be Qoheleth's (the author and/or narrator of Ecclesiastes) final position after struggling with the concept of purpose in a seemingly meaningless world (Ecc 12:9–13). Qoheleth was speaking to an "achievement-driven, entrepreneurial society,"[14] urging his readers to be freed from obsessions of grandeur and striving. Rather, one should be filled with the fear and wonder that comes from wisdom.[15] Closely related to the dependence of God is the recurring theme of the fear of God. The *fear* of God in the wisdom corpus is the " . . . awe-filled and awful wonder of God."[16] God does not elicit horror to the wisdom writers but does illicit a sense of terror. Fear in this context is more akin to the Kantian notion of the sublime. Immanuel Kant differentiates the sublime from the beautiful in that they elicit different sensitivities from the perceiver. Kant writes,

> The beautiful in nature concerns the form of the object, which consists in limitation; the sublime, by contrast, is to be found in a formless object insofar as limitlessness is represented in it, or at its instance, and yet it is also thought as a totality: so that the beautiful seems to be taken as the presentation of an indeterminate concept of the understanding, but the sublime as that of a similar concept of reason.[17]

Things do not possess sublimity as a characteristic, but rather the feeling of sublimity is the rational response to the grandness or might of a thing. For instance, if one were to stand overseeing the vastness of the Grand Canyon, s/he would likely be overwhelmed by the greatness of the canyon. The viewer would not be overcome by its beauty but by its overbearing immensity. When God told Job about the behemoth and the leviathan (Job

---

12. Osborne, *The Hermeneutical Spiral*, 253.

13. Ibid., 244.

14. Brown, *Wisdom's Wonder*, 182.

15. Ibid., 183.

16. Ibid., 20.

17. Kant, *Critique of the Power of Judgment*, 128.

40–41), it was not merely to boast but to restore Job's fear of the Lord. The wisdom writers see God as vast and great. God is mysterious and cannot be fully taken in. God is sublime.

Since the wisdom corpus is committed to passing down practical advice to subsequent generations, it seems that God's authority may be displaced by human experience and observations. After all, the name of YHWH never becomes the source of wisdom in the Hebrew texts. Penchansky writes that the Hebrew sages "reminded the rest of the Israelites that other peoples, not only Israelites, had wisdom and could read the 'book' of nature."[18] Penchansky makes the point that Ben Sira, the writer of the apocryphal book Sirach, was the first person to merge wisdom with the law and the prophets.[19] The Greek wisdom literature of the Apocrypha places God as the authority of wisdom instead of experience and observation. Osborne, however, argues that YHWH's authority is presupposed in the wisdom corpus. God is the indirect authority of the wisdom literature as intrinsic truths are uncovered by God, tradition, and experience.[20]

Finally, Osborne says that wisdom literature bears a creational theology. Creation theology focuses on the order of life, and this is, for instance, at the heart of Job.[21] Humans might find their proper place in creation rather than question the Creator when something seems wrong. The wisdom perspective on creation harkens back to the fear of the Lord, maintaining one must trust that God created the world properly and has ordered everything appropriately. Humans cannot comprehend the divine order and must, therefore, obligingly submit to God's superior wisdom.[22] Job's answer to the problem of evil is actually not a philosophical theodicy. Job seeks for reasons for his misfortunes, but after tarrying with God, he decides to trust God even despite the misfortunes that he does not understand. This is submission to God's wisdom and a true display of the fear of the Lord.

As Osborne outlines the four characteristics of wisdom literature, Brown argues that the epistemological foundation of the wisdom corpus could be summed up as "the wonder of the Other."[23] Brown defines wonder as " . . . an emotion born of awe that engenders a perpetually atten-

---

18. Penchansky, *Understanding Wisdom Literature*, 93–94.

19. Ibid., 93.

20. Osborne, *The Hermeneutical Spiral*, 246.

21. Ibid.

22. Ibid., 247.

23. Brown, *Wisdom's Wonder*, 20.

tive, reverently receptive orientation toward the Other by awakening both emotional and cognitive resources for contemplation and conduct—in short, for wisdom." Wonder contains the elements of perplexity and disconcerted curiosity.[24] Wonder occasions the fear of God as it facilitates inquiry and comprehension in times of crisis and awe. Brown writes, "Wonder . . . oscillates freely between experiences of order and novelty, between fear and fascination."[25] The paradox of wonder is that it often leads not only to a fearful "receptivity of the Other" but also to a desire to know the Other.[26] Wonder therefore incites an openness to what wisdom will reveal. The wisdom writers do not begin their books with trite solutions to big problems, but rather explicate the problems in all their cruelty in order to observe and uncover answers.

Penchansky states that the key to understanding wisdom literature is to acknowledge the wisdom writer's openness and doubt concerning theological issues.[27] For instance, Hebrew wisdom initially claims that God governs the universe fairly and establishes moral principles of wisdom in the hearts of created beings. Job, however, experiences something totally different, and the book sees Job wrestling with the problem of evil and the principles of retribution.[28] How can a good and just God allow an innocent man's suffering? The book of Job ends with Job submitting to God despite his lack of understanding, and God's aversion to the problem of evil. Wisdom literature does not give tidy answers to deep issues, but rather explores the deep issues in order to find contentment. The wisdom writers are happy to revel in the dissonance of conflicting answers and messages, not because they relish obliviousness, but rather because they know that some things in life are mysterious and ultimately insoluble.

Instead of blindly accepting the way things are, the wisdom writers find solace in the exploration. As such, we can often find contradictory voices in a single book. The book of Ecclesiastes, for instance, bears three distinct voices. While Qoheleth, or "preacher," is the writer of Ecclesiastes, Penchansky claims that there are three distinct Qoheleth's in the text. The first voice is the "Pessimistic Qoheleth."[29] This is the voice that begins the

24. Ibid.

25. Ibid., 21.

26. Ibid., 23.

27. Penchansky, *Understanding Wisdom Literature*, 96.

28. Ibid., 48.

29. Ibid., 51.

book stating, "Vanity of vanities, says the Teacher (Qoheleth), vanity of vanities! All is vanity. What do people gain from all the toil at which they toil under the sun?" (Ecc 1:2–3). This is a capricious voice that questions the meaning of life. Berger likens this Qoheleth to the absurdist existentialism of Albert Camus and Lev Shestov.[30] According to Berger, " . . . all three see an unnegotiable gap between our desire for the world to provide us with meaning and that which the inverse is willing to supply."[31] The first Qoheleth is interested in the purpose of his own existence in a seemingly chaotic world.

The second voice is the "Fear God Qoheleth."[32] This voice is consistent with the fear of God motif that was discussed earlier in this chapter. Shrouded in practical advice, Qoheleth maintains the necessity of fearing God. Ecclesiastes 7:16–19 states, "Do not be too righteous, and do not act too wise; why should you destroy yourself? Do not be too wicked, and do not be a fool; why should you die before your time? It is good that you should take hold of the one, without letting go of the other; for the one who fears God shall succeed with both." This Qoheleth seeks to find God's handiwork in the practical customs of life.

Finally, the third voice is the "Enjoy Life Qoheleth."[33] This Qoheleth urges the reader to find joy in the simple pleasures of life. The famous verse Ecclesiastes 8:15 takes its cue from the "Enjoy Life Qoheleth." The verse states, "So I commend enjoyment, for there is nothing better for people under the sun than to eat, and drink, and enjoy themselves, for this will go with them in their toil through the days of life that God gives them under the sun." The main idea here is that God has granted us a good life, so we should enjoy it.

In the book of Ecclesiastes, these three voices oppose each other and fight for interpretive dominance. Some scholars, however, argue that these differing voices actually come from the same narrator and implied author.[34] They claim part of the nature of the wisdom tradition is to portray inner dialogue and the difficulties that surround certain issues. Regardless if there is one implied author or several, each voice takes the experiences of life and draws different conclusions. Penchansky trusts the

---

30. Berger, "Qohelet and the Exigencies of the Absurd," 143.

31. Ibid.

32. Penchansky, *Understanding Wisdom Literature*, 51.

33. Ibid., 51.

34. Bartholomew, *Ecclesiastes*, 79.

Pessimistic Qoheleth as the more authentic voice,[35] but perhaps, the point is to take these differing views together and bask in the dissonance of the voices. Berger writes,

> . . . contradiction seems to guide the thematic concerns of the text. Some scholars have taken the contradictions in the book of Qohelet as an opportunity to flex their exegetical muscles either by forcing all contradictions into tenuous union or simply carving up the text. I have maintained . . . that contradiction is an integral component of the message of the book.[36]

It is this conflict and contradiction that is somehow cathartic for the sufferers. All humans struggle, no matter what religious affiliation. The wisdom corpus does a good job of recognizing that human experience is human experience regardless of context. As wisdom crosses cultures and times, we can all learn from each other. The Hebrew sages were cross-cultural and universal in ideology. However, the later Greek wisdom books, namely Sirach and the Wisdom of Solomon, subsumed all wisdom under the law.[37] This took away wisdom's mystery, and its ability to cope and revel in unanswerable dissonance. The Greek writers were nationalistic, and this gave the formerly universal wisdom a totally Jewish identity.[38] The beauty of wisdom was best seen in the Jewish books. While we don't always have the answers, we can talk about these big problems and empathize with each other. I believe this sapiential persona is akin to folk rock's distinctiveness. Next we will trace the origins and appeal of folk rock in order to see how it too explores life's big questions in fear and wonder.

Bob Dylan and the Wisdom of Folk Rock

The 1950s saw a revival of folk music in the US. According to Simon Frith, this revival would form a community that was " . . . bound by its attitude to music-making itself."[39] The folk clubs would allow anyone to stand up and perform, dissolving the separation of performer and listener.[40] Folk music

---

35. Penchansky, *Understanding Wisdom Literature*, 62.

36. Berger, "Qohelet and the Exigencies of the Absurd," 161.

37. Penchansky, *Understanding Wisdom Literature*, 93.

38. Ibid., 111.

39. Frith, "The Magic That Can Set Your Free," 162.

40. Ibid.

was a form of political propaganda, which sought to entreat solidarity among its listeners to elicit organized responses to civil issues.[41] The political climate in folk music came as a response to the great wars and the anxiety of the Red Scare of the McCarthy era.[42] By the mid-1960s, however, the ideology of these folk communities began to shift to individual discontent with social issues rather than corporate commonality. This helped give rise to the folk rock genre that would emerge around 1965. Frith writes, "The criteria of sincerity began to shift from raw signs to marks of artifice; the resulting separation of artist and audience was confirmed by the development of folk-rock."[43] Bob Dylan would play an integral role to the rise of folk rock as a genre, and his poetic sensibilities are akin to that of the wisdom writers.

In the early 1960s, Bob Dylan was deemed the voice of his generation.[44] Some of his first songs such as "Blowing in the Wind," and "The Times They Are A-Changin'," demark Dylan as a social commentator speaking out against war, violence, and racism.[45] For instance in "The Times They Are A-Changin'" Dylan attempts at an anthem-like declaration that one must be abreast with cultural changes. The lyrics state:

> Come gather 'round people
> Wherever you roam
> And admit that the waters
> Around you have grown
> And accept it that soon
> You'll be drenched to the bone
> If your time to you is worth savin'
> Then you better start swimmin' or you'll sink like a stone
> For the times they are a-changin'[46]

Such lyrics caused Dylan's followers to view him as a spokesperson for an up and coming, socially conscious, American generation. To this end, Krein and Levin write, "Dylan's voice has served as a conscience to the collective soul of America—pointing out injustices we have committed and flaws in

41. Ibid., 163.
42. Wilentz, *Bob Dylan in America*, 19–20.
43. Frith, "The Magic That Can Set Your Free," 162.
44. Bulson, "The Freewheelin' Bob Dylan," 126.
45. Krein and Levin, "Just Like a Woman," 53.
46. Dylan, "The Times They Are A-Changin'."

our worldview."[47] This is a sentiment, however, that Dylan vehemently rebelled against; he did not want to be the poster child of anything. After his initial success in the early 1960s, Dylan hated the voyeuristic consequences of his fame and rather wanted a peaceful life with his wife and children. In his memoirs, Dylan writes, "I wasn't the toastmaster of any generation, and that notion needed to be pulled up by its roots. Liberty for myself and my loved ones had to be secured."[48] The people wanted a prophet coming out of a nationalistic identity. They wanted an Elijah, but Dylan was a Qoheleth. He did not want to be the voice of anyone; he simply wanted to share the wisdom of his own experiences.

Dylan's rebellion towards what is expected caused him to continually redefine himself in subsequent years, both in his music and public image.[49] In the mid-1960s, he retreated from overt political themes in his lyrics, moving away from protest songs and traditional folk melodies.[50] Although Dylan's image and message morphed throughout the years, there was always a common poetic thread found throughout his music. Dylan gravitated towards big questions in his lyrics, rarely giving clearly defined answers.[51] Jordan Rochelau writes,

> . . . Dylan quickly backed away from the role of progressive spokesperson. After the early 1960s, his work emphasizes uncertainties and ambiguities in understanding society and skepticism regarding all ideals. Dylan was booed at folk concerts after the mid-sixties not only for going electric but also for featuring music with ambiguous political content. His trajectory from social critic to skeptical individualist has been compared to that of his own sixties generation.[52]

The two most controversial changes in his career were first his "going electric" at the Newport Folk Festival in 1965, which marked his move away

---

47. Krein and Levin, "Just Like a Woman," 53.

48. Dylan, *Chronicles,* 122.

49. Brake, "To Live Outside the Law, You Must Be Honest," 78.

50. Unterberger, *Turn! Turn! Turn!,* 97.

51. The one exception is Dylan's Christian phase beginning in 1979 where he dogmatically proclaimed Christ as the definitive answer to the world's problems (Wilentz, *Bob Dylan in America,* 176).

52. Rocheleau, "Far Between Sundown's Finish An' Midnight's Broken Toll," 66.

from folk music as a new pioneer of folk rock, and his religious phase when he recorded three consecutive Christian albums.[53]

Dylan's going electric helped mark the genesis of folk rock as a genre. Dylan moved to New York City from Minneapolis as an urban folk singer.[54] Heavily influenced by the music of Woody Guthrie, Dylan would sing covers and protest songs playing his acoustic guitar and harmonica. After signing with Columbia records, he quickly gained fame and notoriety as a folk singer. But with an aptitude for redefining himself, Dylan fused folk songwriting and poetic mindfulness with rock and roll in 1965, marking a pivotal moment for the birth of folk rock.[55] That same year saw the burgeoning folk rock group The Byrds do a rock cover of Dylan's song "Mr. Tambourine Man."[56] With musical acts like Dylan and The Byrds, rock would have the social consciousness and principled inquisitiveness of folk music. Mark Pendelty writes, "As his (Dylan's) 'finger-pointing' folk gave way to artfully crafted rock years later, folk elements remained, including a strong sense of mystery and an ability to perform the full range of human emotion."[57] From this point, Dylan's name would forever be tied to folk rock.

As Dylan is archetypal for folk rock as a genre, he also helped to provide the genre's attributes that resemble those of the wisdom tradition. In Dylan's lyrics one can find conflict and contradiction, and a broad exploration of the big issues of life. Dylan's explorations often change and contrast his earlier assessments. As Rick Furtak writes,

> . . . one of the virtues of his later work is its exploration of these gray areas—that is, bleak emotional landscapes and states of mind which are only a few shades removed from an absolutely black despair. At his darkest of moments, Dylan shows us something about the possibility of finding hope in a blighted world, and he even considers how one might continue to live without hope if necessary.[58]

Furtak likens Dylan's later work to existential absurdism, much in the same way that Berger does for Qoheleth. Dylan at times cannot understand the

53. Spargo and Raem, "Bob Dylan and Religion," 87.

54. Pendelty, *Ecomusicology*, 65.

55. Roberts, *Bob Dylan*, 60.

56. Ibid., 61.

57. Pendelty, *Ecomusicology*, 65.

58. Furtak, "'I Used to Care, but Things Have Changed,'" 16.

world that he is in, but his suffering substantiates his existence.[59] For instance, "Not Dark Yet" from the album *Time Out of Mind* (1997) deals with mortality and existence in a poetic reflection:

> *I was born here and I'll die here against my will*
> *I know it looks like I'm moving, but I'm standing still*
> *Every nerve in my body is so vacant and numb*
> *I can't even remember what it was I came here to get away from*
> *Don't even hear a murmur of a prayer*
> *It's not dark yet, but it's getting there*[60]

Even when Dylan seems hopeless in his lyrics, it is his exploration and his wonder that keep him going. He does not procure definitive answers to life's problems but sees his probing as a satisfying response. Chiariello writes, "If we search through Dylan's work to find his answers to these questions, what we might see is a series of conflicting responses, open questions, and changes of mind."[61] In Dylan we see a life-long pursuit of wisdom. Dylan may not have been the spokesperson of his generation, but he has surely been one of its sages.

The legacy left by Bob Dylan on folk rock is vast. With his lifelong pursuit of music, Dylan was able to educate a new generation of musicians to ask profound questions and to bask in the honesty of unconcluded concerns. Bands like the Los Angeles-based Dawes write songs about the simple things of life like deep friendships and time spent well. They also deal with spiritual themes, particularly concerning the unfulfilled promises of religion.[62] For instance, in their song "God Rest My Soul," Dawes questions the allure of eternal life, a central tenet of Christianity, with these lyrics:

> *Oh you can't throw something out there without watching it fall*
> *Only thing that's scarier than dying is not dying at all*
> *So when I have lost all my control*
> *God will rest my soul*[63]

While at times other indie folk bands appear to relate to religion more positively, contemporary folk rock artists tend to come back with complex

---

59. Ibid., 24.
60. Dylan, "Not Dark Yet."
61. Chiariello, "Bob Dylan's Truth," 105–106.
62. "Exploring Spirituality with Dawes and Cory Chisel."
63. Dawes, "God Rest My Soul."

images of otherwise straightforward subjects. For instance, British folk rock band Mumford & Sons deal with spiritual and existential themes showing both the difficult and hopeful aspects of the issues. As Ulasich writes, " . . . they (Mumford & Sons) manage to ponder Biblical themes like love and grace without a shred of triteness. Instead, they come with a recognition of the struggle in this world. They honestly and authentically acknowledge the tension of light and darkness within our own hearts, all the while keeping hope alive." Like Dylan, Mumford & Sons also, interestingly, plugged in and "went electric" on their third album *Wilder Mind*.

Some bands, however, view church positively as a place for comfort and solace. For instance, The Wallflowers wrote a song entitled "Hospital for Sinners," praising the benevolence of the church. It might be interesting to note that The Wallflowers are led by Jakob Dylan, Bob Dylan's son. Regardless of the position that the bands take on spiritual and existential matters, there is a consistent theme of questioning and tarrying on deep-rooted issues. This is a sensibility that was derived from Bob Dylan at the outset of the folk rock genre and corresponds with the sapiential tradition found in the Bible.

Engaging the World in Fear and Wonder

Because folk rock handles theological and existential matters in a distinctive way, one can begin to shape a transformational theology of folk rock by picking up these themes. It appears to me that there are five particular theological commitments implicit in folk rock that are analogous to ideas found in the wisdom tradition. The first of these concerns the nature of God. Folk rock sees God as infinite and mysterious. God is ultimately incomprehensible, and we can only see glimpses of God's presence. What follows is a mature fear of the Lord, which gives due account of God's infinity. God is vast and great, and the correct way to relate to God is in wonder and humility.

The next commitment deals with creation. We are sentient, introspective creatures residing in a created order that stretches far beyond us. We as humans must, therefore, find our place in the world. This creational and existential focus on life is key to the identity of folk rock. Both the folk rock view of God and creation can, however, lead to incredible anxiety. One can quickly and easily entertain feelings of meaninglessness because of the vastness of creation and the Creator. Indeed, we can see Job and Qoheleth struggle with issues of worth and identity, but in both cases, the inner dialogue and true struggle ended with trust. It is not taboo to have existential struggles in a transformational theology of rock; in fact, the journey of self-discovery is part of its appeal! However, one cannot remain in a state of existential dejection, which leads us to our next commitment: in a transformational theology of rock, we must approach the world in fear and wonder.

One can avoid or beat the existential despair that comes from sublime reflection by approaching the world in fear and wonder. Despair comes from feelings of worthlessness, but if one were to look at the sublimity and greatness of God and creation without immediately contrasting it to the atomicity of his or her own existence, then one can take a step back and delight in the wonder of the created order. Existential despair comes from the crisis moment when one realizes that s/he is not the center of the universe. When one is struck by the beauty of the infinite, it will overwhelm a person. It is the attitude of wonder that will allow this overwhelming-ness to manifest as bewilderment rather than crushing defeat.

The fourth commitment is to be open to what wisdom will reveal. When a person approaches the world in fear and wonder, s/he cannot expect any fixed or rigid denouements. Such an attitude contradicts the openness that wonder requires. Folk rock asks questions and rarely supplies answers. This reveals an openness to new possibilities and shows the priority of the dialogue over and against the resolutions, which leads to the fifth and final commitment: striving for contentment.

The appeal of both wisdom literature and folk rock is its openness and honesty towards the real and challenging parts of life. Saying that a lot of life's issues do not have clear-cut answers is a genuine response that people can identify with. Qoheleth's mission in asking and thinking about life's difficulties was simply to find contentment in the face of unanswerable questions. This is often the only way, as experience shows us, that one can live amidst a world of anxieties. To review what we have discussed thus far, a transformational theology of rock asserts that God is infinite and mysterious, and since we are a part of Creation, we must find our place in this world. We must approach the world in fear and wonder and be open to what wisdom will reveal so as to strive for contentment.

In the last part of this chapter, I would like to concretize the theological implications of folk rock by looking at the music of two prominent contemporary Christian artists: Michael Gungor and John Mark McMillan. American singer-songwriter Michael Gungor is a quintessential example of a folk rock artist who embodies a transformational theology of rock. His music often deals with a creational theology that depicts the majesty of God, the creatureliness of humans, and the trust of God in difficult times. Gungor co-leads the band "Gungor" with his wife Lisa, and the band has gained critical acclaim with the release of their 2010 album titled *Beautiful Things*. *Beautiful Things* deals with the spiritual and physical transformation that can be attained through Christ's redemption with songs like "Dry Bones." The album also deals with creation's proclamation of God's splendor with songs like "The Earth is Yours." The song that best exemplifies the folk rock wisdom themes, however, is the title track, "Beautiful Things." In "Beautiful Things," Gungor deals with trusting God to make something good out of a person's life in the midst of pain and trials. Consider the opening verse of the song:

> All this pain
> I wonder if I'll ever find my way
> I wonder if my life could really change at all[64]

As is evident in the second verse, however, God can make good things come from the hardships of life:

> All around
> Hope is springing up from this old ground
> Out of chaos life is being found in You[65]

Through these lyrics, Gungor explores the intricacies of life and hardship by trusting God in the face of adversity. Gungor answers the existential question of his life's significance by diverting the issue to God's glory.

Like the wisdom writers, Gungor believes that nature can teach us and testify of God's glory. Gungor repeatedly visits themes of creation in his lyrics and, as is evident in his book *The Crowd, The Critic, and the Muse*, believes that the world around us is a suitable source for theological reflection. He writes,

> How could a full human life consist of anything less than a robust, sensual experience of the goodness of creation? To be human is to be aware. Without awareness, which depends on our senses, we would be ignorant of existing at all. If we could not see, hear, touch, smell or taste, how would we know that we were alive? A

64. Gungor, "Beautiful Things."
65. Ibid.

sensual awareness is the conduit between ourselves and the goodness and beauty of the world around us. *Taste and see,* sings the
Psalmist. Every one of our senses is potent enough to wash the
mind in wonder of the extravagant goodness of the universe.[66]

It is not that nature replaces God as the ultimate theological source, but
rather that God can communicate to us, his creatures, through creation.
Consequently, we, by being in touch with nature, can learn of God's goodness and the goodness of God's creation. This is akin to wisdom authors
who believed that one could uncover theological truths by studying nature
and human experiences. As Penchansky writes, "The sages regarded the
world of nature as a sacred text upon which Yahweh has written important
insights about life."[67] Michael Gungor's folk rock exhibits the creation theology commitments of wisdom theology and in this way is functioning in
a sapiential way.

Another artist who displays the folk qualities of a transformational
theology of rock is John Mark McMillan. McMillan is an American singer
and songwriter whose music is recognized for its poetic lyricism and theological depth. His most famous song "How He Loves" was released in 2005
on the album titled *The Song Inside the Sounds of Breaking Down.* The song
has since then received critical acclaim and has been covered by many notable recording artists including David Crowder Band, Jesus Culture, Hillsong United, Kari Jobe, Flyleaf, and The Glorious Unseen. In many ways,
this song became the worship song of a generation as it dealt with loss,
trust, and God's love for people. Consider the lyrics of the first verse:

> *He is jealous for me,*
> *Loves like a hurricane, I am a tree,*
> *Bending beneath the weight of His wind and mercy.*
> *When all of a sudden,*
> *I am unaware of these afflictions eclipsed by glory,*
> *And I realize just how beautiful You are,*
> *And how great Your affections are for me.*[68]

These lyrics show a person dealing with afflictions, yet trusting God through
it all to the point that s/he is overwhelmed by God's affections. While these
lyrics portray a contextualization of a transformational theology of rock, the

66. Gungor, *The Crowd, the Critic, and the Muse,* Location 836.

67. Penchansky, *Understanding Wisdom Literature,* 2.

68. McMillan, "How He Loves."

story behind these lyrics is even more notable. McMillan wrote this song while he was mourning the loss of his childhood friend Stephen Coffey. Coffey died the night after he proclaimed in a staff meeting that he would gladly give his life if his death would inspire a generation to draw close to God.[69] McMillan recounts the anger that he felt in his heart towards God after the incident writing, "He [Coffey] was my best friend. I'd known him since we were children. We were baptized together. Really, what it came down to is I was angry with God. I didn't quite know what to do with those feelings, but through that anger came resentment, [sic] I was able to see the heart of God in it all. God was able to take something terrible and show me something through it."[70] Somehow, in this difficult time, McMillan was able to trust God and allow God to bring peace and contentment to his heart. He was never given an answer as to why this tragedy occurred, but only that God can draw goodness out of any situation, even one as heartbreaking as this. He goes on to say that Christian music should explore hurts and problems in its art. Instead of being concerned with political correctness, one should write from a place of genuine emotion in order to have a dialogue with God. McMillan writes,

> I think people get so concerned with being correct that they end up editing themselves down, but that's not the way King David did it. That's not the way they do it in the Bible. You bring God what you have and let Him deal with you. I really feel like God is not interested with how correct our words are. He doesn't want us to get into weird situations, but I think He'd really prefer something that's incorrect and genuine instead of something that's correct but comes from a robot.[71]

Thus, McMillan affirms one of the main themes of this book–that Christians need to create music from real and genuine places, no matter how gritty or coarse they may seem. Real people deal with real issues in this world, and if Christians do not confront these matters head on, then the world will see Christianity not as "the Way" but as a naïve perspective on life. With "How He Loves," McMillan becomes a folk rock artist and a sage, and Christian artists would do well learning from McMillan's approach to music.

---

69. Selders, "The Heart of John Mark McMillan," 2.

70. McMillan in Selders, "The Heart of John Mark McMillan," 2.

71. Ibid., 3.

Conclusion

The main argument of this chapter was that *folk rock artists, like wisdom tradition writers, revel in the wonder and dissonance of diverging truths.* It is also important to acknowledge the value that such a theological approach can bring to today's hardships. This approach allows people the freedom to express themselves genuinely to each other and to God. It does not make light of tough situations but addresses them head-on. Lastly, it teaches us the virtues of trust and contentment, so we can agree with the writer of Proverbs, "Trust in the Lord with all your heart, and do not rely on your own insight. In all your ways acknowledge him, and he will make straight your paths" (Prov 3:5–6).

This chapter began by investigating the main themes of biblical wisdom literature. We then looked at the influence and formation of folk rock as a genre. Next, we further developed our transformational theology of rock by looking at theological implications drawn from an exploration of folk rock, and I gave examples of contemporary folk rock artists that are portraying these theological characteristics. This chapter is an important contribution to the study of theology and rock because it mines the hermeneutic form of an important musical genre in the Western world. Cultural engagements such as this can help us grasp a better sense of the world we live in. Folk rock is one avenue of creativity that deserves appropriate consideration.

4

The Prophetic Screams of Heavy Metal

I n 2010, Jake Luhrs, frontman of the Christian heavy metal band August Burns Red (ABR), started the nonprofit organization Heart Support. Luhrs saw brokenness and alienation in the faces of many of ABR's young fans. He realized that his levy of influence would one day pass and that his time to positively affect lives was at hand.[1] Heart Support is an online community that provides help for troubled youth. The site receives and answers anonymous questions and offers guidance and resources to help young people overcome troubles that are difficult to face. Heart Support provides help with issues including pornography, sexual abuse, and depression and supports kids that deal with addictions and self-inflicted violence.[2] Luhrs and other members of prominent metal bands (such as Beau Bokan of Blessthefall), regularly sit at Heart Support booths at major metal and hardcore festivals such as Van's Warped Tour to sign autographs and chat with fans.[3]

Luhrs used his platform of fame and notoriety in the heavy metal subculture to launch this holistic ministry of care and restoration. When asked what his ultimate goal for Heart Support was, Luhrs responded:

1. Campbell, "I Want to Bring Unity Back Within the Music Scene," 1.

2. Ibid., 2.

3. Ibid., 1.

I want to bring unity back, especially within this industry and the music scene and this particular genre of music. It's very heavy, negative and dark. . . . This world is a very dog-eat-dog kind of game, and our youth are important. This scene is important to me, and I'd rather it be taken over with positivity and looking out for one another than anything else. That's one of my main goals for Heart Support to really pour into this specific demographic as far as the genre of music and our youth.[4]

What Luhrs and those involved in Heart Support are doing is offering hope to people that desperately need it. This is an indigenous organization that is steeped in the intricacies of the metal subculture. It is a ministry that arose from the metal scene and is exemplar of the sort of ministry that can derive from Christian metal.

Our Western society sees a marginalized group of young people expressing themselves and their desires through the musical outlet of heavy metal music.[5] While these utterances are themselves, in a way, prophetic, I would like to assert that *Christianity is speaking a message of energizing hope to a marginalized group by the ministries of Christian heavy metal bands.* This topic is of particular significance in that it elucidates an unfamiliar yet significant missional ministry that embodies the orthopraxis of our transformational theology of rock. Genres of extreme music tend to attract disenfranchised people, and some young Christians feel called to minister in this realm. I will approach this chapter first by overviewing Walter Brueggemann's principles of prophetic imagination to see how they can be voiced today. Next, I will briefly evaluate metal as a genre. I will argue that metal is already participating in prophetic-like activity and is thus predisposed for the prophetic energizing that Christian metal bands bring to the subculture. Finally, I will show how some Christian metal bands are already doing this. It is my hope that the greater Christian community would embrace this sort of missional ministry.

4. Ibid., 2.

5. I am referring to "heavy metal" broadly as an umbrella title of all the subgenres that comprise the musical genre. I am using the term synonymously with "metal," and not as its own subgenre of heavy music. This is consistent with the way sociologists Walser (*Running with the Devil*, 3), and Weinstein (*Heavy Metal*, 7) use the term.

The Principles of Prophecy

David Peterson defines prophetic literature as "literature that attests to or grows out of (i.e., is generated by) the activity of Israel's prophets."[6] It is not only the words of the Old Testament prophets that comprise prophetic literature, but also the stories about the prophets. Israel's prophets received communication from God in different ways and became the link between God and the people.[7] Peterson says the prophets were intermediaries, "standing between the world of the sacred and secular."[8] The prophets would see the signs of the times and state them in poetic ways and also interpret each event within Israelite religious and ethical mores.[9]

Although the prophetic literature of the Old Testament is diverse, there are some common principles that can be found running throughout the text. Peterson highlights that a "covenantal background" underlies prophetic literature.[10] The covenants made between God and the people, such as those found in Deuteronomy, motivate prophetic reflection concerning their votive relationship. In fact, the later prophets endeavored to find new ways of grasping Israel's relationship with God, forming the semblances of a "New Covenant."[11] The prophets also held an "imperial perspective" of God.[12] The predominant prophetic image of God is God enthroned in a divine council. This perspective shows the international importance of the covenantal theology as God is the God of all nations and kingdoms.[13] Peterson writes, "Israel's prophets serve as heralds for a cosmic God. As such, they offer an international perspective for what happens to Israel even as they affirm the importance of God's covenant with Israel."[14] Thus, while the covenant was made locally between God and the Israelites, it was intended for global developments. Accordingly, one can understand the covenantal and imperial perspectives of God and the people as profiling the theological substructures beneath the prophetic imagination.

6. Peterson, *The Prophetic Literature*, 4.

7. Ibid., 7.

8. Ibid.

9. Ibid., 10.

10. Ibid., 37.

11. Ibid.

12. Ibid., 38.

13. Ibid.

14. Ibid., 39.

Walter Brueggemann describes the prophetic imagination as standing against the comfortable "royal consciousness" of the day. Ancient Israel's royal consciousness was marked by affluence, oppressive social policies, and the establishment of a static religion.[15] Solomon's imperial reign marked the height of this ideology and countered the countercultural Hebrew identity instituted by Moses.[16] Indeed, the prophetic imagination is rooted in the exodus of the Hebrews as God established a new community that would stand against the oppression of Pharaoh.[17]

For Brueggemann, the model of Old Testament prophecy is important for the Church today as the prophet is the child of his or her own tradition, often speaking truth and life into a marginalized group. Brueggemann repeatedly associates today's social situation as being vexed by the royal consciousness. The United States is coming upon a state of despair as the church is entangled by the governing values of American culture. However, the vestiges of hope that arise out of prophetic preaching impede full despondency of the nation.[18] Hope surfaces when a countercultural community stands in opposition of the royal consciousness and disassociates with the oppressive system. In such dire straits, it is the prophetic task to articulate hope that there is the possibility of a good future governed by God.[19] The prophetic voice accomplishes this by following a tripartite agenda.

The first part of the prophetic agenda is to call out the unjust system in power. As Brueggemann writes, "The prophetic task is to expose the distorted view of societal reality sustained by the ideology that breeds unrealistic notions of entitlement, privilege, and superiority."[20] What is important to note is that the system is already unjust. The prophetic voice does not exist merely to cause factious unrest in a community but comes into existence as an emissary for the distressed when a community is in grief. The prophetic voice does not create the conditions of oppression but makes them palpable and reacts to them.[21] Naming the system of oppression leads to its criticism. Prophetic

---

15. Brueggemann, *The Prophetic Imagination*, 27.

16. Ibid., 31.

17. Brueggemann, *The Practice of Prophetic Imagination*, 34.

18. Brueggemann, *Hopeful Imagination*, 7.

19. Brueggemann, *Reality, Grief, Hope*, 119.

20. Ibid., 33.

21. Brueggemann, *The Practice of Prophetic Preaching*, 18.

critique does not merely disparage the royal consciousness but asserts that it cannot keep its promises with its false claims.[22]

The underlying issue is that people do not grieve their current situation of oppression because they are numbed by the organizing principles that were set out by the royal consciousness. This creates a vicious cycle that keeps people in oppression as they have come to accept the only reality that is presented to them. Prophetic critique creates space to grieve by breaking away the numbness that has taken root and allowing people to see the world for a moment as it is affected by the ruse of the royal consciousness. Brueggemann writes, "It is the task of prophetic ministry and imagination to bring people to engage their experiences of suffering and death."[23] Grieving allows reality to sink in and paves the way for a new possibility, but grief can just as easily lead to despair. As such, the prophetic task turns to energizing.

The prophet finally energizes God's people by offering an alternative reality where God is a decisive agent in the world.[24] In this reality, God leads the people to freedom from the oppressors. While the dominant imagination seeks to offer closure and an absolutist impression of its ideological countenance, the prophetic imagination offers another perspective that breaks open the tidy and domineering disposition of the royal consciousness.[25] The prophetic imagination offers hope and newness in the midst of loss and grief. The prophetic imagination is " . . . the declaration that God can enact a *novum* in our very midst, even when we judge that to be impossible."[26] As Leonora Tubbs writes, "I believe that the prophets of God—both in ancient times and today—have been harbingers of hope, naming reality as it is and placing before us a vision of the new future God will bring to pass."[27] The prophet thus advances his or her agenda by offering a new reality in the midst of the inconsolable consequences of the royal consciousness.

By the tripartite agenda of naming, grieving, and energizing, the prophet plays a pivotal role in generating change to a broken society. As prophets speak against the corrupt status quo of the forces in power, they can only exist in the margins of society. Heavy metal is also a social phenomenon that operates from a standpoint of marginalization, and this

22. Brueggemann, *The Prophetic Imagination*, 11.

23. Ibid., 41.

24. Brueggemann, *The Practice of Prophetic Preaching*, 45.

25. Ibid., 32.

26. Ibid.,.

27. Tisdale, *Prophetic Preaching*, xii.

analogous origination causes both the prophet and the "metalhead" to speak a similar language.

Heavy Metal as a Prophetic Act

Two sociologists that have made significant expository contributions towards the genre and culture of heavy metal are Deena Weinstein with her book *Heavy Metal*, and Robert Walser with his book *Running with the Devil*. Their work will shape our understanding of the music and subculture. Forming in the 1970s as an offshoot of rock music,[28] metal has been a controversial genre of music that " . . . stimulates visceral rather than intellectual reaction in both its partisans and its detractors."[29] According to Walser, the genre of metal is most indebted to blues music as its progressions, vocal melodies, and guitar solos all rely heavily on the pentatonic scale.[30] Classical music, however, also plays a major influence to the virtuoso guitar playing that lead guitarists try to emulate.[31] In fact, by fusing musical elements such as soaring guitar solos with the heavily distorted guitars and pulsating blast beats of the drums, the music " . . . articulates a dialectic of controlling power and transcendent freedom."[32] Power is the overriding theme of the metal genre, which is evident in the music. Distorted guitars function as a sign of extreme power and commanding expression.[33]

While power is the leitmotif of metal, there are, according to Weinstein, two organizing metaphors that drive metal's theme of power: namely, the Dionysian and the Chaotic.[34] The Dionysian experience is made manifest by rebellion. As was mentioned in chapter one, all rock genres portray a level of countercultural revolt against the status quo of society. This has been typified by rock's proclivity towards "sex, drugs, and rock and roll." While metal is generally in concert with this Dionysian attitude, it tends to express its rebellion with extreme images of horror, mayhem, death, and the grotesque rather than symbols of sex and drugs.[35] Metal is more often

28. Weinstein, *Heavy Metal*, 11.

29. Ibid., 3.

30. Walser, *Running with the Devil*, 58.

31. Ibid.

32. Ibid., 108.

33. Ibid., 42.

34. Weinstein, *Heavy Metal*, 35.

35. Ibid.

Dionysian in the context of the dynamic rather than the erotic. While this Dionysian metaphor ties metal thematically to the broader context of rock, it is metal's reference to chaos that is unique to the genre. Weinstein writes, "Chaos is used here to refer to the absence or destruction of relationships, which can run from confusion, through various forms of anomaly, conflict, and violence, to death. Respectable society tries to repress chaos. Heavy metal brings its images to the forefront, empowering them with its vitalizing sound."[36] The same images of monsters, mayhem, and the grotesque that are used to portray Dionysian rebelliousness also portray chaos as a form of resistance to injustice.[37] Chaos thus puts a cog in the machine of the oppressive status quo.

Heavy metal as a genre is not only controversial because of its extreme sonic nature but also because of the violent and sometimes satanic imagery that is used. While there are a few instances of metal bands proselytizing satanic beliefs, the vast majority of metal bands do not. Indeed, Weinstein claims that, with few exceptions, metal is rebellious but not anti-Christian.[38] Nevertheless, the devil and hell are regularly mentioned in metal lyrics. However, these two serve symbolically as shorthand for disorder and chaos and are not used in confessional ways.[39] These act merely as symbols within the larger context of power and freedom. Furthermore, Eric Strother points out that metal music often uses themes of chaos and disorder in descriptive rather than advocative ways. In other words, metal bands " . . . draw attention to chaos for the purpose of making others aware of it."[40] Metal sustains a deep agitation towards the corrupt power systems of the world, both political and institutional, but does not call for social or political reform. Instead, metal calls for the individual to overcome these struggles through personal efforts.[41]

Controversy and boundary-crossing are the goals of metal.[42] Hjelm, Kahn-Harris, and LeVine explain that metal music and culture is encoded with transgressive themes in order to use controversy as a critical tool of

36. Ibid., 38.

37. Ibid., 39.

38. Ibid., 262.

39. Ibid., 41.

40. Strother, "Unlocking the Paradox of Christian Metal Music," 111.

41. Weinstein, *Heavy Metal*, 242.

42. Hjelm, Kahn-Harris, and LeVine, "Heavy Metal as Controversy and Counterculture," 7.

social engagement.[43] The authors define controversy as " . . . activities of individuals or groups making public claims about conditions that are perceived as a threat to certain cherished values and/or material and status interests."[44] In this way metal's controversies are "discursive-symbolic" as they raise public awareness through "claims-making" through decidedly symbolic gestures.[45] Metal critiques dominant culture and challenges the "circuits of power and knowledge."[46] As such, the symbolism that metal uses in its music and marketing is purposefully controversial. Hjelm, Kahn-Harris and leVine write, "Metal bands explore themes such as sexual excess, the occult, death, violence and mutilation. They revel in myths that explore humanity's darker side and in stories of human evil and degradation. Metal music has tested the boundaries of music, volume and sound itself."[47] Moreover, as Gabrielle Riches points out, the darker aspects of humanity are symbolically represented in *every* facet of metal culture, including the embodied act of moshing.[48] She writes, "Symbolically, the mosh pit acknowledges the essential conflicts of life and, as one enters the mosh pit, one embraces all the pain, hurt, joy, pleasure and suffering that delineate existence."[49] The mosh pit, then, is a cathartic vehicle of communal identity formation.[50] Such embodied practices allow fans to fully immerse themselves into the live concert experience, which allows them to symbolically reject their dominant society as they are being " . . . reincorporated into an alternative society."[51] Moshing, like other symbolic gesticulations found in metal, is not aesthetically agreeable but serves its greater purpose of controversy. There is no sense in defending metal by attempting to homogenize its character since controversy is its *modus operandi*. Criticizing metal only strengthens the controversial appeal of its ethos. The only way to penetrate a subculture of controversy is to *out-transgress* it. This is an idea that we will discuss further below.

43. Ibid., 6.

44. Ibid., 7.

45. Ibid.

46. Ibid., 7.

47. Ibid., 14.

48. Riches, "Embracing the Chaos," 317.

49. Ibid., 320.

50. Ibid., 316.

51. Ibid., 324.

It's important to note, however, that metal is also prophetic by nature. The metal subculture follows the first two parts of Brueggemann's prophetic convention: naming and grieving. Metal music names and criticizes oppressive institutions by shedding light on society's woeful state of subjugation. It grieves by totally embracing the reality of the present condition. Blogger Dane Train puts it aptly: "People in the metal scene know there is something deeply wrong with the world. And Metal often expresses our outrage. Instead of pretending everything is OK or anesthetizing ourselves with consumerism, self-pity, or poison, metalheads tend to confront things head on."[52] People are attracted to metal culture because they see issues in the world today and are willing to name them and display the grief that they cause.[53] Grief is the prophetic response to the oppression of society's royal consciousness.

However, while grief can lead to a new and hopeful energizing reality, it can contrarily saturate a person's psychological state leading to feelings of hatred and despair. Despair is the natural succession of grief if hope does not inspire the grieving community. Metal tends to wallow in the grief and despair of its disenfranchised state. What is missing from the metal community is hope, and this hope can be grasped by prophetic energizing. Christian metal adds this third important prophetic task: energizing.

Christian Metal as a Voice Of Hope

Christian metal formed in the 1980s as an alternative brand of metal that would spread Christian values.[54] Weinstein calls Christian metal a " . . . well-crafted missionary effort to recruit members and save souls."[55] This is evident in the fact that unlike other Christian music markets that cater to Christians, Christian metal bands performed primarily for secular crowds.[56] Indeed, the spreading of social values from a Christian backdrop was the animus of such a ministry.[57] Eileen Luhr claims that Christians found the evangelical "language of dissent" to be akin to the language of

---

52. Train, "Jesus Christ and the Headbanger."

53. Ibid.

54. Luhr, "Metal Missionaries to the Nation," 103.

55. Weinstein, *Heavy Metal*, 54.

56. Luhr, Metal Missionaries to the Nation," 104.

57. Ibid., 115.

power and struggle found in metal.[58] This gave Christians an entry point for conceptual interchange. One way that early Christian metal bands did this was to promote an inverted rebellion against sin.[59] They often used violent and apocalyptic biblical imagery to present points of salvation.[60] In this way, Christian metal bands shared the gospel in the native tongue of the metal subculture.

From its inception, however, Christian metal faced much adversity. Luhr claims that there was a schism in Christian thought whether Christian metalheads should view metal culture as a lifestyle or merely as a tool for evangelism.[61] When metal was seen as a lifestyle, some Christians worried they would lose their Christian values and be subsumed into the culture. Additionally, metal bands often sought validation from both the metal scene and the church but rarely found support in either. As Strother writes, " . . . Christian metal has found itself uniquely positioned between the Church on one hand and the heavy metal subculture on the other, not exclusive to either, yet desiring to be fully accepted by each."[62] Because of this Marcus Moberg discusses the "double-controversy" in which Christian metal subsists.[63] At the outset of Christian metal, bands strove to demonize their counterparts in a hostile environment in order to distinguish themselves as active participants in spiritual warfare.[64] This led to the ridicule of Christian metal by the secular scene, as early bands like Stryper and Vengeance Rising were often dismissed as imitative. Since many factions of Western Christianity correspondingly criticized the movement, Christian metal arose amid a state of double-controversy as neither poles supported their efforts."[65] While Christian metal began with a strong evangelistic bent, it has since grown to be much more holistic.

This history of double-controversy, however, allowed Christian metal to develop with a thick skin, answering criticisms on both sides. What resulted was a counter-counterculture that resonates among young people

58. Ibid., 107.

59. Ibid., 118.

60. Weinstein, *Heavy Metal*, 54.

61. Luhr, Metal Missionaries to the Nation," 121.

62. Strother, "Unlocking the Paradox of Christian Metal Music," 3.

63. Moberg, "The 'Double Controversy' of Christian Metal," 94.

64. Ibid., 91.

65. Ibid., 89.

as a new approach to Christian spirituality.[66] Moberg writes, " . . . within today's transnational scene, Christian metal is recurrently discursively constructed as constituting an alternative form of *religious expression*, an alternative *means of evangelism,* a fully *legitimate* form of religious expression and evangelism, and a 'positive' *alternative* to secular metal."[67] In this way, Christian metal forms an alternative Christian identity. This would likely not have been possible without Christian metal's discursive history.[68] As is evident in the example given in the introduction of this chapter, Christian metal bands, in many instances, offer a unique countercultural lifestyle to metalheads that is still authentically metal.

Nevertheless, Strother claims that the concept of the "metal missionary" is a fitting one. Both metal bands and missionaries dedicate their lives to the culture that they are ministering to, and adopt their dress, language, and social customs.[69] It should be noted, however, that Christianity has long been an impelling aspect of the metal subculture. There are certainly many in the metal subculture that reject Christian values and look at religion with disdain, but Christian metal has been a consistent stream within the culture from the outset. So, at least in part, Christianity helped to shape the metal subculture. Thus, the analogy of the metal missionary is thus more like a missionary travelling to a foreign country to continue work that has already begun rather than going to a country and sharing the gospel for a first time. Nevertheless, adopting the "metal missionary" convention is helpful as it allows one to see Christian metal as a missional enterprise rather than a euphemistic para-subculture that young Christians can participate in. Christian metal is good when it is authentic and speaks the real language of the surrounding culture.[70] At its best Christian metal presents a new controversy for the already controversial broader metal scene.

Christian metal offers hope to a disenfranchised people. When marginalized people fossilize their conditions of grief, they lose their sense of imagination. They cannot see a way out of their despair and thus comfort themselves with aggression. Anger becomes an opiate. Subsequently, violence emerges as the banal response to grief. The benumbed imagination of the metal subculture needs to be vivified with a vision of hope. *Kerygmatic*

66. Ibid., 95.

67. Ibid., 94–95.

68. Ibid., 95.

69. Strother, "Unlocking the Paradox of Christian Metal Music," 8.

70. Moberg, 96.

affirmations of the coming Christ can inspire hope in the midst of brokenness. Brueggemann writes, " . . . people are changed, not by ethical urging but by transformed imagination."[71] A person can be changed when his or her imagination is brought to life and is able to see a new and hopeful reality in the midst of despair. The prophetic task of Christian metal is thus confessional rather than didactic, holistic rather than proselytizing.

Theologian Jürgen Moltmann claims that hope is actually at the core of Christianity. Christians are an eschatological people. Not only do they await the coming Christ, but they also participate today in the promises that come from the future complete redemption of the cosmos. Moltmann writes,

> . . . eschatology means the doctrine of Christian hope, which embraces both the object hoped for and also the hope inspired by it. From first to last, and not merely in epilogue, Christianity is eschatology, is hope, forward looking and forward moving, and therefore also revolutionizing and transforming the present. The eschatological is not one element *of* Christianity, but it is the medium of Christian faith as such, the key in which everything in it is set, the glow that suffuses everything here in the dawn of an expected new day.[72]

The eschatology of Moltmann can be summed up as a future hope that transforms the present. Christian hope is, as Moltmann puts it, "resurrection hope," and is grounded in the redemption made possible by Christ.[73] Christian hope is concretely established in the life, death, and resurrection of Christ. It was Christ's earthly ministry that established the kingdom of God on earth, and his resurrection gives us the future hope that the kingdom of God will be brought to its culmination.[74] As mentioned in chapter one, it is in this way Christians live in the "already" and "not yet" of salvation history.[75] We are already saved and redeemed, yet the complete redemption is not yet here and will be ushered in with Christ's return. We are now given a foretaste of what is to come. We are given hope for a new day: hope for redemption.

Hope for the Christian is not something that is unlikely–it is not wishful thinking. Rather, hope is something that produces tangible change in

71. Brueggemann, *Hopeful Imagination*, 25.

72. Moltmann, *The Coming of God*, 16.

73. Ibid., 18.

74. Ibid., 11.

75. Ibid.

the world here and now. Hope is a force and a motivation of newness. It is the catalyst that can bring about a new day. Such a hope cannot be founded on a lie. Such a hope is only sustainable if it is rooted in some future reality that has somehow been made palpable for us, even if only for a glimpse. The Spirit gifts the glimpse of a redeemed reality to us. This gives Christian hope a pneumatological substance.

Moltmann states that God stands in the future and draws all of creation to its culmination.[76] As such, it is the Christian's responsibility to share in the ministry Christ started of expanding the kingdom of God on the earth. We are to partner with the God who is coming on this day, because the one who is coming is here and drawing us towards the eschaton. Moltmann writes, "He (Christ) promises a new world of all-embracing life, of righteousness and truth, and with this promise he constantly calls this world in question—not because to the eye of hope it is as nothing, but because to the eye of hope, it is not yet what it has the prospect of being."[77] This is the sort of hope that Christians must instill in people. When a broken and marginalized person walks in the depth of despair, s/he can be filled with the hope of resurrection and the redemption of the world. This is the sort of hope that must be energized by the prophet.

Energizing Hope to a Broken Generation

In what ways, then, do Christian metal bands instill hope to a marginalized crowd? While there are various ministries that aim towards present transformation, such as Heart Support which was discussed at the beginning of this chapter, some Christian metal bands strive to engage in holistic ministry through their onstage message and lyrics.

One of the most vocal leaders in the Christian metal and hardcore scene is Tommy Green, front man of the California and Utah based band Sleeping Giant. Green preaches a message of love and hope to young broken people, in part because he himself came from a place of brokenness. Green has an incredible testimony. As a teenager, he moved to California and became part of the Christian hardcore scene. Even though he was participating in a *Christian* scene, he found himself living a lie and getting into trouble. After high school at age 18, Green had an affair with a married woman. The woman's husband consequently committed suicide.

76. Moltmann, *Theology of Hope,* 39.

77. Ibid., 164.

Astonishingly, the husband admonished Green to stay with his wife in his suicide note, so Green ended up marrying the woman he had an affair with.[78] After a little while, the woman cheated on Green, and somehow, through her infidelity, Green saw the analogy of the church as an unfaithful bride to Christ. He vowed from then on to live for Christ and to try love and forgiveness avoiding anger and loneliness.[79] After trying to restore his marriage, the marriage failed, but Green has since been instilled with a new passion to extend the love and forgiveness that he continually experiences from God to marginalized youth who need hope. Since then, Green also re-married and lives happily with his wife and children in Salt Lake City, Utah.

Green's heart is for youth who have started the prophetic cycle but need to be energized. Green critiques the church for neglecting these young people who desperately need love and hope. He says that the Christianity he sees is "Rated R," meaning that real people have real struggles, and not everything is black and white. Some people are going through terrible struggles but are ignored because their issues and lifestyles seem too extreme for the casual Christian.[80] In this way, the church can be fake. Concerning this, Sarachik writes:

> In the hardcore music scene, Green is around people with piercings and tattoos, and maybe other things that are part of who they are that 'Christians' may frown down upon. If some of these people walk into a church there is a good chance they will feel uncomfortable because people may no be so receptive of them. The same thing with people that are struggling with depression, substance abuse, or whatever else it might be. Green wants people to truly learn to love as Jesus did with open arms for all. This is what he means by "Rated R Christianity," because the real world is not always so pretty.[81]

Green takes the church to task claiming that the true call of the church is to love the unlovable just as Christ loved those on the fringes: the prostitutes, tax collectors, lepers, etc. Instead, the church is governed by fear, rejecting its prophetic calling as an energizer of hope. This can clearly be seen in some of the lyrics from Sleeping Giant's song "Descending Into Hell" off of their album *Sons of Thunder* (2009):

78. Sarachik, "Sleeping Giants Frontman Tommy Green Finds Jesus Through Affair."
79. Ibid.
80. Sarachik, "The Christianity I see is Rated R."
81. Ibid.

These people live so violated and we're concerned with church agendas
Oh My God
Pure religion says I fight this war
The hidden millions in our own back yard, exploited masses
These kids are all alone, waiting for someone
I tell you what's 'biblical' the master came to set the captive free,
and we should be like him, we will worship and pray, then instigate their release![82]

This is a powerful message that is sorely needed by those on the fringes. Christians like Green are doing an incredible work for the kingdom of God, by energizing hope in a world of despair. This is the prophetic ministry of the metal missionary.

Another way that some Christian bands are transforming and redefining the imaginations of people in the metal subculture is by altering the meaning of key metal symbols. Take for instance the pentagram. The pentagram was once understood as a Christian symbol as each of the five points mark one of Christ's wounds from the crucifixion. However, today the inverted pentagram is commonly associated with evil and the occult.[83] It is seen as a blasphemous symbol that is in rebellion against Christianity. A Christian death metal band named Impending Doom re-appropriated the symbol and formed it into a "repentagram" consisting of nine points that symbolize the different aspects of the fruit of the Spirit.[84] The band Oh, Sleeper used a "broken pentagram" symbol for the cover of their 2009 album *Son of the Morning*. This is an inverted pentagram where the two horns are cut off.[85] The new symbol of a desecrated inverted pentagram creates the image of an arrow pointing upwards. It speaks eschatologically of God's victory over the powers of evil, and offers a doubly controversial critique on a symbol intended to elicit chaos. This theme is correspondingly evident in the final lines of "The Finisher," the final song of *Son of the Morning*:

We will sing to a world reborn from suffering.
From the armories the angels sing.
You will see them end this suffering.
From the armories the angels sing.

82. Sleeping Giant, "Descending Into Hell."
83. Jorgensen, "Nature Religions," 320.
84. "Repentagram."
85. Strother, "Unlocking the Paradox of Christian Metal Music," 152.

You will fear them when they lift their wings.
They will sing to a world reborn.
They will sing as I cut off your horns.
I'll cut off your horns.[86]

Christian metal artists, like the exilic prophets, are poets. These poets, according to Brueggemann, want people to re-experience the world under an alternative set of metaphors than the one's supplied by the dominant culture.[87] Cutting off the devils horns seems to be a good start.

Conclusion

In this chapter I argued that *Christianity is speaking a message of energizing hope to a marginalized group by the ministries of Christian heavy metal bands.* First, we discussed the principles of the prophetic imagination and gave particular primacy to the work of Walter Brueggemann. We then looked at the origins and themes of heavy metal as a genre, noticing that metal music is already engaged in prophetic activity. While metal music calls out the oppressive work of our society's royal consciousness, it leaves young people at a state of grief, which can easily turn into despair. Thus, we next turned to the ministries of Christian metal bands and witnessed how they participate in the prophetic energizing of a marginalized crowd. We demonstrated these ideas by taking a closer look at some Christian metal bands that approach their ministries as energizing prophets.

The prophetic ministry of these metal missionaries should inspire Christians all over the world to love the unlovable and reach the broken. Jake Shaefer sums it up best,

> While some Christians can't look past the 'worldliness' of the scene (tattoos, piercings, screaming vocalists, and 'guitar riffs from the devil'), spirit-filled Christian hardcore is certainly a platform in which warriors for the army of Jesus Christ are being strengthened and encouraged to take the name of Jesus seriously and to bare it with pride.[88]

At their best, Christian metal bands are missional ministries that should be supported by the church rather than demonized.

86. Oh, Sleeper, "The Finisher."
87. Brueggemann, *Hopeful Imagination,* 24.
88. Shaefer, "An Interview with Tommy Green."

5

Nationalism and Southern Rock

N eil Young took Southern American pride to task in the 1970 hit song "Southern Man." Here Young speaks against the institutional racism of the American south, and how such an ideology sits intrinsically opposed to the Christian faith many southerners express. The lyrics state:

> Southern man
> better keep your head
> Don't forget
> what your good book said
> Southern change
> gonna come at last
> Now your crosses
> are burning fast
> Southern man[1]

Young hated racism and spoke out against it both loudly and categorically. A couple of years later in 1972, Young released another South-condemning, anti-racism track with the song "Alabama." The chorus to this song states:

> Alabama, you got
> the weight on your shoulders
> That's breaking your back.
> Your Cadillac

1. Young, "Southern Man."

84

has got a wheel in the ditch
And a wheel on the track[2]

The "weight" that Young is referring to is the weight of racism that still stains the fabric of Southern culture. Although Alabama's laws of segregation had been lifted by 1972, the culture still had, so to speak, "a wheel in the ditch" and another on the track. Young's songs hit hard pointing out the double-mindedness and hypocrisy of racism in the allegedly "Christian" region of the American South. But what does Young, a Canadian, know about the South? How can he, from a distance, make such categorical statements about an entire region? This is precisely what irked Ronnie Van Zant, frontman of the band Lynyrd Skynyrd, causing him to invalidate Young's claim through song on the national scale.

Skynyrd responded to Young with the song "Sweet Home Alabama," from their 1974 album *Second Helping*. Interestingly, the defense of Alabama did not come from natives as the men of Skynyrd hailed from Jacksonville, Florida. At least they were Southerners! At any rate, the band seemingly chose to sing about Alabama for a couple of reasons: 1) Young called Alabama out by name, and 2) Alabama represented a sort of ground zero for both Southern culture and the controversies surrounding racism. Alabama thus became the archetype of the south–a symbolic land that encapsulated the history and ideals of the American south. Young reduced the "southland" down to the issue of racism, and it is this generalization that motivated Skynyrd's retort. Thus, the anthem of the south begins with Young being called out by name:

Well I heard mister Young sing about her
Well, I heard ole Neil put her down
Well, I hope Neil Young will remember
A Southern man don't need him around anyhow[3]

Skynyrd appeals to the person on this first verse suggesting that Young cannot speak to the southern situation as an outsider. It should be noted, however, that Young and the men of Skynyrd were actually friends and showed a ton of mutual respect for each other. While they shared some ideological

2. Young, "Alabama."
3. Lynyrd Skynyrd, "Sweet Home Alabama."

differences, they respected each other's sides, covered each other's songs, and at one point, Young even drafted some songs for Skynyrd to perform.[4]

If the issue had been left there, the song would just have been chalked up as part of a feud between two sets of musicians. But "Sweet Home Alabama" became one of the most controversial rock songs ever written as Skynyrd puzzlingly endorsed not only the state of Alabama, but also, seemingly, its destructive racist ideology. Butler writes that Skynyrd projected an " . . . adherence to traditional Southern racial ideals in their glorification of Alabama's segregationist governor George Wallace in 'Sweet Home Alabama.'"[5] Wallace was, of course, the governor who set up the blockade on Luther King's march in Selma, which had to be overturned by President Johnson. Wallace was fiercely against racial equality, articulating in his 1963 inaugural speech as governor of Alabama:

> It is very appropriate that from this cradle of the Confederacy, this very heart of the great Anglo-Saxon Southland, that today we sound the drum for freedom as have our generations of forebears before us time and again down through history. Let us rise to the call for freedom-loving blood that is in us and send our answer to the tyranny that clanks its chains upon the South. In the name of the greatest people that have ever trod this earth, I draw the line in the dust and toss the gauntlet before the feet of tyranny, and I say segregation now, segregation tomorrow, segregation forever.[6]

Skynyrd pays homage to Wallace with the line, "In Birmingham they love the guv'nor," and later on again,

> Sweet home Alabama
> Oh sweet home baby
> Where the skies are so blue
> And the guv'nor's true[7]

So Skynyrd does not only endorse some aspects of Southern culture, but defends it wholesale, warts, and all. To many, however, Wallace should have been disavowed, and the defense of the South should have been more nuanced. Nevertheless, the anthem of the South has forever expressed a jaded past and with pride. Since then, "Sweet Home Alabama" has grown

4. Chong, *Neil Yong Nation*, 249.

5. Butler, "Luther King Was a Good Ole Boy," 46–47.

6. Wallace, Inaugural Speech.

7. Lynyrd Skynyrd, "Sweet Home Alabama."

to become one of the most popular rock songs ever. Today the controversial lyrics are largely forgotten, and the song is sung around the world as an anthem of American pride.[8]

Southern Rock is the only mainstream genre of rock that holds Christianity as an essential characteristic. As Young pointed out, however, this Southern religiosity is not separated from some of the bigoted cultural standards that arose from decades of wayward thinking. While racism has always been a problem in the South, there are other issues that stand against the gospel in more implicit ways, like the South's valorization of war and violence. As such, *the Southern mentality that shapes Southern rock is ripe with theological implications concerning nationalism and Christian identity*. Thus for this chapter we will view a snapshot of Southern rock in order to approach the deeper subject of its theological significance. We will trace the history and characteristics of southern rock, and then discuss how the nationalistic Christianity of the south is something different than the Christianity of the Bible. While the nationalistic Christianity of the South will be critiqued in this chapter, we will also highlight Southern rock's redeeming qualities as it upholds standards of hospitality with a focus on redemption, providing nuance that is absent in both Young and Skynyrd.

A Southern Spin on Rock

Like several of the rock genres we will encounter in this book, the term "Southern rock" is notoriously difficult to define.[9] Duane Allman of the Allman Brothers Band once pointed out that rock and roll, in general, originated in the American South. So why add the adjective "Southern" to differentiate a different genre of music? Allman's exact words were: "Rock was born in the South, so saying 'Southern rock' is like saying 'rockrock.'"[10] In other words, the term "Southern rock" is redundant. This is somewhat misleading, however. While blues and country (rock's predecessors) did come primarily from the south in the 1920s and 1930s, and most of the "originators" of rock came from the south (Fats Domino, Little Richard, Jerry Lee Lewis, Chuck Berry, Buddy Holly, and Elvis Presley), the term "rock and roll" was first used in Ohio by disc jockey Alan Freed.[11] Also,

8. Bernstein, *Sweet Home Everywhere,* Location 1.

9. Gilmore, "Growing Roots in Rocky Soil," 103.

10. Allman, in Pappademas, "Essential Southern Rock."

11. Newfield, "Who Really Invented Rock 'n' Roll."

some integral figures of rock came from different regions of the US as well, like Bo Diddley (Midwest) and Bill Haley (North). So rock's origins were a bit more expansive than the American South. Moreover, one must not forget the significance of the British invasion of the 1960s on rock music. Bands like the Beatles, the Kinks, the Rolling Stones, and the Who would forever change the face of rock music. Nevertheless, there seems to be something superfluous about the title Southern rock.

Furthermore, how can one justify giving international genre appeal to regional music anyways? Southern rock is not *universally* identifiable because the bands often sing unabashed anthems of southern American life. Yet a song like "Sweet Home Alabama" is beloved all over the world and, for many, represents a regional pride that goes beyond the American south. While Southern rock is difficult to define, it does reference a musical movement from a particular time and place, which proved to bear cultural influence and staying power. So tracing the origins and characteristics of Southern rock will be beneficial for understanding an influential regional ideology.[12] For the purposes of this chapter, we will grasp onto Scott Bomar's broad definition. He writes that southern rock is " . . . music that was rooted in a specific time, belonged to a particular place, was created by musicians with similar formative and cultural experiences, and served as a key expression of a uniquely countercultural movement in the South."[13]

Tracing the Origins of Southern Rock

Southern rock first came into existence in the late 1960s and early 1970s in the southern American states of Florida, Georgia, Alabama, and Tennessee.[14] At first the movement was propelled, almost singlehandedly, by record producer Phil Walden who began signing regional rock and roll bands to his newly formed label Capricorn Records in Macon, Georgia.[15] The first signings included the Allman Brothers Band, the Marshall Tucker Band, the Outlaws, Wet Willie, and many more. While the Allman Brothers Band and the Marshall Tucker Band were the best known, all of these bands formed a similar identity and musical style. Shortly thereafter major labels, MCA and Atlantic in particular, began pedaling Southern rock un-

12. Butler, "Lord Have Mercy on My Soul," 75.

13. Bomar, *Southbound,* xv.

14. Ibid., xiv.

15. Butler, "Lord Have Mercy on My Soul," 74.

der subsidiary labels, such as Sounds of the South. Bands would then begin identifying themselves by declaring allegiance to these formative record companies, adopting the musical styles of their marquee bands.[16] Capricorn's first release was the Allman Brothers Band's self-titled debut album (1969), considered by many to be history's first Southern rock record.[17] As such, the Allman Brothers Band is usually credited as the originators of Southern rock. Even before signing with Capricorn, Duane and Greg Allman were playing in other influential bands such as the Allman Joys and the Hourglass, which had semblances of the electric blues rock that would greatly influence the sound of southern rock.[18] Many of the early Southern rock bands and musicians, such as Lynyrd Skynyrd, were already fans of the Allmans from their earlier incarnations.[19] So by influence and timing, the Allmans paved the wave for a new movement of rock.

The Allman Brothers came from the American South at a time when the land was filled with racial prejudice. The band was rather progressive when it came to race relations, enlisting an African American session drummer named Jaimoe Johanson as a founding member, much to the chagrin of their surrounding friends and families.[20] Although they did not really sing about political matters, the band stood as a countercultural force amongst a racist south due to their racially integrated band. As Bartow Elmore writes, "The music of the Allman Brothers Band is unique in illustrating the basic tensions and anxieties that young Southerners faced in the late 1960s and early 1970s—anxieties about racial integration, cultural sterility in an industrialized world, and a changing landscape."[21] Unlike other southern rock bands, the Allman Brothers expressed disinterest in confederate symbols and stereotypes.[22] Lynyrd Skynyrd, on the other hand, wore the symbols with pride by stretching a giant Confederate flag behind the band at live shows as a backdrop.[23] The Allman Brothers' lack of overt socio-political discourse was the exception of Southern rock, and not the rule.

16. Butler, "Luther King Was a Good Ole Boy," 42.

17. Bomar, *Southbound,* 43.

18. Ibid., 26.

19. Ribowsky, *Whiskey Bottles and Brand-New Cars,* 26.

20. Butler, "Luther King Was a Good Ole Boy," 48.

21. Elmore, "Growing Roots in Rocky Soil," 111.

22. Ibid., 121.

23. Ribowsky, *Whiskey Bottles and Brand-New Cars,* 116.

While Duane and Greg Allman grew up in Daytona, Florida, it was another Florida band that would eventually thrust Southern rock to new heights by receiving international fame and chart topping success. Jacksonville based band Lynyrd Skynyrd took their name in 1969 (although they had been playing together since 1964) in homage to a hated high school gym teacher named Leonard Skinner.[24] The original five-piece band was led by Ronnie Van Zant, and although they initially had trouble finding a record label, their then manager Alan Walden (Phil's brother) managed to get them signed to MCA where the band would produce five albums, four of which would end up going platinum. They were known for tight musicianship, catchy songs, and raucous off stage behavior. They often got in fights with others and each other, drank themselves into stupors, and engaged with drugs and women on a regular basis.[25] Skynyrd was like the Allman Brothers' unhinged little brother. The men of Skynyrd were the kings of Southern rock until 1977 when they were involved in a plane crash killing six people including two band members: guitarist Steve Gaines and Ronnie Van Zant.[26] For a while thereafter, Skynyrd called it quits until 1991 when the band reformed with Ronnie's brother (and doppelganger) Johnny Van Zant taking on frontman duties.[27] While southern rock bands still exist today, the great movement of the 1970s essentially came to a close with the disintegration of the original Lynyrd Skynyrd.[28]

While the Allman Brothers and Skynyrd are perhaps the best-known Southern rock acts emerging from the Southern rock movement, there were many other bands and a lot of variance concerning musical style and ideology. Nevertheless, what we have with the Southern rock movement of the 1970s is a snapshot into a regional culture and religiosity that was expressed and rebelled against by rock musicians. As Butler writes,

> The bands that constituted the Southern rock movement in the 1970s expressed lyrical views and opinions during an era when young Southern white males found themselves at a chaotic period in the search for personal and regional identities, examining their traditional patterns of beliefs and behaviors within a rapidly changing South. Through a unique brand of rock and roll music,

24. Ibid., 30.

25. Ibid., 84.

26. Smith, *Rebel Yell,* 100.

27. Smith, *Rebel Yell,* 125.

28. Butler, "Luther King Was a Good Ole Boy," 55.

the Southern rock movement became emblematic of the South's struggle for redefinition in the post-civil rights era.[29]

One thing that can be taken from a survey of Southern rock is how people of the South formed their regional identities, and how and to what extent Christianity played a role in the ideology of the south. Before we explore the religious character of southern rock, let us see if we can pull together the disparate southern rock groups by highlighting a few common characteristics.

Common Characteristics of Southern Rock

In the 1970s southern rock music developed its own sonic particularity. While the drummer typically hits hard with simple boogie rhythms in the pocket with the bassist, the hard rock guitars give Southern rock its unique sound. Guitar riffs are often doubled up (or tripled as in the case of Skynyrd) and played in unison before the band breaks into a verse. The frontman typically sings full voice without falsetto (like other rock bands of the time), and portrays a noticeable Southern twang. Lyrically the songs comprise issues of common life, identity, and Southern pride. These themes are guided by four characteristics that are consistently found in southern rock: the southland, masculinity, white supremacy, and religion.

The first common characteristic, "the southland," embraces the Southern environment as a nostalgic, identity-forming domicile. Southern rock is countercultural as it stands against commercialization and the social homogenization of suburbia.[30] The South, is held up as a sacred land unlike the suburban spread that dominates our late modern setting. It is sacred in its unfettered state, so the "Southland" that Southern rockers yearn for is more of an ideal place—it is a *perception* of the South rather than its reality. Southern pride is thus a call back to the wild.[31] As Elmore writes, "Southern rock . . . is a product of the soil on which it was born, a celebration of the southern wildlands and at times a lament for its rapid degradation."[32] As is evident in the introduction of this chapter, songs like "Sweet Home Alabama" personify Southern pride by romanticizing a locality that serves

29. Ibid., 43.

30. Elmore, "Growing Roots in Rocky Soil," 108.

31. Ibid.

32. Ibid., 125.

as a symbol for a way of life. This first characteristic is one that is found uniformly in all Southern rock acts.

Another nearly universal characteristic of Southern rock is masculinity. In many lyrics, we find the narrator negotiating what it means to be a man in the world. There is a propensity towards working-class labor and a moral ethic that upholds familial loyalty and hard-nosed resilience in the face of adversity. Consider lyrics from the Marshall Tucker Band's song "Am I the Kind of Man":

> Am I the kind of man
> Who believes in peace
> Who'll stand up and fight in a minute
> Over something that he believes
> Loves all his brothers
> Treats his elders with respect
> Never heard me say that I don't give a damn
> What the hell, who gives a heck[33]

Here the protagonist is posing the question to his lover if he is living up to the standards of genuine manhood. The song is full of intentional contradictions as the singer admits to missing the mark. There are also ideological contradictions as the singer proclaims peace, and then admits to "fighting" for what he believes in the very next line. Such is the moral arbitration of Southern ideology. The Southern conception of manhood calls men to be God-fearing, hardworking, hard-nosed, faithful, and morally upright—with the ability to throw a punch. The implications of each of these descriptions often refute each other, but Southern ideology nevertheless holds them together as important components of true masculinity. Southern rockers seek to offer revisions to the "Southern imaginary" all while accepting and dealing with the high ideals of manhood that are expressed in this southern American version of Christianity.[34]

Unfortunately, misogyny and sexism also play roles in Southern masculinity, often rearing their ugly heads in Southern rock. It is common to find songs of men bragging about their sexual escapades, debasing a woman's integrity in the world. Skynyrd's "What's Your Name?" is a case in point as Van Zant sings about coaxing a fan into sex on the road. What is worse is that these stories are often autobiographical and take place in the midst

33. The Marshall Tucker Band, "Am I the Kind of Man."
34. Stimeling, "To Be Polished More than Extended," 122.

of spousal infidelity. What is additionally confounding is that a Southern rock band might have a degrading track on their album followed by a song proclaiming their Christian ideals. Bragging about sexual competence is, apparently, a part of Southern masculinity.

The notion of traditional Southern masculinity also frequently leads to white supremacy.[35] As Bomar writes, "Sadly, some of the Southern stereotypes were not simply media inventions but reflections of real-life bigotry. Highly publicized battles of the civil rights movement, for instance, found high-profile politicians defiantly embracing racist, regressive attitudes that cast a shadow over the entire region."[36] The white man became the champion of Southern ideology and the true inheritors of the sacred "Southland." While some Southern rock bands rebelled against Southern racism by openly paying homage to black blues musicians,[37] apart from only a few exceptions, Southern rock cajoled a white crowd singing songs of white dominance. Some bands also used symbols and imagery that would invoke racist attitudes.[38] Skynyrd has been on record many times defending their use of the Confederate flag as a symbol of Southern pride as opposed to a symbol of racism.[39] Although the band knew that it offended some people, they refused to remove it from their live show in defiance of media in an effort to stick to their laurels.[40] Skynyrd finally stopped flying the Confederate flag at shows in 2012. Nevertheless, many Southern rock bands were egalitarian and demonstrated that one could be a white southern man *and* racially progressive.[41]

One unique facet of Southern ideology is how its Christian religious convictions are wrapped up in every other aspect of life. Southern ideology does not separate its Christian ideals from its worldview, but instead fuses Christian morality with the dogmas of Southern pride. This fusion of Christianity and Southern pride, what we shall call "southern American Christianity," or "SAC," sets up the moral standard that southern rockers adhere to. Southern rockers deal with issues of sin and salvation in their lyrics depicting the struggle of living up to the moral standards of SAC.[42]

---

35. Butler, "Luther King Was a Good Ole Boy," 44.

36. Bomar, *Southbound*, xiv.

37. Butler, "Luther King Was a Good Ole Boy," 47.

38. Ibid., 46.

39. Ribowsky, *Whiskey Bottles and Brand-New Cars*, 116.

40. Ibid., 119.

41. Butler, "Luther King Was a Good Ole Boy," 55.

42. Butler, "Lord Have Mercy on My Soul," 73.

The reason a southern rocker can sing about God and sexual infidelity or drunkenness in the same breath is because these bands are depicting the struggle of sin in their own lives. As Butler writes, "Although southern rock bands openly, vigorously, and frequently indulged in sinful activities . . . they often returned to religious topics and struggled to reconcile their beliefs with their behaviors."[43] The goal of the southern rocker is not to glorify their vices but rather to expose them. In some ways, singing about sin is confessional for the Southern rocker. While some might argue that Southern rockers are too lustful in their confession, perhaps by owning up to their mistakes they take their first steps on the road of becoming a good man. A good example of Southern Christian ideology, masculinity, and morality can be seen in Skynyrd's song "Simple Man":

> *Mama told me when I was young*
> *Come sit beside me, my only son*
> *And listen closely to what I say.*
> *And if you do this*
> *It will help you some sunny day.*
> *Take your time . . . Don't live too fast,*
> *Troubles will come and they will pass.*
> *Go find a woman and you'll find love,*
> *And don't forget son,*
> *There is someone up above.*[44]

To be the "simple" man is to be a good man, which is ultimately the goal of a Southern gentleman.

Peacable Kingdom?

Is the Christianity that Southern rockers sing about really Christianity? Aside from the hypocrisy and carnal living often found in Southern rock, there seems to be a deeper underlying issue that extends beyond the music into American identity itself. Southern rock unabashedly sings about religious themes as their Christianity is wrapped up in their social environment. While it is a good thing to allow one's faith to inform the rest of one's life (more on this below), it is a problem when the so-called "Christian"

43. Ibid., 78.
44. Lynyrd Skynyrd, "Simple Man."

religion is informed by the prejudices of life. In this way the Christianity put forward is not the "pure and undefiled religion" that James yearns for (Jm 1:27), but rather a contextualized Christianity that supports ideologies that are antithetical to Christ's teaching. The themes of war, violence, sexism, and racism sometimes found in southern rock, and American culture at large, go against the Christianity that Christ taught, and the ethics that derive from his teachings. What follows is a short exploration into the claims of SAC, and how its ideals work against the kingdom of God.

Theologian and Christian ethicist Stanley Hauerwas maintains that Christian ethics is narrative in nature. For Hauerwas, Christians should find their identity in the Christian story. First and foremost, Christians must see themselves as participants in God's story, otherwise their faith can become a mere system of beliefs rather than a way of life.[45] Morality is not found in the duty or consequences of biblical rules, such as the Ten Commandments or the Sermon on the Mount, but in the outworking of God's narrative that is seen in the life of Christ through the community. Hauerwas writes, "The Christian savior story and ethic is that of Jesus himself. Jesus determines the story as the crucial person in the story. Thus, his identity is grasped not through other savior stories, but by learning to follow him, which is the necessary condition for citizenship in his kingdom."[46] Christian convictions take form as a set of stories that make up a tradition, and it is the tradition that forms the community.[47] Therefore, morality must come from the true life of a disciple of Christ, as s/he is part of the Christian community, rather than from the ethical implications of belief.[48] In other words, it is a Christian's communal *orthopraxis* and not the *orthodoxy*, which must initiate a Christian ethic. Christian ethics exists first to help people "rightly envision the world," before any norms or principles can be mandated.[49] Christians are an "alien people" who are able to bring change to the world because they see the world in ways that others cannot.[50] Christians see the world through the redemption of the cross and are able to rightly live in the world, helping others to see this same redemption. Thus, Christian narrative forms a Christian's character.

45. Hauerwas, *A Community of Character*, 44.

46. Ibid., 43.

47. Hauerwas, *The Peaceable Kingdom*, 24–25.

48. Ibid., 16.

49. Ibid., 29.

50. Hauerwas and Willimon, *Resident Aliens*, 24.

Furthermore, we do not create our own character, but rather it is constructed as we enter into a community. Our character is, as Hauerwas puts it, "a gift from others which we learn to claim as our own by recognizing it as a gift."[51] Sin is when we believe that we possess our own character—it is the human need of control.[52] This selfishness can bring us into a life of sin and isolation. Sin also arises when a person follows another narrative that is antithetical to God's story. In this way, a person enters into sin as an alternate narrative forms the person's character to look different than that of Christ. These are the narratives that are expressed by the kingdoms of the world, and these alternate kingdoms arise as people fear one another.[53]

As noted in the previous section, the nationalism of the American South has been fixed into its expression of faith. As such, it has created something that is different than Christ's narrative found in Scripture. In its place we have a SAC narrative, with particular suppositions that seem antithetical to Christ's biblical narrative. As Hauerwas writes, "Americans continue to maintain a stubborn belief in a god, but the god they believe in turns out to be the American god. To know or worship that god does not require that a church exist, because that god is known through the providential establishment of a free people."[54] Instead of seeing freedom and liberty as implications of a biblical anthropology evident in the *imago dei,* the ideals of freedom and liberty are deified *as* the American god. Americans have made freedom an end in itself rather than a gift from God to enter into right relationships with God and others.[55] Hauerwas sees America as a prime example of the "project of modernity," which produces a people that claim no story except his or her own chosen story.[56] In other words, freedom is achieved when one "makes" him or herself—when a person adopts his or her own narrative at a time when s/he has no story. It is a radical individualism that ultimately puts trust in its own agency instead of being grafted into God's narrative. This is all a result of the melding of American politics and Christian ideology. This adds to the Christian narrative a modern contextual ideology that ultimately sets up a straw man of the kingdom of God. As such, this perversion of the truth can only be seen as

51. Hauerwas, *The Peaceable Kingdom,* 45.

52. Ibid., 47.

53. Hauerwas, *A Community of Character,* 49.

54. Hauerwas, *War and the American Difference,* 16.

55. Hauerwas, *A Community of Character,* 80.

56. Hauerwas, *War and the American Difference,* 17.

an institution of sin. There needs to be an appropriate separation of church and state: not to keep God and the church out of the US, but to keep the US out of God and the church. As Hauerwas states, " . . . the great difficulty is how to keep America, in the proper sense, secular."[57] Yet America has a long history of seeing itself as a Christian or chosen nation.

American Exceptionalism and the Kingdom of God

In his book *American Exceptionalism and Civil Religion*, John Wilsey traces the history of American exceptionalism and puts it into critical dialogue with the tenets of the Christian faith. American exceptionalism is the belief that the US is in some way a nation that is set apart. The US plays an integral role in God's plan of cosmic redemption as a chosen nation. When exceptionalism is discussed in strong providential terms it includes five characteristics: the US is (1) a chosen nation with (2) a divine commission. It is an (3) innocent nation, with (4) sacred land, and (5) radiates glory.[58] These characteristics together form the notion that the US is a blessed nation and a paradigm of sorts. Of these characteristics, I would like to highlight some difficulties found in the notions of innocence and chosen-ness.

The idea that America (or any nation for that matter) is innocent is, for Reinhold Niebuhr, a great irony. It is ironic for Americans to claim a status of innocence because when it does it can no longer admit to any wrongdoing. The "innocence" that Americans defend is an idea that can only be believed when one has skewed and manipulated its own sense of history, whitewashing the terrible acts committed on the national scale, such as imperialism and slavery. Niebuhr writes, " . . . we are (according to our traditional theory) the most innocent nation on earth. The irony of our situation lies in the fact that we could not be virtuous (in the sense of practicing the virtues which are implicit in meeting our vast world responsibilities) if we were really as innocent as we pretend to be."[59] When the nation claims innocence, it ultimately relinquishes itself from exercising the responsibilities of power. What is needed is a realist perspective that does not claim superfluous titles like innocence for a nation that cannot be.

The concept of chosen-ness is also problematic. Richard Hughes sees two possible biblical precedents for America's "chosen" status: The Old

---

57. Ibid., 6–7.

58. Wilsey, *American Exceptionalism and Civil Religion,* 18.

59. R. Niebuhr, *The Irony of American History,* 23.

Testament vision of Israel being God's chosen people, and the biblical vision of the kingdom of God.[60] Chosen America is likened to the gentiles being brought into the fold of chosen Israel as adopted sons (Eph 1:5). Paul's idea of chosen-ness does not concern an earthly kingdom, but rather the kingdom of God. As Hughes recounts, the kingdom of God is marked by two main attributes: "(1) equity and justice for all human beings, especially the poor, the marginalized, and the dispossessed, and (2) a world governed by peace and goodwill for all human beings."[61] As such, the biblical vision of the kingdom of God is subversive and stands against earthly nations offering the world a counter-vision of a new reality.[62] Wilsey, nevertheless, sees the US as distinctive and blessed by God.

While Wilsey believes the US is a special and unique place as a "haven of freedom, opportunity and material bounty,"[63] it is far from perfect. When these characteristics are adopted uncritically, one develops an unhealthy perspective of America's status in the world. Consequently Wilsey distinguishes between two forms of exceptionalism: closed American exceptionalism, which renders the nation's ideals as canon on par with the gospel, and open American exceptionalism, which sees the US as a blessed nation and critically evaluates its dealings to assure its right relation with God in the world. As Wilsey writes, "American exceptionalism is part of a civil religious belief system. And as an aspect of civil religion, exceptionalism can either deify the nation or present a just political model to emulate. Closed American exceptionalism serves to deify the nation. Open American exceptionalism serves to present a worthy example for the nation to pursue."[64] While closed American exceptionalism leads to idolatry and injustice, open American exceptionalism can lead to " . . . compassion, justice and general human flourishing."[65] Thus for Wilsey, nationalistic pride is attainable and favorable so long as it is approached in a manner consistent with open American exceptionalism.

Closed American exceptionalism is most blatantly expressed in the mid-19th century concept of "manifest destiny." The term "manifest destiny" was coined in 1845 by John L. O'Sullivan to explain "God's unique

60. Hughes, *Christian America and the Kingdom of God*, 30.

61. Ibid., 32.

62. Ibid., 34.

63. Wilsey, *American Exceptionalism and Civil Religion*, 213–214.

64. Ibid., 28.

65. Ibid., 19.

mission for America,"[66] which was essentially to expand the nation from the Atlantic to the Pacific, and in process to form the world's great superpower. It was America's destiny to become a "city on a hill" for the rest of the world to emulate. Under this premise Americans began practicing imperialism reminiscent of Israel's conquests of the Promised Land (Canaan) in the book of Joshua. This territorial expansion was brought to its fruition with the Mexican-American war when the US ended up possessing the North American continent from coast to coast.[67] Politics aim towards bettering a nation, but when the political agenda is fused with religious zeal, not only does the true religion become tainted, but also it forms into a new nationalistic religion that serves the purposes of the government rather than God. Thus the adherents of the new religion confuse patriotism with faithful discipleship, seeing anyone who stands against their nation as someone who stands against God. Wilsey writes,

> Many Christians assume that God chose America to be his special people to do his work in the world. Many uncritically accept patriotic expressions as a part of church worship services. Christians often sing songs linking patriotic devotion with love for God and think little about what the words mean and how those words fit into their overall theological matrix of beliefs. For many Christian people, patriotism equals spirituality because their assumption is that America is God's country. Anyone who stands with America is, therefore, holy, good and just. Anyone who stands against America is scandalous, immoral—perhaps even demonic.[68]

So the pitfall of closed American exceptionalism is idolatry as the US serves as a sign of a higher order that is alien to the biblical witness.

Wilsey, however, still views the American creeds of liberty and equality as high ideals. Since the US is founded on these principles, America becomes the model nation for the rest of the world.[69] Yet, open exceptionalism accounts for the flaws and imperfections of the American nation.[70] Thus, America can be upheld as a model nation only after being critically assessed. When Christians, like Wilsey, put America up as a model, however, they are implicitly making the statement that America is closest to resembling a godly

66. Ibid., 17.
67. Ibid., 66.
68. Ibid., 220.
69. Ibid., 33.
70. Ibid., 220.

nation. Why should anyone embrace a model that is admittedly imperfect? Would it not be better to strive for a model that is perfect? This seems to be Hauerwas' point when he sees the church as a witness to the kingdom of God.[71] Perfect polity is found in the kingdom of God, and the church must strive to adequately reflect the kingdom of God on earth. Christian ethics and polity should derive from the kingdom of God, and not from a good but imperfect nation that has nearly as many vices as it has virtues.

Contrary to Wilsey, Hughes offers a different perspective on nationalistic pride as it concerns the kingdom of God. Hughes states that the church and the kingdom of God cannot be too closely tied to any governmental system, and the US must be understood as separate from the kingdom of God. In fact, the US was not established as a Christian nation but as one that would neither support nor prohibit any particular religion.[72] This is evident in the first amendment, which states, "Congress shall make no law respecting an establishment of religion, or prohibiting the free exercise thereof."[73] Earthly nations are essentially antithetical to the kingdom of God in their social structures. While earthly nations, even the ones that are "Christian" nations, embrace values that exalt the rich and powerful, the kingdom of God raises up the poor, disenfranchised, and dispossessed.[74] Faith and politics concern different things, and when they are merged together we end up following a religion that is neither pure nor undefiled. The atrocities of war and greed are only allowed in such a religion. As Hughes writes,

> When Christians embrace the myth of Christian America but refuse to question the nation when it behaves in ways that are alien—even hostile—to the Christian faith, they implicitly transform their religion into a highly destructible force that erodes justice for the poor and threatens the peace and stability of the world. In this radically perverse scenario, Jesus and the religion that bears his name now sanction war instead of peace, oppression instead of reconciliation, and greed instead of selfless giving.[75]

Earthly nations embrace greed, self-interest, and violence in order to maintain power and privilege in the world, whereas the kingdom of God lifts up the ones who are hurt in the world. Jesus' goal in proclaiming the kingdom

71. Hauerwas, *A Better Hope*, 94.

72. Hughes, *Christian America and the Kingdom of God*, 2.

73. "Bill of Rights."

74. Hughes, *Christian America and the Kingdom of God*, 3.

75. Ibid., 30.

of God is to promote a radically new kingdom where the empire's values are flipped on their heads.[76] This is the kingdom that God intended all along, and the earthly kingdoms are an apparition or a bad dream of life in Christ on earth. If this is the case, and the earthly kingdoms are far away from the kingdom of God, how can Christians engage the world socially and politically?

A Nonviolent Church as a Real Option

The above polemic against a nationalistic Christianity may seem altogether negative, forcing Christians to adopt some form of quietism. This is not my intention, however. Rather, I am seeking how to rightly be Christian in a secular environment. Hauerwas makes similar claims: "I have never sought to justify Christian withdrawal from social and political involvement; I have just wanted us to be involved as Christians."[77] Instead of allowing the world to influence our Christianity, which ultimately leads to a nationalistic Christianity, we must allow our faith to dictate how we relate to the world socially and politically. As individuals, our Christianity must inform our political insight, and not vice versa. This means that we must not blindly follow a politician or political party. We must be critical and discerning, holding every politician's rhetoric and political position to the scrutiny of Christ's message. We need to form something like a checklist of Christ's position on topics and see how well a politician or political position holds up to its standards. This can help inform us on how to vote "Christianly."

When Christians stand against anti-Christian ideals and offer alternatives, then the church will function as light in a dark world. But if the church is subsumed into national identity, then no real alternate option can be given. Hauerwas writes, " . . . the task of Christians is to be the sort of people and community that can become a real option and provide a real confrontation for others. Unless such a community exists, then no real option exists."[78] The church will regain its political significance if it can set itself up as an alternative to things like war and Constantinianism by promoting a commitment to Christian nonviolence.[79]

---

76. Ibid., 63.

77. Hauerwas, *A Better Hope*, 24.

78. Hauerwas, *A Community of Character*, 105.

79. Hauerwas, *War and the American Difference*, 12.

As tragedies will inevitably occur in the world, we must sustain each other through hardships, instead of seeking vengeful retaliation.[80] To retaliate is to foster and enable the vicious cycle that produced the tragedy in the first place. The only way to overcome a systemic evil is to offer a better alternative that can stand against the evils of the world. A Christian's guiding principle in political discourse should be the notion that peace is the means and end of a redeemed society. When peaceableness is the mark of the Christian, then other issues such as the nature of morality, the meaning of freedom, and the reliability of religious convictions gain their appropriate context.[81] So peace must become the hallmark of Christian living before a Christian spotlights other cultural and political issues. Peace cannot be taken by power but is given to us as a gift from God. We receive this gift as we become the community that is centered on the peaceable king who was killed for our redemption and teaches us how to live peacefully in a rebellious world.[82] Peace is an order that is built on the truth of the crucified and risen Christ, whereas coercion is an order built on lies.[83] Both contain order rather than disorder, but the order built from coercion is a perversion of God's intentions for the world. When this order is in power it produces violence and war, often in the name of God, but is ultimately the antithesis of God.

Peace is the hallmark of the kingdom of God, and the church itself is the alternative to war. For Hauerwas the war has already been defeated by Christ on the cross, but since the world does not see that it has been freed it continues to fight. The world is like prisoners who were chained up in a cell. Christ opened the door and loosened the chains of those in prison, but the prisoners were so used to the darkness that they did not realize they were free and stayed put. When the church becomes the alternative to war, then it will shine light on those who have refused to see. Hauerwas writes,

> I do not want to convince Christians to work for the abolition of war, but rather I want us to live recognizing that in the cross of Christ war has already been abolished. So I am not asking Christians to work to create a world free of war. The world has already been saved from war. The question is how Christians can and should live in a world of war as a people who believe that war has been abolished.[84]

80. Hauerwas, *A Community of Character*, 108.

81. Hauerwas, *The Peaceable Kingdom*, xvii.

82. Hauerwas and Willimon, *Resident Aliens*, 47.

83. Hauerwas, *A Community of Character*, 33.

84. Hauerwas, *War and the American Difference*, xi.

Christians should not practice nonviolence only to rid the world of war; for Hauerwas, war is already defeated. Rather, Christians should practice nonviolence because that is what it takes to be a true disciple of Christ. Jesus counseled nonviolence, and so we as Christians must practice it.[85] In so doing, perhaps, the world will see the witness of Christ through his church. The church must reflect what the world can be, in hopes that " . . . the world can and will positively respond to a witness of peace."[86]

Even though war challenges the "intelligibility of Christian practice," it has become a theological necessity for our nationalistic Christianity.[87] Christians should believe that the sacrifice of Christ has brought an end to the sacrifices of war, but instead Americans implicitly proclaim that other sacrifices must be made in order to ensure our freedom.[88] Christ put an end to Israel's sacrificial system of atonement once and for all on the cross. The consequence is that freedom, forgiveness, and atonement is now freely given to us by Christ's sacrifice. Americans, however, have developed their own sacrificial system to replace that of Christ's. For some reason, the ideal of SAC is that Christ's sacrifice was not enough, and countless young men and women must also die to preserve our freedom. Soldiers are asked to become our country's sacrifice, and then we bring them into our patriotic stories so we can remember the dead.[89] Hauerwas austerely states:

> Christians no longer believe that Christ's sacrifice is sufficient for the salvation of the world, we will find other forms of sacrificial behaviors that are as compelling as they are idolatrous. In the process, Christians confuse the sacrifice of war with the sacrifice of Christ.
>
> If a people does not exist that continually makes Christ present in the world, war will always threaten to become a sacrificial system. War is a counter church. It is the most determinative moral experience many people have. That is why Christian realism requires a disavowal of war.[90]

Because America cannot comprehend the possibility of life outside of death, America becomes a "culture of death." [91] In this way, war becomes

---

85. Ibid., 38.
86. Ibid., xii-xiii.
87. Ibid., xvii.
88. Ibid., 38.
89. Hauerwas, *War and the American Difference*, xv.
90. Ibid., 34.
91. Ibid., 19.

America's altar,[92] and we cannot get rid of war because it has fused with the American imagination and " . . . captured our habits and imaginations."[93]

As an alternative to war and violence, Hauerwas calls Christians to practice nonviolent resistance. Hauerwas sees the church itself as the end of the sacrificial system of war, and nonviolent resistance is the end of hate by being the embodiment of love on earth.[94] God is love, so when the church embodies love, it shines a light on the systemic evils that allow for war to manifest from hate. The end of nonviolent resistance is entering into relationship with those who were oppressors. It is to break bread in a community that without love would be impossible.[95] Hauerwas writes, "If Christians leave the Eucharistic table ready to kill one another, we not only eat and drink judgment on ourselves, but we rob the world of the witness it needs in order to know that there is an alternative to the sacrifices of war."[96] The Christian should seek reconciliation, and true reconciliation will only come by peace.

War is against God, so songs about violence and war only glorify a kingdom that stands in opposition to God. Southern rockers often justify their concepts of justice through violence with some sort of "Christian" notion. Take the Skynyrd song "God & Guns" for instance,

> *God and guns*
> *Keep us strong*
> *That's what this country*
> *Was founded on*
> *Well we might as well give up and run*
> *If we let them take our God and guns*[97]

For Skynyrd the American ability to defend itself through violence belong in the same category as Christ. While Jesus said, "Blessed are the peacemakers" in the beatitudes, Skynyrd goes so far to call guns the peacemaker: "you say your prayers and you thank the lord for that peacemaker in the dresser drawer."[98] The God who supports violence and calls guns the "peacemaker" is not Christ, but the God of the empire. Hughes states it aptly:

92. Ibid., 33.

93. Ibid., 54.

94. Ibid., 90.

95. Ibid.

96. Hauerwas, *War and the American Difference*, 69.

97. Lynyrd Skynyrd, "God & Guns."

98. Ibid.

Jesus counseled peace, but the empire practiced violence. Jesus counseled humility, but the empire engaged in a ruthless pursuit of power. Jesus counseled concern for the poor, but the empire practiced exaltation of the rich. Jesus counseled modesty, but the empire practiced extravagance. Jesus counseled simple living, but the empire encouraged luxurious living for those with the means to embrace that way of life. And while Jesus counseled forgiveness and love for one's enemies, the empire practiced vengeance.[99]

The religion of Southern rock does not adopt all of the sentiments of the empire, but it does adopt some, especially when it comes to violence, vengeance, and power. As such, the religious nationalism found in Southern rock is something that must be rejected. "Southern American Christianity" must be replaced with "Christianity" without adjectives. Just as Christ brought the possibility of redemption to the whole world, there too are redeemable qualities of Southern rock that can speak powerfully to our understanding of God in the world. To this task we now turn.

Sin, Redemption, & Southern Hospitality

Southern rockers sing about their past failures and regrets. If the band is singing about sin in order to glorify the acts, which Southern rock bands often do, then they play into a double-mindedness that works against the kingdom of God. If the southern rockers are sincere, then the song becomes a confession—a testament to the world of what destruction sin can bring. While Skynyrd's latter iteration glorified the role of guns, for instance, the band actually portrayed a negative stance on guns in their 1975 song "Saturday Night Special." Some fans attribute "God & Gun's" change of views to the fact that Johnny, and not Ronnie, Van Zant is the main lyricist of the second incarnation of Lynyrd Skynyrd. At any rate, Ronnie Van Zant sang about the mindless violence that guns regularly enable:

> It's a Saturday night special
> Got a barrel that's blue and cold
> Ain't no good for nothin'
> But put a man six feet in a hole[100]

99. Hughes, *Christian America and the Kingdom of God,* 186.
100. Lynyrd Skynyrd, "Saturday Night Special."

This suggests that Van Zant may have had experiences that shaped his reformed stance on gun violence. Perhaps some of the most gripping Skynyrd lyrics deal with a reformed view on drugs and alcohol abuse. Van Zant penned the lyrics to "That Smell" for the band's 1977 album *Street Survivors*. Consider these lyrics:

> *Whiskey bottles, and brand new cars*
> *Oak tree you're in my way*
> *There's too much coke and too much smoke*
> *Look what's going on inside you*
> *Ooooh that smell*
> *Can't you smell that smell*
> *Ooooh that smell*
> *The smell of death surrounds you*[101]

At one point in the song Van Zant sings, "I know I been there before,"[102] counseling the listeners about the dangers of drug abuse from a place of experience. It is in this way that southern rock can be redemptive.

Instead of offering an implicit nationalistic Christian manifesto of why Southern religion and culture is better than others, Southern rockers can be effective in confessional ways. A transformational theology of rock does not wrap its Christianity up with regional nationalism expressing its superiority to other ways of life. Instead, it portrays accounts of a life lived, good and bad, from a regional perspective of insight. As Southern rockers speak from the heart about matters of life, they engage, in part, in their own redemption. As the Southern adage goes, "confession soothes the soul." Moreover, a confessional approach to rock lyrics can also aid the listener as s/he becomes interested in the band's particular context of insight.

Southern rock also portrays hospitality in unique and powerful ways. Many members of Southern rock bands contain siblings (the Allman Brothers Band, Kings of Leon, the Avett Brothers, Thomas Wynn and the Believers, etc.), and the ones that do not often fight like brothers, make up, and show love and solidarity with each other. Joining a Southern rock band is often like joining a new family. Since the family is of utmost importance in Southern rock, family matters constantly come up in Southern rock lyrics. The Grammy-nominated Christian southern rock band, Rhett Walker Band, for instance, formed to make music about their faith, family, and

101. Lynyrd Skynyrd, "That Smell."
102. Ibid.

their country. Their hope is to let those who come to listen join in on the fun. They want to invite you in like a brother and experience life with them, even if only for a moment. The band recently stated in an interview: "We are a southern rock band, so we hope that when you come to a show, you can sit, enjoy music, and forget about the world for a second."[103]

Conclusion

The appeal of southern rock is that it unabashedly speaks about religious matters in powerful and often provocative ways. They prioritize their faith and family, which often comes across in their songs. The danger rises when the band's sense of faith gets distorted beyond recognition. Confessions turn into polemics, and the gospel that is preached becomes one that is alien to that of Christ's. Our transformational theology of rock has much to learn from Southern rock as it comes to matters of redemption and hospitality, but, like every genre of rock, there are things that must be critiqued or even left behind. In the case of Southern rock, the nationalistic Christianity, which supports violence, sexism, and racism, must be rejected.

This chapter engaged in a dialogue concerning the rightful place of the kingdom of God by using southern rock as a case study. Southern rock often portrays a sullied version of Christianity in order to support views that are antithetical to the kingdom of God. We argued for an authentic Christianity that informs our politics and cultural awareness and not vice versa. To this end, we looked at the Christian ethics of Hauerwas, Hughes, and Wilsey in order to develop a better sense of what living Christ-like in the US might look like.

While Southern rock falls into error by joining culture and politics with religion, the next chapter will look at a genre of rock that does the opposite. In many ways, the dissidence of punk rock is the antithesis of syncretistic Southern rock. Moreover, liberation theology is the converse of nationalistic Christianity. While we continue to address the church's role in culture and politics as the image of the kingdom of God on earth, we will next explore punk rock's affinity towards liberation and see how this track rounds out our discussion about politics and the kingdom of God.

103. Berk. "Rhett Walker Shares the Story."

6

Punk Rock Liberation

T owards the end of their career as a band, the Ramones frequented South America playing for massive crowds in cities including Rio de Janeiro, Buenos Aires and São Paulo. The Ramones were so well received and displayed so much solidarity with their fans at these shows that they dubbed South America as *home*—not a *second home*, or *home away from home*, but simply, *home*.[1] These shows went down as some of the best in Ramones history. In fact, they went over so well that 1996 would see the Ramones return to Rio as part of their farewell tour playing in front of crowds of 40,000+ people. Masses of devoted fans would follow the band around on the streets.[2] Why did the South Americans gravitate towards simple punk rock from four white Americans? Drummer Marky Ramone believes that it might have been the Ramones' lack of pretension and come-as-you-are attitude that endeared the band to the South American fan base. He writes:

> It seemed that even with a language barrier, the fans 'got' everything we were about. Not to look a gift horse or a gift nation in the mouth, but I had to wonder why. There were at least a few obvious answers. In a class-conscious country like Argentina, where for centuries there was a caste system, the Ramones might have represented a leveling of the playing field. All you needed were sneakers, jeans, a T-shirt, and a leather jacket and you were one of us. Membership may not have been free, but it was certainly

1. Ramone and Herschlag, *Punk Rock Blitzkrieg*, 347.
2. "End of the Century."

cheap. . . . A rock show—any good rock show—provided a short but huge relief from reality and sent a booming message to authority. A good rock band was a bunch of antiheroes.[3]

The Ramones somehow helped to craft the identity of the impoverished and marginalized youth of South America—at least the ones present at the shows. The punk rock ethos struck a chord with young people who grew up in a national and political system of oppression. Many South Americans have long histories of oppression, and the Ramones were able to speak a sort of liberation to them. With themes of anti-establishment rebellion and a strong sense of working-class responsibility, punk rock, at least in this case, produced the anthem of the poor. There is liberating power in punk rock, a power that is also evident in liberation theology. Perhaps by spending time at the crossroads of punk rock and liberation theology, we can better understand the plight of the oppressed.

Isn't punk rock anti-establishment to a fault? What theological musings can derive from a genre of music that is fundamentally against any sort of power structures? The church as an establishment is a power structure, after all, but perhaps there is a bit more nuance to the liberating labors of punk. Punk rock, as we shall see, is critical and countercultural but in a way that is ultimately liberating rather than merely combative. Liberation is expository and efficacious. It seeks to reveal the unethical relations of the dominant power structure before overcoming it. Liberation is above all a cry for societal justice.[4] As theologian Alejandro García-Rivera writes, "Liberation . . . consists not so much in concretely overthrowing a reigning system of abusive power, but, rather, subverting the foundations of the imagination of such power which perpetuates its 'pseudo-existence.'"[5]

I will argue in this chapter that *the aftermath of the mid-1970s punk rock revolution established liberating principles, which offer insight into how one can express spiritual solidarity with marginalized groups.* In this way, punk is a rock genre in which the song of the poor can emerge. First, we will look at the tenets of liberation theology as articulated by Gustavo Gutiérrez, Miguel De La Torre, and Eldin Villafañe. Next, we will trace the punk rock revolution of 1976–1978 as foundational for the many punk subgenres that would ensue. We will particularly look at the Ramones, the Sex Pistols, and the Clash, as these three bands form what would be known as the punk ethos. Finally, we

3. Ramone and Herschlag, *Punk Rock Blitzkrieg,* 348–349.

4. Beyer, "De-Centering Religious Singularity," 375.

5. García-Rivera, *The Community of the Beautiful,* 186.

will, as mentioned above, spend some time at the crossroads of liberation theology and punk rock to see what sort of themes and theological commitments emerge. I argue that the distinctive counter-countercultural identity formation and do-it-yourself (DIY) communal spirit of punk are invaluable resources for articulating a theology of liberation.

Liberation Theology and the Song of the Poor

Liberation theology puts a new spin on the kingdom of God conversation we began in chapter one. While chapter one discussed several views of the kingdom of God's relation to the world, liberation theology seeks to find out how the kingdom of God actually affects the status of humanity and society. As theologian and originator of liberation theology Gustavo Gutiérrez writes, "We are dealing here with the classic question of the relation between faith and human existence, between faith and social reality, between faith and political action, or in other words, between the Kingdom of God and the building up of the world."[6] Liberation theology is a pragmatic theology that arises from the streets of the people. Since theology is human reflection on God, we must first approach the human situation from whence the reflection is being made. Gutiérrez is a Catholic theologian from Lima, Peru, and his socio-historical context saw destitute Peruvians held into socio-economic oppression. Thus, Gutiérrez knew that he needed to express a new approach to theology that gave appropriate attention to the condition of his people. This brought Gutiérrez to read the Bible with a particular focus on Christ as liberator. In this way, liberation theology seeks to understand and participate in "God's comprehensive liberating action in the world."[7]

The catalyst for liberation theology was Gutiérrez's important book *A Theology of Liberation*. In it Gutiérrez argues that theology must be critical reflection on humankind and Christian praxis in relation to God and the church.[8] As such, theology must criticize the institution of the church and other secular institutions if they aid in the oppression of people. Gutiérrez writes, " . . . theology has a necessary and permanent role in liberation from every form of religious alienation—which is often fostered by the ecclesiastical institution itself when it impedes an authentic approach to the Word

---

6. Gutiérrez, *A Theology of Liberation*, 29.

7. Gutiérrez and Müeller, *On the Side of the Poor*, 14.

8. Gutiérrez, *A Theology of Liberation*, 9.

of the Lord."[9] The real contextual situation of the faith community must be the impetus for theological reflection.[10] To this end, theology has historically ignored the entirety of its people as many marginalized Christians have been unable to articulate their distinctive theological tenets. This is in part due to systemic programs not allowing marginalized voices to enter mainstream ideology and in part to the marginal group's lack of training required to make erudite theological assertions. Furthermore, when theology becomes too cerebral and bookish, it ignores the plight of the poor—the same poor that Christ says are the blessed ones (Luke 6:20).[11] Liberation theology corrects this and offers a new way. Gutiérrez defines this mode of critical reflection as

> . . . a theology of the liberating transformation of the history of humankind and also therefore that part of the humankind—gathered into *ecclesia*—which openly confesses Christ. This is a theology which does not stop with reflecting on the world, but rather tries to be part of the process through which the world is transformed. It is a theology which is open—in the protest against trampled human dignity, in the struggle against the plunder of the vast majority of humankind, in liberating love, and in the building of a new, just, and comradely society—to the gift of the Kingdom of God.[12]

Liberation theology is thus the people's theology—a theology that is informed by the socio-historical and political context of its adherents.

The world is unjust because of sin. While sin yielded human death and destruction, it did so in every aspect of the human condition, including its structures and authorities. Because of this, one cannot hold to a narrow understanding of sin that does not fix upon the social elements that were also affected. Gutiérrez, therefore, accounts for three levels of meaning for the term sin. First, sin marks the breakup of relationship between God and humanity.[13] Every form of inner and outer enslavement stems from this level of meaning. Second, sin thrusts us into an inner slavery to the " . . . powers of unreflective profit-seeking."[14] And finally, sin manifests into an outer slavery that is enabled by corrupt economic and social insti-

---

9. Ibid., 10.

10. Gutiérrez and Müller, *On the Side of the Poor,* 55.

11. Ibid., 16.

12. Gutiérrez, *A Theology of Liberation,* 12.

13. Gutiérrez and Müller, *On the Side of the Poor,* 17.

14. Ibid.

tutions.[15] This last sense imputes the social dimension of sin that is often ignored in other existential theologies. Gutiérrez sees sin as a destructive anti-Christian force that begins within the individual and stretches out to the structures of human governing. To break out of the vicious cycle of sin and oppression, which attempts to keep people subjugated, one must be saved by the liberating Christ.[16]

"Salvation" and "liberation" are synonyms that refer to God's communion with suffering humanity by the redemption found in Christ.[17] However, Gutiérrez likewise distinguishes three levels of meaning for the term liberation that interpenetrate and apprise each other. First, liberation refers to the hopes and ambitions of oppressed people and social classes. This level looks at the socio-economic situation that " . . . puts them [the oppressed] at odds with wealthy nations and oppressive classes,"[18] and sees what the oppressed are eager to be liberated from. Second, liberation situates the poor into a historical context, which broadens the horizons of the sought after social changes.[19] This level sees the plight of the poor as a long-standing systemic issue and looks to the present for the establishment of a more just society. Finally, liberation harkens back to the Bible as Christ is the great liberator of humanity. This is a precedent that was set at creation and powerfully demonstrated in the Exodus as the Hebrews were set free from Egyptian oppression. Christ is the one who liberates people from sin, which is the ultimate cause for all injustice and oppression.[20]

Theologian Miguel De La Torre sets out to articulate his liberation theology as an outworking of a Hispanic reading of the gospels. In his book *The Politics of Jesús*, De La Torre unapologetically teases out a Christology that is created from a contextualized Latino/a[21] framework.[22] He does

15. Ibid.

16. Gutiérrez, *A Theology of Liberation*, 103.

17. Gutiérrez and Müller, *On the Side of the Poor*, 17.

18. Gutiérrez, *A Theology of Liberation*, 24.

19. Ibid.

20. Ibid., 25.

21. Although some scholars like to differentiate the terms "Hispanic" and "Latino/a," I have chosen to follow De La Torre and Edwin Aponte's convention of using the terms interchangeably since both labels fail to express the complexity of Hispanic history and culture (De La Torre and Aponte, *Introducing Latino/a Theologies*, 16.) Hispanic typically means "of Spain" as it references groups of people from Spanish decent. Latino/a has ancient Roman roots so it makes room for other descent apart from Spain (15).

22. De La Torre, *The Politics of Jesús*, xv.

this arguing that all Christologies are already contextual, and Christians construct their own image of Christ given the information that was contextually granted them. Not all of these constructed Christologies, however, can be conceived as liberating for Hispanics. As such, De La Torre does not pretend to find the objective historical Christ but views Christ through the lens of a Hispanic follower, opting for a subjective biography of Jesus.

De La Torre differentiates the Eurocentric "Jesus" with the Spanish rendered "Jesús," hence the title *The Politics of Jesús*.[23] He does this in order to "decolonize" the minds of oppressed Hispanics. De La Torre writes, "Before anyone can speak about the liberation of the marginalized from societal, political, and economical structure of oppression, we must begin by liberating ourselves from our own colonized minds, from equating the apex of rigorous thought with Eurocentric subjectivity."[24] So De La Torre is offering a re-reading of the gospels that will inspire adherents to be liberated from oppressive ideology before pursuing the work of communal and societal liberation. The ideological structures must first be broken because they are the gravity holding the oppressed to the floor.[25] De La Torre warns us, "For those in power to remain in power, a constructed Jesus is needed that either explicitly or implicitly maintains the status quo."[26] Therefore, the oppressed must embrace a different image of a liberating Jesús to free their minds from the vicious cycle of oppression and ideological validation that is evident in the unjust structures.

Jesús was a colonized man. He was born and reared in a circumstance of destitution under the empirical power of Rome.[27] Further removed from respectability and propriety, Jesús was raised in Nazareth. De La Torre writes, "Those who came from Nazareth, like Jesús, were looked down upon, mainly because large portions of the Jews living in the area were Hellenized. Being Hellenized meant being of mixed races. The region's inhabitants were too multiethnic in the eyes of the more pureblood Jews living in Jerusalem."[28] In other words, Jesús was from the "barrio," the poor and diverse community that forms at the outskirts of a society. What is so

---

23. This is also a play off the title of John Howard Yoder's influential book, Yoder, *The Politics of Jesus*.

24. Ibid., 25.

25. Gutiérrez, *A Theology of Liberation*, 77.

26. De La Torre, *The Politics of Jesús*, 12.

27. Ibid., 27.

28. Ibid., 59.

radical about the incarnation, then, is not merely the fact that an infinite God would take on flesh, but that God would take on the flesh of the lowly and outcast.[29] Jesús was a wandering migrant, coming from the bottom so that he may be the brother of us all. No one is too low for Christ. His incarnation is thus a divine response to the inhuman conditions that the oppressed are forced to endure.[30] As De La Torre writes, "Just as Jesús . . . participated in the everyday of his time, so too are we called to engage in politics of our present moment by feeding the hungry, providing healthcare to the uninsured, engaging in bringing about justice."[31] For De La Torre, it is the example of Christ's life, including the circumstances in which he was born, that should inform a Christian's ethics. We are to bring justice in the world because Christ did so first. We are to fight for the poor, not only because Christ commanded it, but also because Jesús was counted among them. God realizes full solidarity with humanity through Jesús, as God learns firsthand the true plight of humanity.[32] As such, it is a Christology of Jesús that can speak to the lives and circumstances of the disenfranchised.

While Gutiérrez focuses on theology proper and De La Torre focuses on Christology, Pentecostal theologian Eldin Villafañe sets out to articulate a pneumatology of liberation from a Hispanic-American perspective. While liberation theology was significant for voicing the concerns of the poor in indigenous, mainly Hispanic, communities, it had more of a profound influence on Western liberal theology than on the everyday spirituality of majority-world Latino/a societies. Instead, the poor communities around the world seem to have gravitated towards Pentecostalism. As Miller and Yamamori write, " . . . while Liberation Theology opted for the poor, the poor opted for Pentecostalism."[33] Villafañe, however, sees liberation theology as an integral part of Hispanic identity and spirituality. In his book, *The Liberating Spirit*, Villafañe situates liberation theology into a larger framework of Hispanic theology, which also adequately addresses the primacy of the Spirit in Hispanic spirituality.

Villafañe defines Hispanic Pentecostalism as " . . . part of that movement of the lower class—the working poor and unemployed—that resolves its economic and class status situation by means of a sectarian religious

29. Ibid., 33.
30. Ibid., 53.
31. Ibid., 52.
32. Ibid., 85.
33. Miller and Yamamori, *Global Pentecostalism*, 12.

affiliation."[34] The church community for Hispanic Pentecostals is the " . . . religious resolution to economic deprivations."[35] Villafañe sees several parameters that shape the indigenous spirituality and implicit theology of Hispanic Pentecostals. Along the lines of Gutierrez, Hispanic Pentecostals adhere to a *contextual theology* (emerging from the *barrios*), and a *liberation theology* as Hispanics seek identity and solidarity with the poor and oppressed. Hispanic Pentecostals also adhere to a *spiritual theology* since their faith and practice is more informed by emotive/spiritual factors than cognitive signs and symbols, and they adhere to a *charismatic theology* as glossolalic experiences color their understanding of spirituality. Insofar as Hispanic Pentecostals see the reality of God as a person in the here and now, they also adhere to an *existential theology* and to an *egalitarian theology* as the glossolalic experience levels the gender disparities found in many societies.[36] Spiritual, charismatic, and egalitarian theologies are all pneumatocentric and are needed in addition to the standards of liberation in order to account for the robust Spirit-filled spirituality found in Hispanic cultures around the world.

Theology should, like Gutiérrez has made clear, correlate holistically with *all* of life because the Spirit empowers and leads us in all areas of our lives.[37] Liberation theology's Christocentric focus tends to ignore the spiritual side of life whereas a pneumatological liberation theology accounts for both the physical and spiritual aspects of human existence. It grieves the Spirit when believers manifest the works of sin and aid in its oppressive structures. The Spirit seeks to restore the fellowship that is broken by sin in a "bond of love"[38] by empowering the people with charismatic gifts to do the important work of kingdom building. It is the Spirit that brings order to chaos and protects and provides for Creation.[39] Liberation can only be truly obtained by the liberating Christ, but this is only done by the power of the liberating Spirit.

Liberation theology offers a fresh perspective on the kingdom of God (Gutiérrez), Christology (De La Torre), and the Spirit (Villafañe) that makes way for concrete Christian action in the world today. It moves

34. Villafañe, *The Liberating Spirit*, 137.

35. Ibid., 138.

36. Ibid., 131–132.

37. Ibid., 165.

38. Ibid., 172.

39. Ibid., 182.

beyond armchair speculation and takes theology to the streets. Since its inception in the 1970s, liberation theology has influenced several other contextual theologies such as black liberation theology and feminist theology. In each instance, the theology starts from the context of an oppressed people group and teases out theological reflection that will bring justice to an unjust situation. For the purposes of this book, however, we can only mention the existence of these important theologies and liberation theology's influence on them. It is worth noting, however, that unlike Gutiérrez's liberation theology, black liberation theologians have been particularly attentive to the relationship between popular music and theology.[40]

Before discussing punk rock's kinship to liberation theology, we should note that liberation theology does not come barring difficulties. For instance, because liberation theology is overly functional, it tends to lose touch with basic human values, which William Dyrness argues are basically aesthetic.[41] This poses a challenge for Hispanic liberation theologies. Does a theology that lacks a nuanced approach to worship adequately represent the spiritual commitments of Hispanic communities? The overtly political nature of liberation theology does well in highlighting important issues of justice but often misses out on a proper evaluation of the songs of the oppressed. Apart from Roberto Goizueta's *Christ Our Companion: Toward a Theological Aesthetics of Liberation* and an essay by James Nickoloff, which contrasts liberation theology with Giuseppe Verdi's *Aida*,[42] very little has been written about the aesthetics of liberation, which is mystifying since music and sensual experience is so important for Hispanic communities. Perhaps, this is partly why Hispanics around the world are gravitating towards Pentecostalism.[43] Pentecostal worship in a Hispanic society emphasizes the transformation of the individual. As Andrew McCoy writes,

> . . . both liberation theology and Pentecostalism tend to instrumentalize worship in response to suffering, but they do it in different ways; whereas liberation theology understands worship as a collective action meant to challenge oppressive structures, Pentecostalism, in contrast, tends to emphasize the transforming possibilities of worship as an *individual experience*.

40. See Cone, *The Spiritual and the Blues*; Thurman, *Deep River and the Negro Spiritual Speaks of Life and Death*; and Beckford, *Jesus Dub*.

41. Dyrness, *Poetic Theology*, 55.

42. Goizueta, *Christ Our Companion*; and Nickoloff, "Gustavo Gutiérrez Meets Giuseppe Verdi," 203–221.

43. Jenkins, *The Next Christendom*, 95.

The connection between Pentecostal worship and liberation theology has not been fully fleshed out either. For instance, Villafañe's *The Liberating Spirit* does not have a section articulating the Pentecostal aesthetics of liberation although he does talk about the cultural responsibility humans have to manifest God's creativity and goodness in the world.[44] There is, however, a song of the oppressed and authentic ways to express the outrage of social injustice. In what aesthetic manner can liberation be adequately vented? I would like to argue that there already exists a genre of rock that vociferously yells the song of the poor: punk rock.

Liberating Rock Music

Mark Andersen eloquently states:

> Punk rock, at its best, has always been a cry for life, for authentic existence past the boundaries and barriers so often nourished by society. A few words scribbled down, spat out with feral force, propelled upward by guitar and drum, full of raw conviction and urgency. As fragments of word and sound collide, the beautiful chaos opens a rupture in life-as-we-know-it, providing a window into worlds of possibility, life-as-it-might-be.[45]

Punk rock has (potentially) a liberating character and focuses on familial community in opposition to the oppressive culture in power. As such, punk has qualities that are reminiscent of liberation theology and, as I will later argue, offers insight into how one can truly express solidarity with marginalized groups. Nevertheless, punk has a raucous origin and developed out of the debris of chaotic and nihilistic roots.

Punk formed as a distinct genre of rock music in the mid-1970s. Precursors to punk began in the late 1960s with boisterous acts such as the Velvet Underground and the Stooges.[46] Later, the early 1970s saw the emergence of artists such as the New York Dolls and Patti Smith, which sported a critical attitude that would perpetuate the punk rock ethos. These artists were anti-establishment, critical of mainstream rock music, and displayed a nihilistic attitude towards dominant power structures with wild antics on and off the

---

44. Villafañe, *The Liberating Spirit*, 188.

45. Andersen, "The Virus that Cures," 184.

46. Cross, 20*th Century Rock and Roll*, 61.

stage.[47] The word "punk" was used by John Holstrom, Legs McNeil, and Ged Dunn as the title to their new magazine, which would focus on various elements of popular youth culture as McNeil recounts, " . . . weird rock & roll that nobody but us seemed to like: the Velvets, the Stooges, the New York Dolls, and now the Dictators."[48] It was here that punk would be associated with the subsequent rock bands influenced by the early 1970s progenitors. The punk movement developed on two main fronts: New York and London. Although several notable acts emerged by 1976, the three best-known and most influential bands were the Ramones, the Sex Pistols, and the Clash. These three bands formed what Alan Cross referred to as the holy trinity of punk.[49] Before looking at these band's distinctive contributions to the punk ethos, it would serve us well to quickly survey the features of punk.

Punk's origin historically divides into two waves. The first wave comes in the mid-1970s where punk bands were nihilistic and shocking and " . . . concerned themselves with disturbance and subversion."[50] This wave marks the birth of punk and follows the trajectories of punks "holy trinity." The second wave, beginning in late 1977, tried to cope with the problematization of constituency[51] with bands such as the Misfits and Bad Religion. Then in the late 1970s and throughout the 1980s punk splintered even further into subgenres such as Oi! (Cockney Rejects, Angelic Upstarts) and hardcore (Bad Brains, Black Flag). The 1990s and early 2000s saw the emergence of more influential subgenres such as post-hardcore (Fugazi, Underoath), emo (Dashboard Confessional, My Chemical Romance), metalcore (As I Lay Dying, Killswitch Engage), ska (Streetlight Manifesto, The Mighty Mighty Bosstones), and pop punk (Green Day, Blink-182). Many of these subgenres came about by fusing with other musical genres, like metal, pop, or reggae, to create new identities.

Punk as a movement reacted against several facets of society. It was a movement of defiance, which embraced " . . . everything that cultured people, and hippies, detested."[52] Its first goal was nihilistic—the breakdown and destruction of the status quo.[53] While rock music began as a counter-

---

47. Ibid., 61.

48. McNeil and McCain, *Please Kill Me,* 203.

49. Cross, *20th Century Rock and Roll,* 61.

50. Davies, "The Future of 'No Future,'" 15.

51. Ibid., 16.

52. Savage, *England's Dreaming,* 133.

53. Andersen, "The Virus that Cures," 184.

cultural response to dominant mainstream culture, punk saw rock and roll as the new mainstream. Grossberg writes, "Punk called into question the affective power of rock and roll; it attempted to incorporate its own possibility of incorporation, and its only strategy for survival was constantly to proliferate its own excorporative practice. It tried to celebrate rock and roll even as it acknowledged its conceit."[54] Punk set out to destroy rock as an establishment from within. It became the first genre of rock that was self-critical against its own roots. Mainstream rock, contends Iafrate, " . . . did not speak to the socio-political conditions in which they (punk rockers) found themselves and tended to function as more of a distraction from 'real life.'"[55] Punk epitomized rebellion and donned contrarian symbolism and antics to excite and enrage the masses. Savage writes, "Punk was trafficking in taboos at the same time as it sought to illuminate and dramatize deep-seated contradictions with a sophisticated, ironic rhetoric."[56] The punk ethos spanned farther than its music, encapsulating a new attitude towards the world—one that was critical and subversive.

Aesthetically, punk tried to cut back from the glamour and pretentiousness of mainstream rock. Regev writes that punk had " . . . an artistic ideology of primitivism and minimalism."[57] Punk is sonically loud and fast paced, and early punk reduced down to simple 4/4 drumbeats accompanied by three or four chord progressions on guitars. Punk bands did not showboat with sweeping guitar solos or elaborate drum fills, but sped through two to three-minute anarchistic anthems. Vocal melodies were typically catchy and the lyrics were confrontational. This minimalistic bent was, however, intentional and served as a source of connection to the common person. Davies writes, "Their [punk bands] lack of musical skill itself removed barriers between performer and audience, demystified artistic production."[58] Punk, especially hardcore, offers what Maskell calls a "kinesthetic imagination" that includes thrashing, moshing, and hardcore dancing as a way of " . . . performing history and contemporizing its effects."[59] Like in metal, these actions are initiatory and identity forming.

54. Grossberg, "Another Boring Day in Paradise," 247.

55. Iafrate, "More Than Music," 40.

56. Savage, *England's Dreaming*, 243.

57. Regev, "Producing Artistic Value," 94.

58. Davies, "The Future of 'No Future,'" 22.

59. Maskell, "Performing Punk," 414.

The Unholy Trinity of Punk

Although we certainly can trace earlier roots, the prototypical punk sound was advanced by the Ramones. The Ramones formed in New York in 1974 as a group of novice musicians who wanted to play forceful and energetic rock for the growing East Village scene centered on the famous concert venue CBGB. The Ramones played hard and fast, stripping rock and roll down to its unassuming essence. Bassist, Dee Dee would start every song with a count-in, and then the band would follow the formulaic conventions of late 1950s rock and roll but at hyper speed. Music editor Michael Hann says, " . . . anything unnecessary—anything that distracts from the rush of excitement—is excised. The aim of a Ramones song is not to make you admire the musicianship or the arrangement. It's to take you from a standing start to fever pitch in 120 seconds or less."[60] This simplicity, speed, and dynamism would forever shape the sonic dimensions of punk. The Ramones released their debut album *Ramones* in 1976 after spending $6,400 and a week to record it. This album would put punk rock on the map and set a precedent for cheap, efficient, and minimalistic productions.[61] As Joey Ramone says, "It kicked off punk rock and started the whole thing—as well as us."[62] *Ramones* boasted several hits, but "Blitzkrieg Bop" forever entered the consciousness of punk, and lyrically portrays what the Ramones are all about: getting hyped and letting loose to the rhythm of straightforward rock music. Consider the opening lines of the song:

> *Hey ho, let's go! Hey ho, let's go!*
> *Hey ho, let's go! Hey ho, let's go!*
> *They're forming in straight line*
> *They're going through a tight wind*
> *The kids are losing their minds*
> *The blitzkrieg bop*[63]

Those four words, "hey ho, let's go," became the new punk rock anthem.

As a cultural force the Ramones added other ideological and aesthetic elements to the punk ethos. For instance, each member adopted the surname "Ramone," in homage to Paul McCartney who used the surname as

60. Hann, "RIP Tommy Ramone."
61. Savage, *England's Dreaming*, 156.
62. Ramone in *Please Kill Me*, 229.
63. Ramones, "Blitzkrieg Bop."

an alias when checking into hotels. This grafted the members into a brother-hood of sorts, displaying the importance of community in punk rock. John Cummings, Jeffrey Hyman, Douglas Colvin, and Thomas Erdelyi would be known as Johnny Ramone, Joey Ramone, Dee Dee Ramone, and Tommy Ramone. After recording three studio albums with the band, Tommy left the band to pursue a career as a music producer. His replacement was Marc Bell (Marky Ramone), former drummer of Dust and Richard Hell & the Voidoids. Although other members popped in and out as replacements and short-lived bandmates, only Johnny, Joey, Dee Dee, Tommy, and Marky were inducted to the Rock and Roll Hall of Fame in 2002.

The Ramones also established a punk look. Although this is not the only or even the best recognized aesthetic of punk, their uniform guise would prove influential. They wore tight t-shirts with leather jackets and tight ripped jeans and sported shaggy hair. This look, in a way, codified the ideas of familial unity and rebelliousness. It was difficult to work out what the Ramones politics were as they wore and promoted militarism and right-wing imagery.[64] John is famous for being a conservative Republican, but the rest of the band was, for all intents and purposes, more prone to chaos and ambigu-ity than political party affiliation. Their lyrical content was not as rebellious or political as the British punk bands that would follow. Nevertheless, their style, sound, and presence, made the Ramones one of the most influential progenitors of punk, and one of the most influential rock bands of history.

The early nihilism of punk is best exemplified by the Sex Pistols. The Sex Pistols were a London-based punk rock band, which was put together by visionary manager Malcolm McLaren. The Ramones' sound, attitude, and early success inspired a new generation of English musicians to form bands, and inspired business minded entrepreneurs to cash in on a new movement of rock.[65] McLaren formed the Sex Pistols, and Bernie Rhodes formed the Clash.[66] These two bands would prove to be the most influential of the bud-ding London underground music scene. The Sex Pistols and the Clash arose in a time when England was struggling politically. The economic situation of 1976 was the worst it has been since the 1940s with climbing unemployment and difficult working conditions.[67] While the Ramones expressed political thought only implicitly and focused on fun, rebellion, and minimalism in

---

64. Savage, *England's Dreaming*, 138.

65. Ramone and Herschlag, *Punk Rock Blitzkrieg*, 118.

66. Savage, *England's Dreaming*, 169.

67. Ibid., 108.

their music, the British bands took politics head on. Punk displayed a style of music that the disenfranchised working class easily identified with. The natural progression for punk in the UK scene was to merge the raucous sonic elements of the Ramones with political critique and anarchy. The Sex Pistols were the first to lead this front, shifting the emphasis from a hostile, yet playful rebelliousness, to a deep anarchistic nihilism and cynicism.[68] Punk grew more violent and the Sex Pistols, led by Johnny Rotten, were bent on destroying the institutions of power.

Publicity both quickly propelled the Sex Pistols into international stardom but also rendered them notorious around the globe.[69] Unlike the Ramones, the Pistols detested the mainstream history of rock and sought to counter the counterculture of rock music.[70] As such, the Pistols were the first punk band to proclaim the "end of rock 'n' roll" and, as Davies states, " . . . the first to self-destruct when they were about to become just another rock 'n' roll band."[71] The destruction of rock by the wayward son of "punk" served symbolically as an image of youth revolting against the greater governing powers of the UK.

Musically, the Sex Pistols were also contrarian. They tried to capture the energy of their furious live show in their recordings driving a " . . . wedge into musical standards of the time."[72] The music was simplistic, and Johnny Rotten emphasized his cockney accent. Likewise Joey Ramone, although American, often sang with a faux English accent. This set a precedent in punk rock to emphasize rather than hide the sounds and language of common people. The Sex Pistols would only exist for two and a half years and produced only one full-length album *Never Mind the Bollocks, Here's the Sex Pistols* (1977). Despite their short existence, their influence was immense and helped to spearhead a decade of politically infused, nihilistic, and postapocalyptic rock. One of their greatest songs "God Save the Queen" sums up the Sex Pistols' agenda of nihilism and destruction:

> *When there's no future*
> *How can there be sin*
> *We're the flowers*

68. Ibid., 196.

69. Ibid., 172.

70. Regev, "Producing Artistic Value," 94.

71. Davies, "The Future of 'No Future,'" 12.

72. Savage, *England's Dreaming,* 206.

In the dustbin
We're the poison
In your human machine
We're the future
You're future
God save the Queen
We mean it man
We love our Queen
God saves
God save the Queen
We mean it man
There is no future
And England's dreaming[73]

While the Sex Pistols came first in England, the Clash is the best example of British punk developing its own sociology. As Savage writes, "The Sex Pistols uncompromisingly set themselves apart while the Clash were warmer and more of the people; if the Sex Pistols implicitly and then explicitly advocated the destruction of all values, the Clash were more human, closer to the dialogue of social concern and social realism—more in the world."[74] The Clash gave punk rock their creative urge. Savage says that they were " . . . the construction to the Sex Pistols' nihilism."[75] Put differently, while the Sex Pistols were bent on raising anarchy and destroying the status quo, the Clash had a sense of rebuilding a better reality after the demise of the status quo. It is the Clash, therefore, that best displays Marxist-like action and social concern evident in liberation theology. Davies tells us that " . . . the Clash wore their crudeness as a badge of working-class pride."[76] Although the Clash became heroes of the working class, the band signed major label deals with CBS, Epic, and Sony. Some of their fans saw this as selling out while others saw it as the band changing the structures of the mainstream rock business from within.[77] The Clash did lobby about keeping record and concert prices low for the sake of their fans and kept singing and exploiting their critical socio-economic themes. The Clash

73. Sex Pistols, "God Save the Queen."
74. Savage, *England's Dreaming*, 231.
75. Ibid., 239.
76. Davies, "The Future of 'No Future,'" 11.
77. Cross, *20th Century Rock and Roll*, 64.

promoted left-wing politics, and protested against the aristocracy and England's monarchy. Unlike the Sex Pistols, they were not nihilistic but were actually involved with liberation movements such as the Anti-Nazi League and Rock Against Racism.[78]

The Clash formed in 1976 by frontman Joe Strummer and released six studio albums in an eight-year span before disbanding. While they were part of the first wave of punk rock, their influence came politically as a true band of the people and musically as they fused different genres like reggae, rockabilly, and pop into their sound. Their most acclaimed album was *London Calling* (1979), which went platinum in both the UK and the US. London Calling was a double album with nineteen tracks experimental and musically diverse post-punk.[79] The lyrical content, however, continued to focus on socio-political issues in the UK. The title track of the album sums up their cynical view of England's future:

> *London calling to the faraway towns*
> *Now war is declared and battle come down*
> *London calling to the underworld*
> *Come out of the cupboard, you boys and girls*
> *London calling, now don't look to us*
> *Phony Beatlemania has bitten the dust*
> *London calling, see we ain't got no swing*
> *'Cept for the ring of that truncheon thing*
> *The ice age is coming, the sun is zooming in*
> *Meltdown expected, the wheat is growin' thin*
> *Engines stop running, but I have no fear*
> *'Cause London is drowning, and I, I live by the river*[80]

The first wave of punk came and went in two years and was already displaced by a second wave of punk by 1979. With the sound of the Ramones, the nihilism of the Sex Pistols, and the social consciousness of the Clash, a new powerful genre for the people formed. After assessing the good, bad, and ugly of the punk rock ethos, one might begin to wonder: What elements of punk rock can become resources for a transformational theology of rock?

---

78. Naylor, Mugan, Brown, and Cripps, "Rock Against Racism."

79. Cross, *20th Century Rock and Roll*, 64.

80. The Clash, "London Calling."

Counter-Countercultural Identity and the DIY Community

Ideologically, both liberation theology and punk rock seek justice for marginalized groups. They both look to tear down oppressive power structures by critical engagement, and, at their best, both offer alternative visions of what a better reality can look like. Liberation theology begins by changing the social consciousness of its adherents and then tries to move politically to promote social change. The church often models this new redeemed reality for the rest of society. Punk, on the other hand, tries to change social consciousness and institutions as well but does so concretely in different ways than liberation theology. Both can learn from each other as far as eliciting social change is concerned, and in many cases, both are already adopting each other's methods. For this section I would like to focus on punk rock's "counter-countercultural" identity formation and the DIY community as resources for a transformational theology of rock.

In his helpful article entitled, "More Than Music: Notes on 'Staying Punk' in the Church and in Theology," Michael Iafrate contends that punk rock does not merely reject all organized religion, but rather punk's relationship with religion is more complex.[81] In fact, many Christian youth in the 1980s and 1990s gravitated towards punk as they felt alienated by both their church and mainstream culture. Iafrate writes, "Punk rock communities provide safe spaces for marginalized youth who felt that they did not fit the mold of the socially conservative values of society and of right-wing Christianity."[82] Punk rock and hardcore inserted a sense of religion and spirituality to its followers, as the punk rock ethos required both devotion and authenticity. Unlike other genres of rock, punk developed a social ethic that requires its members to follow in order to be considered punk. For instance, to be punk you must stand against oppression and be radically individualistic (an ironic proposition). Punks must be loyal to their causes and "stick to their guns"[83] in the face of adversity. It does not matter where you come from; it only matters if you're authentic and truly sold out to the cause. If you claim the name of punk, you must truly be punk. Otherwise,

---

81. Iafrate, "More Than Music," 38.

82. Ibid., 40.

83. This is incidentally also the name of a popular hardcore band.

simply "unclaim." Thus, the Punk rock ethos moved beyond mere amusement. The ethical devotion to a style of life is religious in character.[84]

For instance, some Christian punk bands engage in identity formation by offering an alternative way to do life in the midst of dominant systems. As stated earlier, punk developed stylistically as a counter to rock music. Rock music was *the* counterculture of 1950s and 1960s youth, but punk rockers saw Rock as being absorbed into the dominant power structure. As such, punk came into being as a "counter-countercultural" phenomenon. Whenever a counterculture grows to be too popular, there will always be a punk there to counter it. Ideologically, any passionately believed set of principles could become the impetus of a counter-counterculture so long as the principles agitate and stand against a dominant culture. Thus, anything subversive can be punk. Would a conservative faith claim in the midst of a mostly anti-religious genre be subversive? Totally. That was the approach of bands like Relient K and MxPx early in their careers.

Christian bands often call on their listeners to stand firm in their faith in the midst of adversity. For instance, Ohio-based band Relient K wrote a song entitled "Baloon Ride" from their self-titled debut album (2000), which addressed being ridiculed for your faith:

> *I strive towards infinity.*
> *Though sometimes I don't know what to do.*
> *When other people laugh at me*
> *All I do is look towards You.*[85]

Other times Christian punk bands are polemical with their beliefs. For instance, Washington-based MxPx released an album entitled *Pokinathcha* (1994),[86] and one of the more popular songs from that album was "PxPx." Consider some of the dogmatic lyrics found in the song:

> *He's meaningful to us*
> *but not to you*
> *He's the one true center of our lives*
> *his light is shining through*
> *and on to you*
> *It's your choice*

---

84. Iafrate, "More Than Music," 47–48.
85. Relient K, "Balloon Ride."
86. This is a stylized way to say, "poking at ya."

He'll always be there waiting
Pokinatch! Punx![87]

Here, MxPx is proclaiming their faith while upholding the listener's free-dom of choice and dignity. While MxPx is being subtle about their religious leanings, there is room in punk for in-your-face, bombastic banter. Being punk means staying true—subtly or not. A great example of a counter-counterculture, which formed in punk and has been influential for faith-based groups, is straightedge.

Straightedge formed as a punk sub-culture in Washington, DC in the early 1980s as " . . . a philosophy and a lifestyle characterized by abstinence from alcohol, drugs, casual sex, and even meat and animal products in some cases."[88] This movement was catapulted into the punk nation by a band of teenagers named Minor Threat, who refused to consume drugs and alcohol.[89] Minor Threat's outspoken frontman was Ian MacKaye, and many young people from the DC area were attracted to his frank message of men-tal and physical control.[90] MacKaye decried the notion that substance abuse was integral for punk rock, pointing out that drugs and alcohol cause a person to relinquish control of his or her life to outside elements. Take, for instance, lyrics from the song "Straight Edge" from the EP entitled *Minor Threat* (1981):

> *I'm a person just like you*
> *But I've got better things to do*
> *Than sit around and smoke dope*
> *'Cause I know I can cope*
> *Laugh at the thought of eating ludes*
> *Laugh at the thought of sniffing glue*
> *Always gonna keep in touch*
> *Never want to use a crutch*
> *I've got the straight edge*[91]

As is evident, MacKaye condemned the Dionysian lifestyle that often comes along with rock music by debasing its participants. MacKaye ridicules drug

---

87. MxPx, "PxPx."
88. Wood, *Straightedge Youth*, 1.
89. Iafrate, "More Than Music," 42.
90. Wood, *Straightedge Youth*, 8.
91. Minor Threat, "Straight Edge."

abusers placing himself and his ideology above them. The real moralism for straightedge was egoistic and saw drugs and alcohol as deterrents of personal potential. Straightedge subsequently became more than a musical subgenre and emerged as a " . . . lifestyle choice involving a rejection of common forms of alleged vice."[92] Since a strong common moralism, such as that found in straightedge, is needed for community building, a straightedge punk is accepted into the punk sub-community if s/he subscribes to the straightedge moral ideology.

Wood writes, "Straightedge emerged from a largely nihilistic punk scene that often championed the very lifestyle choices most straightedge individuals claim to abhor. As straightedge became conscious of their identity at a more collective level, they sought to establish an identifiable set of boundaries for their scene and subculture."[93] Straightedge punks would mark their wrists with an "X," which would identify them as part of the straightedge community. While there was much unity within the straightedge community, the movement became fragmented when some groups became "hardline," resulting in infighting concerning how strict the straight edge rules should be followed.[94] In several cases, straightedge bands aligned themselves with particular religions as they saw moral commonality between those factions. Wood recounts one of the more popular religious fusions with straightedge to emerge in the early 1990s was known as Krishna-core. Krishna-core was a straightedge movement that promoted the ideas of the Hare Krishna movement and was initiated by the New York band Shelter.[95] While Krishna-core holds to the same moral rules as straightedge, it also sees nature and material existence as illusory and something to be overcome.[96] While Krishna-core was likely the most popular religious straightedge movement, straightedge also merged suitably with Christianity.

I find it odd that Robert Wood could write an expansive sociological study on straightedge punk (*Straightedge Youth*) but fail to discuss Christian straightedge—a subgenre that grew to prominence in the late 1990s. Because of the moral conservatism found in Christianity, virtually every Christian punk and hardcore band was able to align with straightedge. Only

92. Wood, *Straightedge Youth,* 33.

93. Ibid., 42.

94. Ibid., 45.

95. Ibid., 55.

96. Ibid.

a few bands, however, emerged from the hardcore scene speaking about straightedge in the recognizably humanistic manner of MacKaye. Perhaps, the best-known Christian straightedge band was the Florida-based hardcore band Call to Preserve. Consider the lyrics to the title track of their album *Life of Defiance* (2010):

> *Waking up from an apathetic life*
> *The last of the malcontent*
> *Won't be held back by a failed cowardice*
> *Won't dig our own graves*
> *Won't dig our own graves*
> *We won't dig our own graves*
> *Won't sleep in the daylight or abandon the lost in the dark*
> *We'll be the cause of the stir*
> *A return to a life of defiance*
> *Won't sleep in the daylight or abandon the lost in the dark*
> *We'll be the cause of the stir*
> *A return to a life of defiance*[97]

With the chant-like line "we won't dig our own grave," Call to Preserve is standing against the abuses the world has to offer, but they do so in a way that is indebted to their Christian faith. This is evident with the line "Won't sleep in the daylight or abandon the lost in the dark," which alludes to Christ's great commission. So, punk can be counter-countercultural in the way straightedge is: forming identities and communities. These themes pave the way for a rich dialogue between punk and Christian theology. The last theme I would like to address is punk rock's DIY mentality, and how this reflects the active aspect of the liberation ideology of punk.

Andersen describes punk's fundamental axiom as " . . . do whatever you can, with whatever you have, wherever you are, right now."[98] This is certainly true in the music as many punk bands form with minimal musical training between its members, and often play on cheap equipment. But, it is also true as a way of life for the punk mentality. Iafrate writes,

> The DIY approach to music-and culture-making (forming bands, producing records and labels, and organizing concerts and touring networks) found in various expressions of punk rock spills

97. Call to Preserve, "Life of Defiance."
98. Andersen, "The Virus that Cures," 185.

over into the personal ethics and politics of punks, constituting not only a style of and approach to music but an entire way of life that shapes personal and communal identity and that can be explored theologically.[99]

The politics and personal ethics of punk concern a blue-collar perspective on self-reliance and prudence. The punk mentality begins with social criticism and is then followed with concrete action. Instead of making demands for political leaders to engage in social change, the DIY approach attempts to create its own system, as " . . . alternative social forms that prefigure the types of communities punks want to see in the world."[100] The punk scene sought alternative ways to find exposure and do business that was not relying on the powerful organization of the major record label. The solution was to develop its own form of marketing and distribution with the DIY record label.

DIY labels typically provide their own printing, manufacturing, and distributing of punk music in a way that relies on personal interaction and community. As locality plays an important role in its distribution, DIY labels are typically confined to specific music scenes. The labels would make short runs of albums and circulate the music through local shops and outlets. The bands would also be responsible of making their music known and available at concerts and tours. The labels would typically split profits with the bands, allowing bands a greater percentage of revenue than they would get with major labels.[101] While the DIY label was important for circulating punk music in a given scene, they also played another vital role: community building. Kevin Dunn writes, "The respected DIY punk labels tend to be those that, regardless of size, treat their bands and other labels well by fostering a sense of community."[102] The label owners would often be friends of the bands on the label, and as such, the artists were treated with more respect and autonomy than they would with a major label.[103] The DIY labels are, in a sense, the organizers of the local punk rock scene. Iafrate writes that this DIY culture is " . . . community-centered, even communitarian,"[104] because the scene that develops consists of like-minded individuals who

99. Iafrate, "More Than Music," 38.

100. Ibid., 46.

101. Dunn, "If it Ain't Cheap, It Ain't Punk," 224.

102. Ibid., 224.

103. Ibid., 227.

104. Iafrate, "More Than Music," 42.

spend a lot of time together and share a similar set of values and social ethics. This DIY community is reminiscent of the Marxist principles found in liberation theology that focus on social action. As Dunn writes, " . . . *being* DIY and independent is far more effective than *talking* about being DIY and independent. It is a form of cultural production that can turn passive consumers into produces in their own right."[105] As such, the community building penchant found in the DIY ethic is coupled with the identity formation of the counter-countercultural ideology as important principles found in both punk rock and liberation theology that can inform our transformational theology of rock.

Conclusion

In order for rock music to be transformational, it must offer a new way to see the world and the possibility of a new identity. As discussed in chapter four, heavy metal criticizes dominant culture in order to establish a new reality. Punk rock functions similarly to metal in that it begins with critique, but unlike metal, punk establishes a hard-nosed, DIY resolution. Punk rock creates the new reality that it seeks, requiring commitment and participation from all its members. Like punk rock, liberation theology is also participatory and derives from the plight of the people. Iafrate writes, "Liberation theologies . . . have called for participatory theology, or people's theology, in which the people take the lead and the professionals do the reporting."[106] A "punk" take on theology allows for everyone to have a theological voice and for theology to come from the context of community.[107] Each genre of rock displays a unique way to see the kingdom of God and to approach matters of theology and existentiality. I have tried to show by tracing the major themes of liberation theology as pronounced by Gutierrez, De La Torre, and Villafañe that liberation theology answers life's big questions analogously to punk rock. After tracing the characteristics of punk, we saw that the counter-countercultural image making and communal DIY spirit are especially characteristic of the orthopraxis of liberation theology.

What good can come from a theology of punk rock? This question is reminiscent of Nathanael's question about Jesus in John 1:45–46: "Philip found Nathanael and said to him, 'We have found him about whom Moses

105. Dunn, "If it Ain't Cheap, It Ain't Punk," 234.

106. Iafrate, "More Than Music," 52.

107. Ibid., 53.

in the law and also the prophets wrote, Jesus son of Joseph from Nazareth.' Nathanael said to him, 'Can anything good come out of Nazareth?' Philip said to him, 'Come and see.'" As De La Torre has taught us, Nazareth was a marginalized space, like an ancient Middle Eastern barrio.[108] What good came from Nazareth? God incarnate, and ultimately personal and cosmic salvation found in Christ. What good came from liberation theology? An appeal for God's justice made manifest on earth. What good came from punk rock? Come and see.

---

108. De La Torre, *The Politics of Jesús*, 65.

7

Grunge Rock and
the Authentic Self

Nirvana frontman Kurt Cobain once said, "I'd rather be hated for who I am, than loved for who I am not."[1] This phrase reveals Cobain's central appetency: authenticity. Cobain's life can be summed up as a struggle to find himself in a world that routinely attempts to form people through disingenuous values of power and reputation. Yet Cobain's search for identity was not merely a rebellion against the status quo, but rather an existential problem that consumed his creative output and eventually his life. Cobain died at the age of 27 by apparent suicide joining the infamous "27 Club," a list of popular musicians who coincidently died at the age of 27 at the height of their careers.[2] In his life, Cobain made an image of himself that he thought was genuine, and he desperately wanted others to see that image. Cobain partook in a very real struggle that many young people deal with today. As we continue our investigation of a transformational theology of rock, we must engage with the existential questions of identity, and see how both rock music and theology approach the topic. To this end, while many rock bands deal with issues of identity, we will engage Cobain's rock genre grunge as a springboard for our theological discussion. Whereas punk rock

1. Although this quote is usually attributed to Kurt Cobain, there is some debate whether it was Marilyn Monroe who said it first, or if either of them took from the French novelist Andre Gide.

2. The list includes many notable musicians such as Jimi Hendrix, Janis Joplin, and Jim Morrison, Robert Johnson, and Amy Winehouse.

had a communal focus, *grunge rock turned inwards towards deep introspection in attempt to uncover the authentic self.*

We will begin this chapter by surveying the sound and ethos of grunge rock, which will lead into a discussion of Cobain and how his influence fits into the grunge rock culture. Then we will explore theologian Paul Tillich's work on authenticity in his existential theology and use Augustine's *Confessions* as an example of existential enquiring that is rightly directed. Finally, we will continue our search for a transformational theology of rock by looking at the Christian rock band Skillet as a case study. Skillet is a band that navigates similar existential issues as Cobain but ends in affirmation rather than nihilism. In this way we will add an important anthropological element to our transformational theology of rock.

Grunge Rock's Ugly Aesthetic

Punk rock changed the game for rock music. Punk gave permission for would-be rockers to pursue expressiveness over and against musical aptitude. Any group of kids could become the next punk rock band as the only requirements were minimal equipment and the right attitude. As punk moved from New York and London to the West coast of the US, it inspired other rock movements with its DIY ethic and minimalistic aesthetic. Grunge rock, one of the more significant rock movements of the post-punk era, developed in the Pacific Northwest in the early 1980s. Grunge was an influential movement based mainly out of Seattle, which forever changed the identity of rock music in a way analogous to punk. While punk rock was countercultural and antiestablishment, grunge was countercultural but introspective. Grunge dealt with issues of existential authenticity and what it means to be true to oneself in a pretentious world. The poster child of this existential struggle is Nirvana frontman Kurt Cobain, who was deemed the voice of Generation X as Bob Dylan was for 1960s youth and John Lennon was for the 1970s generation.[3] Before diving into Cobain's influence and existential predicament, however, let us briefly survey the history and influence of grunge rock.

---

3. Mazullo, "The Man Whom the World Sold," 730.

A Brief History of Grunge Rock

Grunge rock is a reflection of the "diverse urban personality" of Seattle's varied music scene.[4] The genre began as several post-punk garage bands formed a distinctive scene in the greater Seattle area. Grunge kept the lo-fi recording quality of punk, and like punk, celebrated the marginalized sectors of both the social class and the musical mainstream.[5] These bands superseded punk by changing its sonic dimension. First off, punk existed on pure adrenaline with short songs played at break-neck speeds. Grunge, however, slowed the tempo down to a sludgy pace. Grunge utilized " . . . low-pitched and distortion-heavy instrumentals, gravelly, raspy singing, and a pulse slower than that of hardcore punk."[6] Grunge was deeper and darker than punk but kept the same haphazard or "untrained" flair in its music. One sonic element perfected by Nirvana was the contrasting of dynamics within the same song. Cobain would often sing the verses of his songs with a low melancholic voice accompanied by clean guitar riffs and a simple drum beat, but when the chorus came in, the band would erupt with heavily distorted power chords, harder hitting drums, and higher pitched vocal screeches.[7] The dynamics were extreme, and the contrast gave their live shows another element of power that sometimes eluded punk.

The grunge look also differed from that of punk. Punk rock had several stylistic iterations sporting variations of ripped jeans, cut-off shirtsleeves, metal chains, wild hair (mohawks!), leather jackets, and dark clothes. Grunge, on the other hand, stripped away these outsider affectations in favor of a mundane everyday style. Seattle grunge rockers wore on stage what they wore at home: t-shirts, flannel, and ripped jeans. Grunge bands donned a slacker style that was prevalent in the 1980s Pacific Northwest and did not try to complement a distinctive visual dimension to their sound.[8] Since authenticity is a key principal of grunge rock, the bands and their fans opted to bring in the same ocular features that shaped their everyday lives. Interestingly, however, this low-key style from the Pacific Northwest became a fad in popular culture as grunge entered the mainstream.

4. Tow, *The Strangest Tribe*, 3.

5. Wood, "Pained Expression," 333.

6. Ibid., 333.

7. Mazullo, "The Man Whom the World Sold," 721.

8. Ibid., 718.

Like punk, grunge models an ugly aesthetic. Matthew Kieran argues that the incoherent and ugly ethos adopted by these fringe rock genres exist in contra-distinction to the " . . . highly stylized, slick, and formal emphasis on elegance that was taken to be predominant at the time."[9] While it seems counterintuitive to enjoy an ugly aesthetic, Kieran argues that one can afford pleasure from it if s/he understands the music in a certain light.[10] In other words, the ugly aesthetic of grunge is enjoyable because it is a reflection of the ugliness of the world. It is a countercultural indictment of mainstream pretensions and aims to shed light on the way life really is—in all of its abject wonder. The sonic qualities of grunge and the slouch look and mentality are thus appropriately fitting for the spirit of the day. This also allows the bystander to peer into a situation that was in some way hidden to the rest of the world. Kieran writes that ugly art and music affords us the ability " . . . to explore repulsive, grotesque and incoherent apparitions and situations in a way we could not in the real world."[11] Grunge helps us to see the depths and depravity of our present reality. This is evident not only in the sound but also in the lyrics of many of the songs. Consider Mudhoney's "Touch Me I'm Sick," which was released as their debut single with Sup Pop in 1988. The song utilizes deranged imagery and sexual innuendo, which depicts both a broken world and a fragmented self-image:

> *Ooh wow ooh*
> *I feel bad, and I've felt worse*
> *I'm a creep, yeah, I'm a jerk*
> *Come on*
> *Touch me, I'm sick, wow*
> *I won't live long, and I'm full of rot*
> *Gonna give you-girl-everything I got*[12]

While Mudhoney's song is, in a way, a forbearer of the grunge attitude and aesthetic, Nirvana's music rests at the height of grunge ideology. For instance, Nirvana's song "Lithium" from *Nevermind* (1991) is about a man who found faith after his girlfriend's suicide and depicts irony and ugliness in order to deal with dark issues:

9. Kieran, "Aesthetic Value," 384.

10. Ibid., 385.

11. Ibid., 388.

12. Mudhoney, "Touch Me I'm Sick."

I'm so happy 'cause today
I've found my friends
They're in my head
I'm so ugly, but that's okay, 'cause so are you
We broke our mirrors
Sunday morning is everyday for all I care
And I'm not scared
Light my candles in a daze
'cause I've found god[13]

Both cases raise existential issues and deal with reality in an introspective way. Grunge appropriates a nihilistic view of the self and the world and seeks to find identity in the midst of a broken civilization. As such, the dark and ugly aesthetic of grunge is part and parcel to the ethos of the post-punk movement.

Grunge emerged from Seattle's urban punk scene in the early 1980s.[14] U-Men was a transitional Seattle-based art-rock/punk hybrid band, whose dirty sound acted as a forerunner to grunge.[15] The U-Men toured the US extensively in their eight-year career and developed a cult following in the Seattle area that would eventually become the grunge scene. Later on, new bands such as Green River and Soundgarden surfaced establishing a new, heavier sound quickly gaining popularity in the surrounding areas and on college radio stations.[16] One of the main early catalysts of the grunge movement was the C/Z Records compilation album titled *Deep Six* (1986). This album consisted of music from six popular Seattle-area bands including: Soundgarden, Green River, Malfunkshun, The Melvins, Skin Yard, and the U-Men.[17] While this compilation did not achieve massive financial success, it helped to establish a definitive scene in Seattle. As Stephen Tow writes,

> The release of *Deep Six* represents a seminal moment in Seattle music history, both contemporaneously and in retrospect. The record signified not only the existence, but the viability of this generation of urban punk bands playing heavy, metal-infused

---

13. Nirvana, "Lithium."

14. Tow, *The Strangest Tribe*, 79.

15. Ibid., 67.

16. Ibid., 100.

17. Ibid., 100–101.

music. For urban punks who were closet metal fans, *Deep Six* was a coming-out party.[18]

There was then a new sound and attitude coming from the Pacific Northwest that was not quite punk, and not quite metal—it was grunge.

Perhaps the greatest factor that brought the nascent grunge scene to the mainstream was the work of the record labels. As the grunge scene grew, entrepreneur Bruce Pavitt transformed his fanzine entitled "Sub/Pop" (short for Subterranean Pop) to a Seattle-based record label.[19] Pavitt released a successful compilation disc entitled *Sub Pop 100* (1986) before teaming up with Jonathan Poneman to release single artist releases by seminal grunge bands such as Green River, Soundgarden, TAD, Mudhoney, and Nirvana. Remarkably, after more than twenty years, the label is still in existence today. Soundgarden was the first of the Sub Pop bands to sign with a major label, signing with A&M in 1988. Many of the Sub Pop bands followed suit and gained international fame after signing with major labels. Nirvana began with Sup Pop but became disenchanted with their deal after releasing their debut album *Bleach* (1989), opting instead to sign with the major label DGC, which produced the enormously profitable *Nevermind* (1991) and *In Utero* (1993). Although Pearl Jam was never a Sub Pop band, they hit the mainstream in 1991 with their major label debut album *Ten* through Epic Records. With this new wider exposure, grunge took the world by storm in the early 1990s.

Kurt Cobain's Existential Predicament

Nirvana was not part of the original grunge scene, but they did offer an accessible version of grunge that was easily palatable for the mainstream with their album *Nevermind*.[20] It was this album's pop element that allowed the band to breakout of the Seattle scene into the mainstream.[21] While the album did not shy away from the grunge distinctions mentioned above, the songs were catchy and memorable enough to appeal to a wider audience. However, this newfound success had a paradoxical effect on Nirvana's frontman and principal songwriter Kurt Cobain. Mazullo writes,

18. Ibid., 118.
19. Prato, *Grunge is Dead,* 127.
20. Tow, *The Strangest Tribe,* xiv.
21. Mazullo, The Man Whom the World Sold," 720.

While Cobain's music has been received as an authentic expression of himself (his feelings, his values, and his political and cultural beliefs), at the same time it is habitually acknowledged that Cobain's identity was made fragile, perhaps even fatally depleted, on account of his celebrity. In fact, the veritability of the second comment renders the first an impossibility: if Cobain was indeed not in control of his own identity, how could he have been expressing his authentic identity in his music?[22]

Cobain wore his heart on his sleeve and dealt with deep-rooted issues from his past and present through music. Music was supposed to be the vehicle from which Cobain would find and articulate his authentic self, but the adverse effects of sudden fame proved to be his undoing. Pressure from the industry, fans, and family pushed Cobain further away from his existential journey.[23] His new fame made him wonder if he had lost his authenticity by selling out to the mainstream.[24] As he continued putting out music, he began to realize that the person he was writing about was somebody different than the person trying to find his identity. He created a façade, a mask to hide behind. Interestingly, however, while Cobain struggled to find authenticity in his own music, the music of Nirvana inspired thousands of young people to find theirs.[25] Cobain became the voice of a new angst-ridden generation, but it was this pressure coupled with the ailments of physical and social discomfort that caused him to take his own life in 1994.

Cobain had a troubled youth. While his early years were good, his family quickly fractured putting an end to Cobain's stable childhood.[26] His parents divorced at a young age, and he was forced to move from household to household living with various friends and family members.[27] Part of this was his fault as Cobain fell into drugs and rebelliousness. He dropped out of high school and even had a few stints living on the streets.[28] Cobain internalized the pain from his turbulent childhood years, which is evident in many of his song lyrics and journal entries. As an example, consider the

22. Ibid., 738.

23. Ibid., 741.

24. Wood, "Pained Expression," 333.

25. Mazullo, The Man Whom the World Sold," 741.

26. Cross, *Heavier than Heaven,* 22.

27. Ibid., 61.

28. Ibid., 62.

lyrics of one of Nirvana's early recordings "Even In His Youth," which seems to be about Cobain's childhood:

> Even in his youth [x3]
> He was nothing
> Kept his body clean [x3]
> Going nowhere
> Daddy was ashamed [x2]
> He was something
> Disgrace the family name [x2]
> The family name, he was something[29]

Cobain was always gifted artistically. He was a talented visual artist (well-rendered drawings can be found throughout many pages of his journals), a creative lyricist, and a good musician.[30] He played in a few bands while he was in high school, and even spent some time touring with the Melvins as a roadie.[31] He formed the band Nirvana in 1987 with his high school friend Krist Novoselic on bass guitar and Aaron Burckhard on drums. Burckhard only lasted a few months and Nirvana went through several drummers, of which Chad Channing and Dave Grohl had the longest tenures. Cobain used drugs throughout his adolescence and early adulthood but developed a strong dependency on heroin in his later years. He married Hole frontwoman Courtney Love and they had a daughter named Frances Bean.[32] Towards the end of his life, his heroin dependency was at an all-time high, until April 8th, 1994 when he got high and shot himself in the head.[33] Cobain already attempted to overdose once earlier in the year, and there were already suicide tendencies in his family as two of Cobain's uncles previously took their own lives.[34] The tragic end to Cobain's story suggests that in his intense search for authenticity, Cobain was left dejected and incredulous.

Cobain's authenticity in his music came out in a couple of ways. Jessica Wood argues that the "sick body" was a repeated metaphor throughout his journals and music.[35] Apparently, Cobain struggled with chronic stomach

29. Nirvana, "Even In His Youth."
30. Cross, *Heavier than Heaven,* 29.
31. Ibid., 75.
32. Ibid., 237.
33. Ibid., 355.
34. Ibid., 59.
35. Wood, "Pained Expression," 332.

troubles throughout his life and underwent tremendous anxiety concerning his small body frame and stature.[36] As such, depicting and exploiting his marginal body through drawings and lyrics was one way that Cobain voiced authenticity.[37] His output is also littered with scatological language and shamed expressions. It seems that Cobain's unfiltered countenance was a way to express a genuine confession. He was not hiding who he was, or sugarcoating his feelings and compulsions. Everything was on display with disregard to social correctness. Scatological language is a way to express authenticity as it displays a " . . . 'primally sincere' mode of writing."[38] Nothing was off limits for Cobain's artistic communication because his ultimate goal was only to express authenticity. In so doing, Cobain wanted to give off an attitude of carelessness as if fame just came upon him and everything he did was haphazard. This was not the case. Cobain cared deeply about his music and the state of his band. Cobain even agonized over the aesthetic qualities of his writing. Wood writes, "His multiple drafts of lyrics and letters, as well as his experiments with alternate spellings, indicate his interest in language's aesthetic and communicative potential, even in its conflicted and arbitrary aspects."[39] So in a way, Cobain's attempt to look authentic was actually manufactured. When one looks inwardly without direction, one can easily get lost. Unbridled exploration into one's own darkness may lead to a nihilism that seems inescapable. Such nihilism will take the form of an extreme skepticism that ultimately renders life meaningless. This seems to have been the case for Cobain. Mazullo states it well: "In the end, the idea of cultural authenticity stifled and devoured Kurt Cobain."[40] The case studies of grunge rock in general and Kurt Cobain in particular leads to the inevitable question: is there a way to find one's authentic self and explore it without falling into despair? It is to this question that we now turn.

The Authentic Self & Confessions

To answer Cobain's predicament of authenticity, we will now turn to the existential theology of Paul Tillich. When dealing with issues of being and existence, Tillich emerges as the quintessential existentialist theologian.

36. Ibid., 337.
37. Ibid.
38. Ibid., 335.
39. Ibid., 343.
40. Mazullo, The Man Whom the World Sold," 742.

Tillich was a German-born Lutheran theologian who sought to understand God in a new way that is distinct from the classical Judeo-Christian concept of God and foundational for any concept of ultimate reality. For Tillich, he very task of theology is to reflect on what concerns us ultimately (I.4).[41] In other words, the ontological issues of our own authentic existence should guide our theological reflection. Tillich writes, "Theology formulates the questions implied in human existence, and theology formulates the answers implied in divine self-manifestation under the guidance of the questions implied in human existence (I.12)."[42] Therefore, theology is not merely reflection on ancient Near Eastern Scripture and tradition but is rather the task of finding oneself, finally, in relation to God's ultimate reality. Our ultimate concern thus precedes reflection on God, reflecting, rather, on what " . . . determines our being or not-being (I.4)."[43] The ultimate concern of humanity concerns our ultimate destiny. We care about the infinity that we belong to and yearn for, the totality of true being, and the conditions that subsist beyond all the present conditions around us (I.4).[44] Theology and philosophy are related in that they both ask questions of being. While philosophy is concerned with the ontological structure of being, theology concerns itself with the meaning of being (I.7).[45] Cobain's questions of authenticity are theological concerns. Cobain yearns to comprehend the meaning of his being and what it means to be authentically alive amid all of the distracting conditions surrounding him. While Cobain's problems are existential, the answers to his problems are theological.

In his book *The Courage to Be*, Tillich states the human problem is the threat of non-being. A person's most basic form of anxiety comes from his or her recognition of mortality.[46] The possibility of death puts us face to face with questions of fate, giving us anxiety about the meaning of our actions. There is also the anxiety of guilt when we realize that our being is inadequate[47] and the anxiety of meaninglessness when we feel we have no place in the world.[48] Surely, it was the anxieties of guilt and meaning-

41. Tillich, *Systematic Theology*, 12.

42. Ibid., 61.

43. Ibid., 14.

44. Ibid.

45. Ibid., 22.

46. Tillich, *The Courage to Be*, 41.

47. Ibid., 43,

48. Ibid., 49.

lessness that drove Cobain to his suicide. Cobain's sense of guilt, however, seemed to be more of a "guilt before the demands of the age," rather than a "guilt before God." Nevertheless, it seems that Cobain struggled with his feelings of adequacy regarding his being. Cobain's search for authenticity, unfortunately, led him to the dire conclusion of meaninglessness.

For Tillich, the appropriate answer to anxiety is courage. Courage is both an ontological and an ethical concept. Ontologically courage is the self-affirmation of one's being, which is ethical when " . . . man [sic] affirms his own being in spite of those elements of his existence which conflict with his essential self-affirmation."[49] In other words, courage is the choice to affirm the self in the face of anxiety. We display courage when we self-affirm our being in the midst of any of these forms of anxiety. We display courage in the face of death and fate when we encounter God in something like a religious experience.[50] Tillich prefers to view God as the "Ground of all Being" or "being-itself (1.3)."[51] For Tillich, God must be equivalent to being itself, or God would be subservient and subordinate to being.[52] Since God as creator is necessarily foundational, God must be the root to everything both in its being and becoming. When a human encounters being-itself, which is manifested in the *logos* of being,[53] then s/he displays a "courage of confidence" that s/he is an individual self in her or his "encounter with God as person."[54] Courage is displayed in the anxiety of guilt when we first identify our sin and the source of our guilt and come to a real understanding that we are accepted despite our shortcomings. Tillich writes, " . . . the courage to be is the courage to accept oneself as accepted in spite of being unacceptable."[55] This alludes to the Christian doctrine of grace when God loved us "while we were yet sinners" (Rom. 5:8). As such, we must display the courage to accept acceptance.[56] Courage is displayed in the face of meaningless when we exhibit "true faith," which is " . . . the acceptance of the power of being, even in the grip of nonbeing."[57] The "power of being" is

---

49. Ibid., 5.

50. Ibid., 150.

51. Ibid., 79.

52. Kuzmič, "To the Ground of Being and Beyond," 48.

53. Tillich, *Systematic Theology*, 79.

54. Tillich, *The Courage to Be*, 150.

55. Ibid., 151.

56. Ibid., 152.

57. Ibid., 162.

God, so ultimately, it is a true and absolute faith in God that will help one overcome the anxiety of despair.

Tillich's project is a response to the modern problem of existence. We cannot go back to a pre-modern era (the fundamentalist agenda) and cannot reject theology or our understanding of God because of the modern anxiety and displacement of the long-standing Judeo-Christian conception of God. Instead, we must see "God above God."[58] We must understand God in a way that breaks through the previous constructs. This is not to find a contextualized God, like in liberation theology, but to seek a God who is ultimate reality. When we find our authentic self, we reject alienation and exist in right relation to the ultimate reality, which is God. While Cobain offers a case study of anxiety leading to actual non-being, let us consider a case where anxiety leads to the courage to be. There has been a long tradition within Christian theology and moral thought to uncover the authentic self by delving into deep introspection and self-criticism. Self-criticism allows one to be cathartic while truly engaging the world. Discussing one's painful journey of sin and redemption not only offers lessons of Christian living to an audience but also allows one to speak about reality in a way that is not sugarcoated or romanticized. Perhaps, the greatest critical self-reflection is *Confessions* by Saint Augustine.

Towards the end of the 4th century CE, Augustine wrote his *Confessions,* a semi-autobiographical book that was started in 397 CE shortly after his appointment to become the Bishop of Hippo. The book is considered semi-autobiographical because it mixes his personal story with theological and philosophical musings about the nature of God and the world. In fact, the book is split up into two parts. The first nine books are Augustine's story through his conversion, and the last four books contain philosophical reflections concerning God, time, memory, and creation. Sorabji has argued, however, that these latter philosophical books belong with the former set because they complete Augustine's reflections on the soul's journey towards salvation.[59] This book is also not a memoir because Augustine does not recount his entire life—in fact, he lives for more than 30 years after its publication! Augustine set the books up as prayers to God, recounting stories of his youth along the way and giving the reader a glimpse of his inward struggle in his journey towards God. As Dyrness writes, " . . . Augustine, especially in the *Confessions,* turned inward in his search for God.

58. Ibid., 171.

59. Sorabji, "Time, Mysticism, and Creation," 215–216.

Throughout his turbulent youth, in what he came to see as his long journey to God, he realized that the deep longings of his soul were in fact calls from God."[60] He recounts his life in order to show his own conversion from sinful living within a heterodoxical Christian subset known as Manichaeism, into a life of devotion and fidelity to God.

Although Augustine writes in great detail, he does not recount every aspect of his life, and at times, gives unequal attention to various events. For instance, while Augustine shares personal stories about his father in order to build a sort of character profile, he hardly mentions his death. Robin Lane Fox points out, however, that it is not necessarily the case that Augustine had a strained relationship with his father. Rather, the *Confessions* are singularly focused on Augustine's relation to God, so his father Patricius, a pagan until his later years, did not play a major role in Augustine's faith.[61] Augustine does make mention of his father's financial sacrifice in giving Augustine an exemplary education, but that is nearly the extent of Patricius' influence on his religious life (*conf.* 2.3.5).[62] Augustine's mother Monica, on the other hand, had a profound effect on Augustine's spiritual upbringing. She raised him in a Christian home and fervently prayed and petitioned for Augustine's conversion when he went astray in his youth. As such, Monica's death is recounted in detail, displaying a great deal of grief (*conf.* 9.11.25).[63]

Scott MacDonald points out that in the *Confessions*, Augustine makes every point to extrapolate on his past sins and what the nature of sin is. In a way, Augustine is obsessed with both the concept and personal circumstances of sin.[64] Because it is sin that he confesses and is ultimately liberated from, Augustine recounts his sin in great detail in order to show its pervasiveness in his life and his struggle to overcome it. MacDonald writes, "Augustine wants us to see the sinful state from which his journey back to God must begin. But he also intends the autobiographical elements to provide a backdrop for important philosophical and theological themes. In particular, he intends reflection on his own sins to yield theoretical understanding of the nature of sin in general."[65] Augustine recounts particular sins of his youth and early adulthood to show how rooted sin is in the

60. Dyrness, *Poetic Theology*, 41.

61. Fox, *Augustine*, 41.

62. Augustine, *Confessions*, 26.

63. Ibid., 177.

64. MacDonald, "Petit Larceny, the Beginning of All Sin," 45.

65. MacDonald, "Petit Larceny, the Beginning of All Sin," 46.

constitution of one's human condition. For instance, Augustine recounts a childhood story about stealing pears. As a boy, he and some friends stole pears from a neighborhood orchard (*conf.* 2.4.9–2.5.12).[66] He did not need the pears and did not steal them to alleviate his hunger. Instead, Augustine stole the fruit solely for the purpose of entertainment. He became a petty thief only because it was an iniquitous deed, and this act of sin enticed his carnal self. The "theft of pears" story exists so Augustine can show us three things about moral depravity: 1) one can love something wicked solely for the sake of the wickedness, 2) the motive of such depravity is unintelligible, and 3) we can see the effects of the Fall in Augustine's personal pilgrimage.[67] Augustine's worldly desire at the supposed age of innocence caused him to articulate the doctrine of original sin. Williams Mann describes Augustine's notion of original sin writing:

> Adam and Eve's fall ushered into the world *original sin*, which is not an event but rather a condition. . . . It is the condition imposed by God as punishment on Adam and Eve for disobedience. According to Augustine the condition includes dispossession from a naturally perfect environment, the loss of natural immortality, and the acquisition of susceptibility to physical pain, fatigue, disease, aging, and rebellious bodily disorders, especially sexual lust.[68]

Original sin is thus the condition that all people are born into. It is not an individual act against God but rather the condition of living opposed to God as a result of the Fall. Augustine uses the stealing of pears story as evidence of such a condition, and subsequently, the concept of original sin has become a first order issue in theology and the impetus for countless theories of atonement.

Augustine's condition of sin reached its heights during his late adolescence and early adulthood when he became sexually active. In this period, Augustine "ran wild in the shadowy jungle of erotic adventures (*conf.* 2.1.1)."[69] Consequently, lust and sexuality plagued him from his youth to adulthood. Augustine makes mention of an unnamed concubine who lives with him for nearly fifteen years, bearing him an illegitimate son named Adeodatus.[70] After his schooling, he began teaching rhetoric in Thagaste

66. Augustine, *Confessions*, 30–31.

67. MacDonald, "Petit Larceny, the Beginning of All Sin," 49.

68. Mann, "Augustine on Evil and Original Sin," 81.

69. Augustine, *Confessions*, 24.

70. Ibid., xvi.

(*conf.* 4.2.1).[71] This is another part of his life that Augustine found deplorable because he was selling lies by teaching people to win cases through eloquent speech. He also was caught up in the gnostic Manichaean doctrine and became one of its great spokespersons. Even then, however, Augustine thought deeply about philosophical and theological issues and did not accept things readily without criticism. So Augustine was a brilliant young man, enraptured by his lust and hungry for truth.

It was not until encountering Ambrose that the tides of faith began to change for Augustine. Ambrose would teach Augustine how to approach the Bible hermeneutically in more complex ways, opening up a new avenue for spiritual growth and formation (*conf.* 8.1.2).[72] In fact, Augustine's deeper reading of scripture and the example of devoted Christians led Augustine to his conversion. Augustine's conversion was not merely concerning belief. It took some time until Augustine reasoned and came to a deep understanding of God in order to satisfy his intellectual pursuit before fully committing to the ways of Christ. During this time he was not ready to give up his worldly pleasures. Augustine recounts his famous prayer from this time: " . . . at the beginning of my adolescence when I prayed you for chastity and said: 'Grant me chastity and continence, but not yet (*conf.* 8.7.17).'"[73] For Augustine, conversion meant total devotion to Christ and the church, giving up all sexual immoralities and living a chaste life. Before finally converting, Augustine wrote " . . . my two wills, one old, the other new, one carnal, the other spiritual were in conflict with one another, and their discord scattered my soul (*conf.* 8.5.10)."[74] Augustine would convert leaving behind his lustful youth for a life of celibacy and Christian devotion.

Augustine's story displays the courage to be in a couple of ways. While Augustine does not deal with the anxiety of meaninglessness like Cobain, he certainly does suffer from the anxiety of guilt and, to an extent, the anxiety of fate. The issue of guilt for Augustine is a moral dilemma whereas his issue of fate is an intellectual one. Augustine is so caught up with his own sin that he finds himself thoroughly disgusting.[75] He comes face-to-face with his depravity, recounting the deep roots of sin all the way to his infancy. This realization, according to Tillich, is the first part of accepting

71. Ibid., 53.
72. Ibid., 152.
73. Ibid., 145.
74. Ibid., 140.
75. Wolterstorff, "Suffering Love," 107.

acceptance. It took Augustine quite a while to see his own corruption as a destructive force of non-being, and his true conversion bears the mark of ultimate faith as he totally rejects non-being in order to uncover his authentic self in relation to being-itself. This moral courage is depicted in the first nine books of the *Confessions*. The latter books on time, memory, and creation show Augustine confronting God's infinity. Augustine reflects on the nature of creation in relation to the transcendent God, and these reflections are the apologetic articulations of his own encounter with an infinite God. In this way, Augustine once again affirms himself as rooted in the ground of being. As such, Augustine's story in *Confessions* is an example of existential struggle that leads to self-affirmation rather than destruction. Augustine understood his issues were theological and thus recounted his long journey to authenticity by seeking God.

Smoke & Mirrors

There is no doubt that Cobain strove for authenticity. He had visceral reactions against those that he thought were inauthentic and had a complex relationship with fame and status. Nevertheless, he crafted an image of himself that he wanted the world to see. A crafted image is a second order reality—a simulacrum of the authentic self. Cobain's haphazard and disheveled persona was carefully crafted rather than truly arbitrary. Cobain cared about his record sales and about how many times his videos played on MTV. He might have hated this about himself, but if he were true to himself, he would have admitted his preoccupation with fame and notoriety. But, the image that he fed the media was a different vision. Perhaps, this struggle is in part what led Cobain to his escapist drug addictions and ultimate suicide.

Cobain's story is a tragedy. The fact that he took his own life is certainly tragic but so is his example of nihilism that was fed to the masses. Cobain had real human struggles of identity and authenticity—the same existential predicaments that countless thoughtful youth deal with through their maturation. He earned fame and fortune through his creative output but was unable to garner peace with his newfound cultural authority and fiscal wealth. However, Cobain's expression of existential angst was a good thing. Young people need to understand that they are not alone in their feelings of estrangement, and having a hero to look up to and guide them through these issues is undoubtedly a desirable convention. The issue was that Cobain was not disposed to be a role model, guide, or mentor. Cobain needed the very thing that he became for many young people: a hero and guide. Many rock icons like Elvis, Dylan, and Lennon used their influence to shape their respective cultural eras. Sometimes, like in the case of Dylan, they were reluctant to embrace the title "voice of a generation," but through their music and cultural authority, they were nevertheless able to help shape youth culture and help many young people find their identity. A transformational theology of rock would follow Cobain's lead and embrace issues of identity and confront them head on, but there would be a dialectical mediation of identity in a world that was created by a higher order—a God whose very existence is the root of all other being. This is the attentive introspection that was displayed to us by Augustine's *Confessions*. Is there a case study example of a band that displays such a theological engagement with identity? I believe the band Skillet fits the bill.

Skillet is a Memphis based hard rock band that formed in 1996 and is still active today. Although they are not a grunge band, it is hard to find any hard rock band that formed in the 1990s that was not influenced by Nirvana and the grunge rock movement. Skillet was formed as a trio consisting of frontman John Cooper (the only original member left in the band), Ken Steorts, and Trey McClurkin. The band began as a post-grunge rock band but constantly shifted musical identity between albums testing out various sounds ranging from alternative rock to electronica. With the band's sixth studio album, *Collide* (2005), Skillet settled into a hard rock fusion sound sporting elements of industrial, metal, and grunge. Since the band has existed for over twenty years, making it one of the longest-tenured successful Christian rock bands in the US, it went through several member changes. The members typically leave on cordial terms, citing a desire to change lifestyles as the usual reason. The current lineup sees John Cooper as frontman and bassist, Kori Cooper (John's wife) on guitar and keys, Seth Morrison on lead guitar, and Jen Ledger on drums. The band is one of the most successful Christian rock bands of all time selling over two million CDs in the US alone.[76] Skillet is also well known for its relentless touring, never differentiating between Christian and secular crowds and venues. Throughout Skillet's entire existence as a band, Cooper has been singularly focused on portraying a positive Christian message to a fan base of youth that desperately seek existential validation.

Skillet's eighth studio album *Rise* (2013) is a concept album that deals with a young person finding himself in the midst of a difficult and sometimes

76. Law, "Skillet Band Shed Christian Title."

tragic world. Cooper describes the album's protagonist as, "... coming into adulthood ... faced by the horrors that we see every day—floods, bombings, earthquakes, school shootings. He's also faced with his own problems from his family life. It's about his path to salvation, and wanting to be significant in some way. The record has a lot of ups and downs, all leading to this salvation experience."[77] Through his music, Cooper embraces the role of mentor that was unfairly grafted onto Cobain. Cooper has sensed a calling and a purpose in his life from a young age, and so feels it is his duty to help others find their authentic selves.[78] Through their lyrics and offstage accessibility (they constantly do signings and make themselves available on social media), Skillet turns out to be the good older brother to a youth in crisis. Consider the lyrics of "Sick of It" from *Rise* (2013):

> When everything you do
> Don't seem to matter.
> You try but it's no use
> Your world is getting blacker.
> When every time you fail
> Has no answer.
> Every empty promise made
> Is a reminder.
> No one can make this better
> Take control, it's now or never!
> Are you sick of it?
> Raise your hands,
> Get rid of it!
> While there's a fighting chance.[79]

This song identifies the problem of existential angst but calls the listener to stand up and take control of the situation at hand. This contrasts starkly with Mudhoney's irony in "Touch Me I'm Sick," and Nirvana's nihilism in "Even In His Youth" discussed earlier. Skillet tackles the problems of existence and authenticity head on but offers transformative rather than nihilistic solutions. For instance, the song "Salvation" from the same album gives the answer to finding authenticity: a right relationship with God. The

77. Cooper in Price, "Skillet Just Keeps Getting Hotter with Rise."

78. Law.

79. Skillet, "Sick of It."

song's lyrics are ambiguous, but the Christian overtones become overt with the title of the track. At one point in the song Cooper sings,

> *Been out from under who I am*
> *And who I want to be*
> *Held you tightly in my hands*
> *Why are we unraveling*[80]*?*

These lyrics state that the person who the protagonist truly is and wants to be only exists when he is in right relations with God. This is like Augustine in *Confessions* when he sees God as the source of his life and the means of finding authenticity. When we are seeking to find ourselves in relation to God, then we can stand with Søren Kierkegaard and say, "Now with God's help I shall become myself."[81] Being apart from God causes us to be further away from an authentic existence because we are displaced from the ground of being. Skillet is exemplar of a transformative rock band that grapples deeply and theologically with such matters of being.

Conclusion

As we survey grunge rock and notice its existentialist and intensely individualistic identity, the questions may arise: are these issues contrary to the concerns of punk rock and liberation theology? Is there a tension between liberation and existential theology? It seems that both have conflicting premises, which lead to radically different conclusions. On one hand, liberation theology speaks to a communal situation. When there is a systemic evil that keeps people oppressed with a vicious cycle of domination and self-validation, then people must rise up together to overcome this evil. Punk rock and liberation theology seek liberation from an oppressive system. The system affects entire groups of people, so a song of liberation is a communal song. Punk rock is rock music's logical conclusion as it is the counterculture standing against the status quo that is not only antediluvian but also oppressive.

On the other hand, existential theology speaks to a humanistic audience. Existential theology arose from Western power and dominance, so its adherents were not oppressed by a systemic evil. In fact, the first world existentialist theologians may have been oblivious or indifferent to the majority world troubles that birthed liberation theology. The West, however, reacted

80. Skillet, "Salvation."

81. Kierkegaard, *Papers and Journals,* 295.

against Enlightenment humanism and post-war estrangement. When the West was ravaged by two world wars, it did not see a long-standing economic systemic evil like Latin American countries, but rather it saw evils being committed against groups of people because of differences in identity. Jews and minorities were seen as less than human by the Nazis in WWII and were, thus, exterminated in the Holocaust. When the wars ended and the dust settled, the questions of concern for Westerners were "What have we become?" and "Who are we?" The Western mind had to rediscover itself in a rapidly changing post-war context. Hence, the existential issue became the starting point for many Western theologies. Grunge rock came about in the 1980s, way after the world wars, but the existential concern was still of interest in 1980s America. Despite all of its problems, the US does not have an economic system of oppression analogous to that of the Latin American countries from which liberation theology arose. The struggle for youth culture concerned identity in a world where boredom reigned supreme, and the status quo seemed duplicitous at best.

It is not that liberation and existential theology oppose each other, but rather they answer different questions and address different social problems. Both theologies bear in mind the end goal of cosmic and personal transformation and see God as the answer to their problem. Both views are needed for a transformational theology of rock, but greater emphasis will be given to the one that better speaks to the plight of its fan base's context. While a transformational punk band would be more effective in 1980s, Peru, a transformational grunge band, would be more effective in the 1990s Pacific Northwest.

In this chapter we addressed the issues of identity and authenticity by putting grunge rock in dialogue with the existential theology of Paul Tillich. Kurt Cobain's life was surveyed as an example of an existential search leading to nihilism, whereas Augustine's life displayed the same type of search leading to religious authenticity. We then saw how the pursuit of authenticity can aid our transformational theology of rock and looked at the lyrics and ministry of the band Skillet as a case study. For our final chapter, we will once again look at identity and see what theological issues emerge from alternative rock.

8

The Otherness of Alternative Rock

The Arctic Monkeys are heralded as one of the first ever bands to gain worldwide success through social media and alternative marketing strategies.[1] The band formed in England in 2002, and after some gigging, they began to record and produce their own music at a local recording studio. They burned copies of their demos onto discs and handed them out for free at concerts.[2] Fans uploaded the music to the web, and through file-sharing and social media sites like MySpace, the band amassed a huge following.[3] Once they landed with Domino and English record label, they recorded and released their debut album in 2006, *Whatever People Say I Am, That's What I'm Not*. Because of the media hype and the band's cult following, the record became the fastest selling debut album of all time on British charts selling over 360,000 copies in the first week.[4] The band has since released four more full-length studio albums and is widely regarded as one of the world's premiere alternative rock bands. While theirs is a success story of an independent artist making it big, Artic Monkeys also epitomize the new aesthetic of contemporary alternative rock.

1. Skancke, *The History of Indie Rock,* 76.
2. Ibid., 77.
3. Sackllah, "Arctic Monkeys' Whatever People Say I Am."
4. Ibid.

Developments in technology changed rock music in the 21st century. The DIY mentality of punk, grunge, and other alternative genres has profoundly shaped the way music is made today. Bands and musicians have come to realize that they do not need a major record label to record, market, and distribute their own music. While the indie record label was the first move away from the dominant mainstream marketing of major labels, it has now become customary for bands to record their own music with local or home studios, press their own albums through local or online manufacturers, and sell physical copies of their albums at concerts and digital copies through online distributors. Furthermore, advancements in online social marketing allow bands to market themselves and build worldwide fanbases. While a few bands, like Arctic Monkeys, skyrocketed to international success utilizing these contemporary DIY methods, most bands and musicians will never see a tremendous amount of success, giving credence to the internet meme, "on the web, everyone will be famous to fifteen people."[5] Nevertheless, the vehicle for self-expression without reliance on dominant culture allows for a new diversity in rock and, in a way, a re-emergence of rock's original countercultural ethos. This turn towards artistic independence in rock is described invariably with the loaded terms "alternative" and "indie."

Alternative and indie rock are two closely related rock genres that are difficult to grasp as definitive movements. This is largely because "alternative" and "indie" are such fluid and ambiguous terms that one might see them as meaningless or useless for his or her understanding of culture. Yet, I believe that their propensity towards negation can tell us something important about theology. For this chapter, we will trace what these movements are, and how they came about in order to understand an essential principle about our transformational theology of rock, namely, that *our theology is a fluid concept that fluctuates as culture and history changes*. We will begin this chapter by attempting to define the terms alternative and indie, and what they have come to mean in today's rock culture. Then, after noticing alternative and indie's propensity towards negation, we will look at theological ideas, like the "otherness" of God, which are presented through an approach of negation. Finally, we will make the point that theology must remain fluid so as to engage the ever-changing world.

5. This phrase is a play off of Andy Warhol's "fifteen minutes of fame."

Fluidity and Alternative Rock

Indie is a subgenre offshoot of alternative rock. Both of these aliases, however, are ambiguous and notoriously difficult to define. These labels came into existence not as a label to group the entirety of a musical *style*, like that of punk, grunge, Southern, or folk rock. Rather, these labels came to designate a *way of doing* rock. For instance, "alternative" came about as a negation of mainstream rock. Basically, alternative rock is rock that is unconventional and can be listened to as a substitute to mainstream rock. Alternative is thus a *fluid* designation. When an alternative band gains mainstream success and influences a movement, then it becomes the new status quo, and the new alternative is whoever negates this new mainstream. Likewise, indie is a fluid label that designates independent artists. Once the artist signs a recording contract, however, are they no longer considered indie? What if an *indie* record label signs them? As it happened, both "alternative" and "indie" developed into stylistic categories of music while maintaining the particular ethos that accompanied the unique way of doing rock. Alternative rock is the alternative to whatever is dominating culture. In our present day, for instance, alternative rock is turning back to 1960s and 1980s rock sounds in order to subvert the highly technical innovations in music and mass consumption. The indie mentality and the alternative ethos thus form a tight bond in recapturing what it means to be "rock and roll." In this section, we'll evaluate both the terms "alternative" and "indie" and attempt to come to an understanding of these pivotal movements in rock.

What Alternative Rock is Not

As discussed above, "alternative rock" or "alt-rock" is a catchall phrase that describes any type of rock music throughout the decades of rock's history that stands against the mainstream of rock and roll. As such, there are many tremendously different concepts of what alternative rock is and what bands endure as quintessential alternative rock bands. As Cross notes, "Alt-rock has the added complication of being so diverse in sound and scope that it can be infinitely customized, allowing each individual fan to find a niche all his own."[6] If you asked ten people which bands were the greatest and most influential alternative rock bands of all time, you would likely get ten vastly different answers. Nevertheless, we will attempt to trace (in a very

6. Cross, *20th Century Rock and Roll*, 6.

basic outline) the historical meanderings of what has become known as alternative rock.

The origins of alternative rock are often traced back to the pre-punk era of the 1960s. Bands such as the Velvet Underground were making music that was intentionally crude and bombastic. The Velvets were comprised of avant-garde, art school musicians that performed " . . . bleak, in-your-face rock and roll that challenged (and ultimately destroyed) the wide-eyed innocence of rock and roll."[7] For instance, the song "Heroin" from the influential album *The Velvet Underground & Nico* (1967) embraced the complexities of heroin-use without outright condemning it. In fact, the song venerates the feelings that come from the high of heroin as a needed escape from the insincerity of the world. Consider these lyrics:

> *Heroin, be the death of me*
> *Heroin, it's my wife and it's my life*
> *Because a mainer to my vein*
> *Leads to a center in my head*
> *And then I'm better off and dead*
> *Because when the smack begins to flow*
> *I really don't care anymore*
> *About all the Jim-Jim's in this town*
> *And all the politicians makin' crazy sounds*
> *And everybody puttin' everybody else down*
> *And all the dead bodies piled up in mounds*[8]

While "Heroin" does not mince words concerning the cruelties of this world, it also sonically devolves into a mess of chaotic distortion as the song escalates to a final halt. The Velvet's courage to experiment with sound and tackle taboo subjects lyrically secures them as a true alternative to the dominant rock scene. Thus, the Velvets became one of the first bands to form a counter to rock music's countercultural ethos. The idea is that while rock began as a counterculture of mainstream music, its popularity and commercial success made rock the new mainstream. Although the Velvets were supported and managed by famed art superstar Andy Warhol, they never sold very many records or acquired international fame. Their influence, however, was undeniable. As the old quip attributed to Brian Eno

---

7. Ibid., 8.
8. The Velvet Underground, "Heroin."

states, "The first Velvet Underground album only sold 10,000 copies, but everyone who bought it formed a band."[9]

The mantle of alternative rock was then carried by other proto-punk acts such as the Stooges, Patty Smith, and the New York Dolls. Each of these acts experimented with their sounds and performances in such a way that they would agitate the mainstream. For instance, the Stooges, with their leader Iggy Pop, were prone to wild stage antics and destruction,[10] Patty Smith mixed spoken-word poetry with proto-punk rock music earning the title "the Queen of Punk,"[11] and the New York Dolls were a group of cross-dressing men who would perform in full makeup and women's attire, becoming the first band to wear spandex on stage.[12] This nascent alternative movement was closely associated with visual art and other artistic avenues. Along with the Velvet's connection to Warhol, Patty Smith was a close friend to photographer Robert Mapplethorpe, and Iggy Pop became lifelong friends with David Bowie. A new alternative way of life was forming and expressing itself inventively through avant-garde art and rock music.

As discussed in some detail in chapter six, punk rock formed as the first full-blown alternative rock subgenre in the mid-1970s. The punk rock influence was enormous and as discussed in the previous chapter, influenced grunge and every other alternative rock subgenre that would subsequently take shape. One highly influential alternative rock subgenre was known as "college rock" and formed in the 1980s. The major rock stations played mainstream rock and pop, causing alternative rock bands to rely only on concerts and word of mouth to gain public exposure. College radio stations were extremely influential for the spreading of alternative rock music because they, unlike the mainstream rock stations of the day, played any type of music they wanted. Thus, college radio stations became the sole outlet for indie and alternative rock radio airplay.[13] College radio played a variety of post-punk alternative bands including Sonic Youth, the Pixies, and the Smiths. Some of the college radio bands would gain huge followings and eventually breakout into the mainstream. The greatest example of this is R.E.M.

---

9. Jovanovic, *Seeing the Light,* xii.

10. Cross, *20th Century Rock and Roll,* 16.

11. Ibid., 40.

12. Ibid., 52.

13. Skancke, *The History of Indie Rock,* 39.

R.E.M. was formed in the 1980s as four University of Georgia students began jamming together.[14] With the help of college radio and frequent performances at local bars around Athens, Georgia, R.E.M. developed a huge local following. The band eventually signed to the indie label I.R.S. records, released a debut album entitled *Murmur* (1983), and toured the country relentlessly. The band experienced a slow climb to stardom until 1987 when they released their fifth studio album *Document*. This album had two singles "The One I Love," and "It's the End of the World as We Know It (And I Feel Fine)" that propelled them to international prominence.[15] From then on, the band toured the world for many years, released ten more studio albums, and cemented their names as one of the progenitors of 1990s alternative rock. In fact, R.E.M. helped to solidify a particular sound for the alternative rock genre.

1960s alternative was noisy, art-school rock, 1970s alternative was largely shaped by punk, and 1980s alternative was shaped both by the heavier sounds of hardcore and grunge and by the synth-heavy sound of post-punk. R.E.M., on the other hand, did not fit the sound of the other alternative bands of the 1980s. The band played catchy, upbeat songs with the usual rock band instrumentation. They typically played twangy but not heavily distorted electric guitars and also used acoustic guitars. Concerning the song "It's the End of the World," Kallen writes, "With its rapid-fire lyrical delivery, dynamic beat, and catchy chorus, 'It's the End of the World' helped spark a back-to-the-garage movement that spawned dozens of indie bands." R.E.M.'s influence helped shape 1990s alternative rock as a distinct genre that was the next craze in mainstream rock. Bands like Oasis, U2, Fastball, Third Eye Blind, Goo Goo Dolls, Gin Blossoms, Live, and Radiohead dominated the 1990s airwaves forming a softer, less synth-laden sound with more sensitive lyrics than alt-rock's previous incarnations. Lyrically, alternative rock music spans a wide range of subjects including love, sex, fantasy, social and political issues, spirituality, etc. At times alternative bands would sing about identity and display a sense of exclusion and otherness in their lyrics. Consider Radiohead's famous song "Creep" from the album *Pablo Honey* (1993) about a self-loathing protagonist who feels invisible when he is snubbed by a girl:

> *I don't care if it hurts*
> *I want to have control*

14. Kallen, *The History of Alternative Rock*, 64.
15. Ibid.

I want a perfect body
I want a perfect soul
I want you to notice
When I'm not around
You're so very special (clean version)
I wish I was special
But I'm a creep
I'm a weirdo
What the hell am I doing here?
I don't belong here[16]

While "Creep" speaks of the difficulties of those who do not quite fit in, alternative rock is lyrically diverse, often demanding poetic and multilayered readings. Unlike punk or grunge, there is no clear lyrical agenda in alternative rock.

1990s alternative rock spawned off various subgenres in the 2000s. With bands like My Chemical Romance, Further Seems Forever, and Taking Back Sunday, "Emo" mixed influences from 1990s alternative rock, punk, and goth rock. "Post-hardcore," with bands like Underoath, The Devil Wears Prada, and Pierce the Veil, was another alternative subgenre that mixed metal and hardcore into the fray. Mainstream stations played pop rock and nu-metal. But if one were to listen to an alternative rock station today, s/he would likely be listening to music influenced by the so-called "post-punk revival."

The post-punk revival began in the early 2000s when bands such as the White Stripes, the Strokes, and the Yeah Yeah Yeahs began to make major noise in rock radio circuits. The new millennium saw a group of rock bands being influenced both from the stripped down rock and roll sound of 1960s garage rock bands like the Kinks, the Stooges, and the Sonics, and the reverb-heavy synth rock of 1980s post-punk from bands such as Joy Division, the Talking Heads, and the Cure. What emerged was an upbeat, danceable form of alternative rock that sounded both retro and fresh at the same time. Kravitz describes the movement as containing the " . . . indie rock spirit and love of guitar pop that inspired musicians for decades."[17] Bands like the Killers, Interpol, and Arctic Monkeys gained quick notoriety but stood the test of time as they all are still among the world's most

16. Radiohead, "Creep."
17. Kravitz, "Revisiting the Post-Punk Revival."

popular bands a decade later. While alternative rock is still a fluid concept, post-punk revival bands like the Arctic Monkeys seem to truly represent the new alternative. I think it is more than coincidental that their debut album was named *Whatever People Say I Am, That's What I'm Not*. That title is about as alternative as it gets!

What Indie Rock is Not

According to Novara and Henry, "indie rock" gained its name from 1980s UK when the first charts for independent artists appeared. The term, like alternative rock, is difficult to define because it also spreads across many subgenres and divergent styles.[18] The designation of "indie" as its own musical genre, however, developed in the mid-1990s and gained popularity in the 2000s as record labels began marketing indie as a distinct style of music.[19] What characterized indie music in the 1980s, however, was not a sonic commonality, but the DIY ethic of self-promotion and self-production. Indie rock took a very important lesson from punk: anyone can be in a band, learn together, and even make a record. As Cohen writes, " . . . the line between fan and performer was paper-thin."[20] Indie music developed a " . . . bold start-up ethos, intensively nurtured networks of the like-minded and the innovation-from-below."[21] The independence of "indie," however, is not a straight up resistance to dominant culture like punk but rather a "negotiation" with dominant culture.[22] The post-punk relationship with dominant culture is thus more ambiguous and intricate than its punk predecessor. Rock music is countercultural in its essence, and from generation to generation, the counterculture is defined and redefined. The rock counterculture was epitomized by garage and psychedelic rock in the 1960s, punk in the 1970s, hardcore and college rock in the 1980s, and grunge and alternative rock in the 1990s.[23] Skancke writes that indie rock " . . . seems to be the latest phase in the cyclical nature of youth-oriented

18. Novara and Henry, "A Guide to Essential American Indie Rock." 816.

19. Skancke, *The History of Indie Rock*, 62–63.

20. Cohen, "How Indie Rock Changed the World," 86.

21. Ibid.

22. Bannister, "Loaded," 78.

23. Skancke, *The History of Indie Rock*, 12.

rock-and-roll music."[24] Therefore, indie is the latest authentic expression of "rock as counterculture."

Indie began as the designation for "independent artists" who made rock music independently instead of using record labels.[25] This mode of production allows bands to be idiosyncratic and not have to conform to pop guidelines for mass appeal. As such, indie rock, in all its forms, allows for sonic experimentation that may not be suitable for the major label market. Skancke writes, "Indie rock has gained a reputation for being the ideal way of making music because indie rock artists tend to experiment, write their own music and lyrics, and avoid overproduction."[26] This artistic freedom, however, often comes at the price of limited success as indie bands regularly struggle to attain general exposure. Indie record labels popped up as outlets for indie artists to keep their distinctive musical freedom while they benefit from a wider audience. Indie labels typically worked regionally, and while they did not have the same reach as major labels, they did help promote bands and distribute their albums to local markets. These labels typically develop friendships with the bands and encourage their artistic freedom. Furthermore, these labels usually split profits with the bands allowing the artists to get a greater percentage of revenues.[27] Sub-Pop and other grunge labels were and are to this day *indie* labels that prided themselves on homespun in-house productions with a regional emphasis. It should be noted that indie labels often forge distribution agreements with major labels to gain further exposure or are bought out by major labels. The major labels want to capitalize on the success of the indie labels, but the idea is that the indie ethos is ever-present in the production.[28] The major labels usually leave the indie label's staff and production methods intact.

However, just as alternative rock formed its own distinctive sound in the 1990s and later as "post-punk revival," indie developed its own sonic commonalities as well. Novara and Henry write, "The hallmarks of this sound include: the careful balancing of pop accessibility with noise, playfulness in manipulating pop music formulae, sensitive lyrics masked by tonal abrasiveness and ironic posturing, a concern with 'authenticity,'

24. Ibid., 87.

25. Ibid., 9.

26. Ibid., 11.

27. Ibid., 59.

28. Skancke, *The History of Indie Rock*, 63.

and the cultivation of a 'regular guy' (or girl) image."[29] Bannister makes the interesting claim that the indie and alternative use of reverberation (the prolongation of a sound) actually creates a form of separation from the mainstream allowing artists to critique culture from a higher vantage point. Bannister writes, "Reverberation achieves a sense of distance and vastness, at the expense of personality. It creates majesty, at the expense of intimacy. It is cool, rather than warm. It is cerebral, rather than visceral. It's like the big picture but at the expense of detail."[30] This "distance" accounts for a de-sexualizing in indie and alternative music as opposed to the intimacy that can be found in R&B or blues-based rock.[31] This is a way that indie and alternative rock orient themselves towards authenticity. As they become detached from emotional engagement in music, the music becomes " . . . free of illusion and can see things as they 'really' are."[32] So indie rock approaches the notion of authenticity in a different way than grunge. Instead of nihilism and scatological imagery, indie rock disengages itself from dominant culture through the use of reverb and social detachment.

Nevertheless, true indie rock formed as alternative bands like Nirvana gained huge mainstream success. This is also when indie began to dissociate itself with alternative.[33] Novara and Henry write:

> 'Indie rock' also came to refer to a more-or-less self-sustaining network of communities, or 'scenes,' of artists that coalesced most frequently in major cities or small college towns. The indie scenes evolved into places for experimentation and, ironically, as havens for musicians with straight-ahead pop sensibilities (as opposed to the 'edgy,' testosterone-driven sensibilities of post-*Nevermind* alternative rockers).[34]

Indie is typically softer than alternative and embraces more pop and folk sensibilities. Indie rock today seems to elicit old-fashioned pop, folk, and soft rock styles in ways that are new, fresh, and edgy.[35] These two "genres" tend to be difficult to distinguish. In fact, many bands today would be considered both indie and alternative. Nevertheless, both alternative and

29. Novara and Henry, "A Guide to Essential American Indie Rock." 816.

30. Bannister, *Positively George Street,* 72.

31. Bannister, "Loaded," 90.

32. Ibid., 91.

33. Novara and Henry, "A Guide to Essential American Indie Rock." 824.

34. Ibid., 818.

35. Ibid., 830.

indie are genres that represent an antithesis to whatever is dominant. These bands are often nostalgic as they try to recapture the countercultural "essence" of rock. Lately, instead of blazing completely new trails, many bands are harkening back to old sounds and repackaging them for today's youth culture. So while alternative rock is not as completely alternative to mainstream music as it once was, the spirit of negation is still there. Alternative rock is known for what it is not and exists as a substitute for what it is rebelling against. In our day of progress, technology, and overproduction, the new alternative strips all of that away and goes back to the roots of rock and roll: the garage.

The Wholly Other

As alternative rock exists in negation to popular music, there is also a long history of theology from negation. Some areas of theology are impossible to talk about in any real way. For instance, how can anyone make sense of God's infinity? Negative, or *apophatic* theology attempts to describe God by way of negation. Boesel and Keller say that negative theology " . . . presses toward the pause and the silence within language. . . . It falls speechless before a mystery that inspires more speech in the next moment."[36] In other words, negative theology takes serious the limits of our knowledge and discourse about God.[37] Although we can never grasp God's infinity, perhaps, we can know things about God by eliminating those things that God is not. As Jacobson and Sawatsky write, " . . . negative theology makes an important point: nothing we can say about God comes close to capturing the awesomeness of God's being."[38] So negative theology is not a bad thing, but rather it is a tool that we can use to get a better sense of ultimate things.

An intuitive notion of Christian theology is that God is not the creation. God is the creator and is, therefore, separate from creation. God is transcendent beyond created reality and, to harken back to Tillich, is the source and root of all existence. Creation is fallen due to sin, and God's

---

36. Boesel and Keller, *Apophatic Bodies*, 1.

37. Apophatic theology can also bear insight for our knowledge of our neighbor and the world. Boesel and Keller write, "The coupling of apophasis and bodies, then, forges a heightened, ethically nuanced tension of obligation split between linguistic gestures toward a transcendent divinity on one hand, and flesh-and-blood commitments to the embodied life of creatures on the other" (Boesel and Keller, 7).

38. Jacobson and Sawatsky, *Gracious Christianity*, 31.

incarnation in Christ is the redemptive answer to the Fall. The incarnation is thus the in-breaking of the transcendent God into created reality. What we have in orthodox Christian theology is a story of deliverance: God is transcendent and utterly apart from creation, yet has chosen to become part of creation in order to save it from its fallen state.

Our human understanding of God is set up as a dialectic of positive and negative claims. For instance, if God is transcendent beyond our reality, then God's reality is metaphysical and totally unknowable. How can we breach the limits of physical reality? The very notion of going beyond or underneath what can possibly be known is nonsense. Indeed, it is inappropriate even to use words like "beyond" or "underneath" as they imply some spacial reality. Nor is God "prior to" or "before" time because there would be no moment *before* time. A transcendent God would be, for lack of a better term, outside space and time. To know God as transcendent is thus an exercise in negative theology. If God is transcendent, then we know God is not bound by anything, including space and time. Therefore, by way of negation, we can know that God is not physical and does not suffer the limitations of finitude.

On the other hand, we can also make positive (*cataphatic*) claims about God because of the incarnation. As Paul tells us in Colossians 1:15–17: "He (Christ) is the image of the invisible God, the firstborn of all creation; for in him all things in heaven and on earth were created, things visible and invisible, whether thrones or dominions or rulers or powers—all things have been created through him and for him. He himself is before all things, and in him all things hold together." We can truly know God because the transcendent God has been made fully known in Christ. Jesus is the visible image of the invisible God, so in Christ we know about God's character, personality, hopes, and vision. We can answer the question "What would God be like if God were here with us?" because God indeed was and, by the Spirit, is here with us. God was and is present in our reality. In Christ, God walked our streets and suffered our hardships. God poured out those divine attributes of limitlessness (*kenosis*) in order to rescue us from our fallen state (Phil 2:5). God the creator became part of the creation in order to save it. The positive claims we can make about God are those that God revealed to us specially and ultimately in Christ.

Karl Barth brought this dialectic front and center in his *The Epistle to the Romans*. One of the leading themes in Barth's work is that God is transcendent and "Wholly Other" to creation.[39] Barth's persistence of God

---

39. Barth, *The Epistle to the Romans*, 49.

being Wholly Other came as a response to liberal theology that reduced God to either a construct of the modern mind[40] or a transcendentalist pantheistic God that can be known fully in nature. As Barth writes, " . . . the power of God can be detected neither in the world of nature nor in the souls of men. It must not be confounded with any high, exalted force, known or knowable."[41] When God becomes nothing more than a construct of the mind or a perfectly knowable presence in nature, God is not the creator, who spoke the universe into existence. God's separateness is part and parcel with the biblical message (see Isa 55) and is an implication of the creedal formulations of God as creator. For Barth, we must begin with negation in order to preserve God's distinctiveness as Wholly Other " . . . beyond all human knowledge and understanding, beyond human categorization as an object or thing."[42] But if God is totally unknowable, then how does Barth, or anyone for that matter, come to any understanding of God? This is where Barth shifts his focus to the incarnation.

Any divine revelation from God to a person or group of people is a special revelation. It is not a revelation that is available for all people at all times but is rather a revelation that is made specifically in a given time and place. God has revealed Godself to humanity through these special revelations. Barth writes, "In His [sic] utter strangeness God wills to make Himself known and can make Himself known. He, whom none of us is able to comprehend, does not deprive any single human being of witness to Himself."[43] Christ is the ultimate special revelation, the "revelation of Revelation," as he is God's full self-revelation to the world.[44] Before Christ, revelations were like premonitions or signs from God, but in Christ, the revelation *is* God. There is a chasm between time and eternity that separates God from humanity, and Christ is the link or tangent that relates us back to God.[45] Christ's death and resurrection also allows for the Spirit to beckon our hearts leading us back towards God. This is a new special revelation as the Spirit reveals the Son to us individually in our own lives today.

---

40. For instance, Schleiermacher alleged that God is the "feeling of absolute dependence," which made God a psychological rather than metaphysical reality. See Proudfoot, "Immediacy and Intentionality in the Feeling of Absolute Dependence," 33.

41. Barth, *The Epistle to the Romans*, 36.

42. Brazier, "Barth's First Commentary on Romans (1919)," 394.

43. Barth, *The Epistle to the Romans*, 70.

44. Ibid., 263.

45. Ibid., 29.

God is known through negation as we reflect on what God is not, and then positively as we reflect on the testimony of Christ. Just as alternative rock can be known through a dialectic of positive and negative reflection, there is a useful dialectic that is set up to know God. While this dialectic may be useful for getting a sense of multifaceted concepts, we must keep in mind that no objective definition can be made of God or alternative rock for that matter. Because God is transcendent, God must also, by definition, transcend any definition or linguistic construct one tries to capture God in. God will never be fully known because God is infinite. As we reflect on the glory of God in the eschaton, we will forever be in fear and wonder of God as new revelations of God's splendor perpetually emanate onto us. While God cannot be defined because of God's transcendence, alternative rock cannot be defined because it is a necessarily fluid concept. Alternative rock exists as an outlier, and once it is brought into the fold, it becomes something else. While alternative subgenres have formed, alternative rock can never truly have one distinctive style—its style is "whatever's not mainstream." In both the case of God and alternative rock, there is an indefinability built into the ontological presence of each.

The Fluidity of Theology

A common problem in theological reflection is forgetting that God is infinite, mysterious, and beyond our ability to fully grasp. God has become known in Christ, but even still, our finite minds can only understand the fullness of God in part. Negative theology is a great tool for thinking about God because it acknowledges both our limitations and the mystery of God. An important rule that we can acquire from negative theology is that our theology must remain fluid. The principal ideas and creedal formulations of theology do not need to change, but how these notions are understood in our given context must be flexible.

If we do not allow growth in our theologizing, we run the risk of canonizing ideas that are not integral to the faith or important for our relationships with God. For instance, in the seventeenth century, the Roman Catholic Church famously ruled Galileo a heretic because of his defense of the heliocentric model of the universe. The church had fossilized antiquated beliefs about the cosmos into their theology. This egregious mistake caused the church to overlook irrefutable science and mathematics that proved the earth revolves around the sun and not vice versa. If the church had a fluid theology, then it would have realized that the basic Christian belief is that God lovingly created everything *ex nihilo*. The scientific concerns of *how* the cosmos works and came into being should be of little concern to the theologian because scientific findings cannot disprove the belief that God was the root cause of it all. This is of course a faith claim. Theologians begin with metaphysical questions whereas scientists work within the physical reality. Theology can continue to be a worthwhile endeavor if, and only if, it knows its limitations.

Conclusion

Negative theology and alternative rock share an indefinability that takes seriously the important aspects of reality that must be left open. Theology is at its best when its method is adaptable to the concerns of the respective times. Barth is quoted saying, "We must hold the Bible in one hand and the newspaper in the other."[46] A transformational theology of rock must speak to the present reality of those inhabiting the world or it will become a futile endeavor. Just as alternative rock adapts and changes as the times change, theology is most fruitful when it speaks to the social, existential, and economic issues that surround a given culture. Because of its fluidity, alternative rock will exist as long as rock exists. In the same way, if theology remains fluid, it will exist as long as ultimate questions exist.

In this chapter, we attempted to understand the ever-changing concepts of alternative and indie rock, which aided our conversation about theology's fluidity. We began by mapping the history and characteristics of alternative and indie rock and saw that the notion of fluidity was key to understanding these movements. Next, we looked at theology that begins with negation just as alternative rock exists as a negation. We saw that negative theology and Barth's view of God's "otherness" were important concepts that respect the ineffability of God. This brought us back to the question of fluidity. We were able to attest that a fluid theology allows for relevance in today's world, but also makes space for the mystery of God. As such, this chapter argues for openness and fluidity when reflecting about theology and culture (particularly rock culture).

---

46. Although this quote is commonly attributed to Karl Barth, the Center for Barth Studies at the Princeton Theological Seminary has not been able to pin down exactly if and when Barth said this. See "Quotes by Barth."

CONCLUSION

A Transformational Theology of Rock in Outline

R ock is more than just music. Rock is a culture and an ideology, which carries its own ethos. It is forcefully countercultural and exists as a bane in the sight of dominant Western culture and ideology. Rock is a way of life that acknowledges there is something wrong with the world. Rock raises awareness of the marginalized voice and offers an alternative mode of existence within present reality. As rock engages and critiques culture, it invariably encounters issues of meaning that are existential and theological. A transformational theology of rock begins with those existential and theological issues raised by and within rock music. A transformational theology of rock, therefore, consists of theological reflections that involve the concerns of marginalized voices of the West. While rock raises some theological questions, a transformational theology of rock attempts to respond to these queries in a way that is faithful to the gospel of Jesus Christ and the work of the kingdom of God on earth. As such, we have mined our long theological tradition to see what cohesive responses can be made to the issues raised by rock music. As different rock genres engage the world differently, we evaluated some of the more prominent genres of rock music, listened to the theological issues that preoccupied the genres, and put the genres into dialogue with theological movements that were concerned with similar issues. When we put together the theological reflections from the different genres, we can begin to notice certain themes and trends that run throughout. These trends are the contents of a "transformational theology of rock in outline." By teasing out the theological issues found in rock, we are able to synthesize our findings and create a distinctive cultural theology that is sensitive to the plight of the marginalized in the West.

A transformational theology of rock first acknowledges that the world cannot be fixed into the simple categories of good and evil. Such categorizations are reductionistic and do not account for the nuanced and multifaceted work of the Holy Spirit in a world that needs salvation. There is no axis of evil that stands entirely opposed to the earth's good and godly regiment. The world is not black and white, rather it consists of different shades of grey. As Barth taught us, no good social or political system is devoid from all evil, and no social evil is beyond redemption. The Spirit is at work in the world setting things right. The Spirit works in the hearts of humans individually and works in the world communally. God's transformation is both inward and personal, and outward and social. In other words, God is after a holistic transformation and seeks to bring light to the darkness in every sector of reality. This is God's mission in the world until all things will be made right in the eschaton.

Since God is Lord over all the earth, there is no cultural place that is off limits for the gospel. Rock is a robust cultural form that deals with many of life's tough issues, and a Christian engagement with rock will thus need to be thick-skinned enough not to shy away from or be consumed by some of the more difficult aspects of culture. To be transformative, our theology must meet people where they are. Radical enculturation and radical separation are opposite but equally inappropriate responses to Christian cultural engagement. Instead, a transformational theology of rock will take an approach that is sensitive to the concerns of culture, while still upholding the integral tenets of the Christian message. A median type approach, like the ones dictated in Niebuhr's *Christ and Culture,* and Howard and Streck's "transformational approach," are more suitable methods for cultural engagement. After establishing the groundwork for a transformational theology of rock, the book approached different rock genres to see how each style of music deals with theological and existential issues in their own way. The chapters on folk rock and heavy metal both deal generally with the human responses to evil and hardships, the chapters on Southern and punk rock both concern themselves with the kingdom of God's relation to the state and social evils, and the chapters on grunge and alternative rock (as written above) both deal with the human understanding of identity and authenticity in a fallen world.

Music that is informed by a transformational theology of rock will come from a genuine place. As the wisdom writers have shown us, it is not wrong to express doubt and dissonance. After all, faith can only exist in the midst of doubt. A transformational theology of rock empowers people to grapple with the tough issues that vex contemporary life. If one truly has faith, one should not be afraid of what is uncovered by an exploration of the issues at hand. If one truly believes that God is all in all, then no pervasive theory will strip away God's lordship. In other words, if we acknowledge that God is God even when times are tough, then exploring doubt-forming issues will never lead us astray. It is the acknowledgment of God's lordship in the midst of doubt that constitutes our faith, and it is the acknowledgement of the mystery of God that allows us to find contentment in times of hardship. A transformational theology of rock would approach difficult subjects head on, in honesty, and would not shy away from the places that the Spirit leads them. Folk rock artists such as Gungor and John Mark Mc-Millan are doing just that.

Grief is the human response to life's hardships. Grief in and of itself is not bad. For instance, as Brueggeman has shown us, the Old Testament prophets utilize grief as an integral aspect of prophetic energizing. The prophet calls out the corrupt system that is dominating the society's marginalized voices before grieving over the merciless situation. At this point, the prophet offers the grieved person a new hopeful vision of a possible reality that is offered by God. If the grief is left unchecked and a new vision is not granted, then grief can lead to a person's despair. Heavy metal follows the same patterns of prophetic energizing but often leads the metal head to his or her despair. A transformational theology of rock would follow the prophetic steps that lead to a new and energizing hope. Christian metal bands like August Burn Red and Impending Doom do just that.

A transformational theology of rock will give credence to the regional area from which the music comes. Music that engages culture, after all, must be in dialog with its own culture. When the region and its values are deified and tied up with Christian ideology, it forms a pseudo-Christianity that weakens and alters the teachings of Christ. Southern rock's lionization of the southland has often fallen victim to concocting a pseudo-Christianity that celebrates Christian values mixed with Southern values that are antithetical to the Christian message. A transformational theology of rock will engage cultures fully and even sing of regionalism with pride, but will not allow cultural values to syncretize with Christ's message, but the familial and regional identity found in southern rock can be celebrated in a nuanced way that does not affect the Christian message. Rhett Walker's music is an example of this.

When the culture's regional identity is affirming and fruitful, then one needs only to avoid deifying its values, but if the region is socially oppressive, then action must be taken. A transformational theology of rock is holistic, so it does not only attempt to change a person's perceptions but also his or her physical wellbeing. When an oppressive social or governmental system is in power, then it is working against God's vision of grace and freedom. While heavy metal and the prophetic imagination concerns themselves with human perceptions in the midst of oppression, both punk rock and liberation theology attempt to incite real and tangible societal change. As punk and liberation theology ultimately work towards the liberation of marginalized people, they begin by calling out the system of oppression, but then work towards living in alternate systems as counter-cultural rejoinders. The punk DIY work ethic and community is akin to the ecclesial communities that form in poor nations that seek liberation. Bands like MxPx offer alternative ways to live life in a manner that is consistent with a transformational theology of rock.

Of course not everyone lives in a corrupt or oppressive system. While there are always systemic evils in society, a transformational theology of rock also offers ways for people to overcome personal evil and find true and authentic existence. Grunge rock dealt with the existential issues of authenticity and meaning, and asked similar questions to those raised by existential theology. Tillich, however, taught that true authenticity is found when one is rooted to the ground of all being, which is God beyond designations. A transformational theology of rock not only allows for but also encourages deep introspection. Self-scrutiny can lead to nihilistic dejection, but it can also lead to a deeper understanding of our finitude in relation to God's infinite reality. A transformational band like Skillet will thus guide fans to find their ways and their authentic selves.

Finally, a transformational theology of rock will elude strict and stifling definitions. For a theology to be progressive and keep up with the times and changing culture, it cannot have aspects that are cemented into the status quo. Christianity already has a scriptural canon, and creedal formulations of basic Christian beliefs, so there is no need for a theology that canonizes its own tenets. Theology, when properly engaged, is a dialogue that leads us to a deeper understanding of God. This God that we study is ultimately "Wholly Other" and cannot be put into neat doctrinal categories. Just as alt rock exists as an alternative to the status quo, let's allow our transformational theology of rock to be an alternative to stuffy theologies that place second order issues above the issues that actually matter in the lives of Christians. When our transformational theology of rock begins to fossilize, let's have the courage to change our precepts. When our transformational theology of rock no longer helps us understand God and what it means to be a disciple of Christ in this world, then let's have the courage to abandon it altogether. Whatever new theology arises from the dust of our transformational theology of rock, whatever the next phase, new wave, or dance craze . . . it's all rock and roll to me.

Bibliography

Allman, Duane. Interview in Alex Pappademas, "Essential Southern Rock." *SPIN* (2004). http://www.spin.com/2004/01/essential-southern-rock/ (accessed, 3/25/16).'

Andersen, Mark. "The Virus that Cures: The Revolutionary Alchemy & Eternal Relevance of Punk." In *Beyond the Music: How Punks are Saving the World with DIY Ethics, Skills, & Values.* Joe Biel. Portland: Cantankerous, 2012.

Altschuler, Glenn. *All Shook Up: How Rock 'N' Roll Changed America.* Oxford: OxfordUniversity Press, 2003.

Augustine. *City of God.* Trans. by Henry Bettenson. 1467 repr. London: Penguin, 2003.

———. *Confessions.* Trans. by Henry Chadwick. Oxford: Oxford University Press, 2009.

Bannister, Matthew. "'Loaded': Indie Guitar Rock, Canonism, White Masculinities." *Popular Music.* Vol. 25, No. 1 (2006) 77–95.

———. *Positively George Street: A Personal History of Sneaky Feelings and the Dunedin Sound.* Auckland: Reed, 1999.

Barth, Karl. *Church Dogmatics, II.2.* G.W. Bromiley and T.F. Torrance, Eds. 1957 repr. Peabody: Hendrickson, 2004.

———. *Evangelical Theology: An Introduction.* New York: Holt, Rinehart and Winston, 1963.

———. *The Epistle to the Romans,* 6th Ed. Repr. 1933, Oxford: Oxford University Press, 1968.

Bartholomew, Craig. *Ecclesiastes.* Grand Rapids: Baker Academic, 2014.

Beaudoin, Tom. "Introduction: Theology of Popular Music as Theological Exercise." In Tom Beaudoin, Ed. *Secular Music & Sacred Theology,* Collegeville: Liturgical, 2013.

Beaujon, Andrew. *Body Piercing Saved My Soul: Inside the Phenomenon of Christian Rock.* Cambridge: Da Capo, 2006.

Beckford, Robert. *Jesus Dub: Theology, Music and Social Change.* London: Routledge, 2006.

Berk, Nancy. "Rhett Walker Shares the Story Behind Southern Rock Sensation the Rhett Walker Band," (2014). http://parade.com/351982/nancyberk/rhett-walker-shares-the-story-behind-southern-rock-sensation-the-rhett-walker-band/ (accessed, 4/2/2016).

Bernstein, Jonathan. *Sweet Home Everywhere: The Life and Times of an Unlikely Rock and Roll Anthem*. Montgomery: The New South, 2014. Kindle Electronic Edition.

Beyer, Peter. "De-Centering Religious Singularity: The Globalization of Christianity as a Case in Point." *NUMEN*, Vol. 50 (2003) 357–382.

"Bill of Rights," Charters of Freedom: A New World is at Hand. http://www.archives.gov/exhibits/charters/bill_of_rights_transcript.html (accessed, 3/21/16).

Bloesch, Donald. *The Last Things: Resurrection, Judgment, Glory*. Grand Rapids: InterVarsity, 2004.

Boesel, Chris and Catherine Keller, Eds. *Apophatic Bodies: Negative Theology, Incarnation, and Relationality*. New York: Fordham University Press, 2010.

Bomar, Scott. *Southbound: An Illustrated History of Southern Rock*. Milwaukee: Backbeat, 2014.

Brake, Elizabeth. "'To Live Outside the Law, You Must Be Honest': Freedom in Dylan'sLyrics." In Peter Vernezze and Carl Porter, Eds. *Bob Dylan and Philosophy*. Chicago: Open Court, 2006.

Brazier, Paul. "Barth's First Commentary on Romans (1919): An Exercise in Apophatic Theology." *International Journal of Systematic Theology*. Vol. 6, No. 4 (2004) 387–403.

Brown, William. *Wisdom's Wonder: Character, Creation, and Crisis in the Bible*. Grand Rapids: Eerdmans, 2014.

Brueggemann, Walter. *Hopeful Imagination: Prophetic Voices in Exile*. Philadelphia:Fortress, 1986.

———. *Reality, Grief, Hope: Three Urgent Prophetic Tasks*. Grand Rapids: Eerdmans, 2014.

———. *The Practice of Prophetic Imagination: Preaching an Emancipating Word*. Minneapolis: Fortress, 2012.

———. *The Prophetic Imagination*, Second Edition. Minneapolis: Fortress, 2001.

Bulson, Eric. "The Freewheelin' Bob Dylan." In Kevin Dettmar, Ed. *The Cambridge Companion to Bob Dylan*. Cambridge: Cambridge University Press, 2009.

Bultmann, Rudolf. *Jesus Christ and Mythology*. New York: Charles Scriber's Sons, 1958.

Butler, J. Michael. "Lord Have Mercy on My Soul: Sin, Salvation, and Southern Rock." *South Cult*, Vol. 9, No. 4 (2003) 73–87.

———. "'Luther King Was a Good Ole *Boy*': The Southern Rock Movement and White Male Identity in the Post-Civil Rights South." *Popular Music and Society*, Vol. 23, No. 2 (1999) 41–62.

Call to Preserve. "Life of Defiance." (2010). http://www.darklyrics.com/lyrics/calltopreserve/lifeofdefiance.html (accessed 2/13/2016).

Calvin, John. *Institutes of the Christian Religion*. Trans. by Ford Lewis Battles. 1536 repr. Grand Rapids: Eerdmans, 1986.

Carson, D.A. *Christ and Culture Revisited*. Grand Rapids: Eerdmans, 2008.

Carter, Craig. *Christ and Culture: A Post-Christendom Perspective*. Grand Rapids: Brazos, 2006.

Chiariello, Michael. "Bob Dylan's Truth." In Peter Vernezze and Carl Porter, Eds. *Bob Dylan and Philosophy*. Chicago: Open Court, 2006.

Chong, Kevin. *Neil Yong Nation: A Quest, an Obsession (and a True Story)*. Vancouver: Greystone, 2005.

Clash, The. "London Calling." (1979). http://www.azlyrics.com/lyrics/clash/londoncalling.html (accessed 2/6/2016).

Clayton, Philip. *Transforming Christian Theology: For Church and Society*. Minneapolis: Fortress, 2010.

Cohen, Deborah. "How Indie Rock Changed the World: Two Steps Ahead of Nerds with Computers, Geeks with Guitars Helped Jump-Start Our Social-Media-Driven DIY Culture." *The Atlantic* (June 2015) 85–95.

Cone, James. *God of the Oppressed.* 1975 repr. Maryknoll: Orbis, 1996.

———. *The Spiritual and the Blues: An Interpretation.* Maryknoll: Orbis, 1972.

Cooper, John. Interview in Deborah Price. "Skillet Just Keeps Getting Hotter with Rise." Billboard (2013). http://www.billboard.com/articles/news/1567896/skillet-just-keeps-getting-hotter-with-rise-exclusive-album-preview-video (accessed, 5/14/2016).

Couenhoven, Jesse. "Law and Gospel, or the Law of the Gospel: Karl Barth's Political Theology Compared with Luther and Calvin." *Journal of Religious Ethics.* Vol. 30, No. 2 (2002) 181–205.

Cross, Alan. *20th Century Rock and Roll: Alternative Rock.* Burlington: CG, 1999.

Cross, Charles. Heavier Than Heaven: A Biography of Kurt Cobain. New York: Hachette, 2002.

Davies, Jude. "The Future of 'No Future': Punk Rock and Postmodern Theory." *Journal of Popular Culture,* Vol. 29, No. 4 (1996) 3–25.

Davies, Philip and John Rogerson. *The Old Testament World,* 2nd Edition. Louisville: Westminster John Knox, 2005.

Davis, Erik. "I'd Like to Dedicate This Next Song to Jesus: The Freaky Origins of Christian Rock." Slate (2007). http://www.slate.com/articles/arts/music_box /2007/07/id_like_to_dedicate_this_next_song_to_jesus.html (accessed 8/6/2015).

Dawes. "God Rest My Soul." (2009).http://www.azlyrics.com/lyrics/dawes/godrestmysoul.html (accessed 6/26/15).

De La Torre, Miguel. *The Politics of Jesús: A Hispanic Political Theology.* Lanham: Rowman & Littlefield, 2015.

De La Torre, Miguel and Edwin Aponte. *Introducing Latino/a Theologies.* Maryknoll: Orbis Book, 2001.

Detweiler, Craig and Barry Taylor. *A Matrix of Meanings: Finding God in Pop Culture.* Grand Rapids: Baker Academic, 2003.

Dhumway, David. "Bob Dylan as Cultural Icon." In Kevin Dettmar, Ed. *The Cambridge Companion to Bob Dylan.* Cambridge: Cambridge University Press, 2009.

Dunn, Kevin. "'If it Ain't Cheap, It Ain't Punk': Walter Benjamin's Progressive Cultural Production and DIY Punk Record Labels." *Journal of Popular Music Studies,* Vol. 24, No. 2 (2012), 217–237.

Dylan, Bob. *Chronicles: Volume One.* New York: Simon & Shuster, 2004.

———. "Not Dark Yet." (1997). https://www.bobdylan.com/us/songs/not-dark-yet (accessed 1/30/16).

Dyrness, William. *Poetic Theology: God and the Poetics of Everyday Life.* Grand Rapids: Eerdmans, 2011.

Elmore, Bartow. "Growing Roots in Rocky Soil: An Environmental History of Southern Rock." *Southern Cultures,* Vol. 16, No. 3 (2010) 102–128.

Eskridge, Larry. *God's Forever Family: The Jesus People Movement in America.* Oxford: Oxford University Press,2013.

Exploring Spirituality with Dawes and Cory Chisel." The Brown Tweed Society (2010). http://thebrowntweedsociety.com/2010/02/13/exploring-spirituality-with-dawes-and-cory-chisel/ (accessed 5/12/15).

Fillingim, David. *Redneck Liberation: Country Music as Theology.* Macon: Mercer University Press, 2003.

Foreman, Jon. Interview in Tim Challies, "Another Switchfoot Concert" (2004). http://www.challies.com/music-movies/another-switchfoot-concert (accessed, 9/5/15).

Fox, Robin Lane. *Augustine: Conversions to Confessions.* New York: Basic, 2015.

Frith, Simon. *Performing Rites: On the Value of Popular Music.* Cambridge: Harvard University Press, 1996.

———. "'The Magic That Can Set Your Free': The Ideology of Folk and the Myth of the Rock Community." *Popular Music*, Vol. 1 (1981), 159–168.

Furtak, Rick. "'I Used to Care, but Things Have Changed': Passion and the Absurd in Dylan's Later Work." In Peter Vernezze and Carl Porter, Eds. *Bob Dylan and Philosophy.* Chicago: Open Court, 2006.

García-Rivera, Alejandro. *The Community of the Beautiful: A Theological Aesthetics.* Collegeville: Liturgical, 1999.

Goizueta, Roberto. *Christ Our Companion: Toward a Theological Aesthetics of Liberation.* Maryknoll: Orbis, 2009.

Green, Keith. *A Cry in the Wilderness: Twelve Bold Messages About UncompromisingFaith.* Nashville: Sparrow, 1993.

———. *Make My Life a Prayer: Glimpses of God from the Ministry and PersonalJournals of Keith Green.* Eugene: Harvest House, 2001.

Green, Melody and David Hazard. *No Compromise: The Life Story of Keith Green.* Chatsworth: Sparrow, 1989.

Grossberg, Lawrence. "Another Boring Day in Paradise: Rock and Roll and the Empowerment of Everyday Life." *Popular Music*, Vol. 4 (1984) 225–258.

Gungor. "Beautiful Things." (2010). http://www.azlyrics.com/lyrics/gungor/beautifulthings.html (accessed 7/3/15).

Gungor, Michael. *The Crowd, the Critic, and the Muse: A Book for Creators.* Denver: Woodsley, 2012, Kindle Electronic Edition.

Gutiérrez, Gustavo. *A Theology of Liberation: History, Politics, and Salvation.* 1971 repr. Maryknoll: Orbis, 1992.

Gutiérrez, Gustavo and Gerhard Müeller. *On the Side of the Poor: The Theology of Liberation.* Trans. by Robert Krieg and James Nickoloff. Maryknoll: Orbis, 2015.

Hauerwas, Stanley. *A Better Hope: Resources for a Church Confronting Capitalism, Democracy, and Postmodernity.* Grand Rapids: Brazos, 2000.

———. *A Community of Character: Towards a Constructive Christian Social Ethic.* Notre Dame: University of Notre Dame Press, 1991.

———. *The Peaceable Kingdom: A Primer in Christian Ethics.* Notre Dame: University of Notre Dame Press, 1983.

———. *War and the American Difference: Theological Reflections on Violence and National Identity.* Grand Rapids: Baker Academic, 2011.

Hauerwas, Stanley and William Willimon. *Resident Aliens: A Provocative Christian Assessment of Culture and Ministry for People Who Know that Something is Wrong.* Nashville: Abingdon, 1989.

Hjelm, Titus, Keith Kahn-Harris, and Mark LeVine."Heavy Metal as Controversy and Counterculture." *Popular Music History*, Vol. 6, No. 1 (2011) 5–18.

Howard, Jay. "Contemporary Christian Music: Where Rock Meets Religion." *The Journal of Popular Culture,* Vol. 26, No.1 (1992): 123–130.

Howard, Jay and John Streck. *Apostles of Rock: The Splintered World of Contemporary Christian Music.* Lexington: University Press of Kentucky, 1999.

Hughes, Richard. *Christian America and the Kingdom of God.* Chicago: University of Illinois Press, 2009.

Iafrate, Michael. "More Than Music: Notes on 'Staying Punk' in the Church and in Theology." In Tom Beaudoin, Ed. *Secular Music & Sacred Theology.* Collegeville: Liturgical, 2013.

Jacobson, Douglas and Rodney Sawatsky, *Gracious Christianity: Living the Love We Profess.* Grand Rapids: Baker Academic, 2006.

Jenkins, Philip. *The Next Christendom: The Coming of Global Christianity*, Third Ed. Oxford: Oxford University Press, 2011.

Johnston, Brian. "Constructing Alternative Christian Identity: An Ethnography of Jesus People USA's Cornerstone Festival." PhD Diss., University of South Florida, 2011.

Jorgensen, Danny. "Nature Religions: American Neopaganism and Witchcraft." In Jacob Neusner, Ed., *World Religions in America: An Introduction*, Fourth Edition. Louisville: Westminster John Knox, 2009.

Jovanovic, Rob. *Seeing the Light: Inside the Velvet Underground.* New York: St. Martins, 2010.

Keuss, Jeffrey. "Tom Waits, Nick Cave, and Martin Heidegger: On Singing of the God Who Will Not Be Named." In Tom Beaudoin, Ed. *Secular Music & Sacred Theology.* Collegeville: Liturgical, 2013.

Kieran, Matthew. "Aesthetic Value: Beauty, Ugliness and Incoherence." *Philosophy*, Vol. 72 (1997) 383–399.

Kierkegaard, Søren. *Papers and Journals: A Selection.* Trans. by Alastair Hannay. London: Penguin, 1996.

Knowles, Christopher. *The Secret History of Rock 'N' Roll: The Mysterious Roots of Modern Music.* Berkely: Viva, 2010.

Kramer, Michael. *The Republic of Rock: Music and Citizenship in the Sixties Counterculture.* Oxford: Oxford University Press, 2013.

Kravitz, Kayley. "Revisiting the Post-Punk Revival." Huffpost (2012). http://www.huffingtonpost.com/kayley-kravitz/post-punk-revival-b_2003987.html (accessed 6/11/16).

Krein, Kevin and Abigail Levin. "Just Like a Woman: Dylan, Authenticity, and the Second Sex." In Peter Vernezze and Carl Porter, Eds. *Bob Dylan and Philosophy.*Chicago: Open Court, 2006.

Kuzmič, Rhys. "To the Ground of Being and Beyond: Toward a Pentecostal Engagement with Ontology." In Nimi Wariboko and Amos Yong, Eds. *Paul Tillich and Pentecostal Theology: Spiritual Presence & Spiritual Power.* Bloomington: Indiana University Press, 2015.

Law, Jeannie. "Skillet Band Shed Christian Title." Breathecast (2014), http://www.breathecast.com/articles/skillet-band-shed-christian-title-i-leave-christian-out-i-don-t-want-to-alienate-says-lead-singer-video-15622/ (accessed, 5/14/2016).

Leibovitz, Liel. *A Broken Hallelujah: Rick and Roll, Redemption, and the Life of Leonard Cohen.* New York: Norton, 2014.

Livingston, James and Francis Schüssler Fiorenza. *Modern Christian Thought: The Twentieth Century*, Vol. 2. 2nd Edition. Minneapolis: Fortress, 2006.

Luhr, Eileen. "Metal Missionaries to the Nation: Christian Heavy Metal Music, 'Family Values,' and Youth Culture, 1984–1994." *American Quarterly*, Vol. 57, No. 1(2005) 103–128.

Luther, Martin. *A Commentary on St. Paul's Epistle to the Galatians.* In John Dillenberger, Ed. *Martin Luther: Selections From His Writings.* Trans. by J.J. Schindel. New York: Anchor, 1962.

Lynyrd Skynyrd. "God & Guns." (2009). http://www.azlyrics.com/lyrics/lynyrdskynyrd/godguns.html (accessed 3/26/2016).

———. "Saturday Night Special." (1975). http://www.azlyrics.com/lyrics/lynyrdskynyrd/saturdaynightspecial.html (accessed 4/2/2016).

———. "Simple Man." (1973). http://www.azlyrics.com/lyrics/lynyrdskynyrd/simpleman.html (accessed, 3/26/2016).

———. "Sweet Home Alabama." (1974). http://www.azlyrics.com/lyrics/lynyrdskynyrd/sweethomealabama.html (accessed 4/2/2016).

———. "That Smell." (1977). http://www.azlyrics.com/lyrics/lynyrdskynyrd/thatsmell.html (accessed 4/2/2016).

MacDonald, Scott. "Petit Larceny, the Beginning of All Sin: Augustine's Theft of the Pears." In William Mann, Ed. *Augustine's Confessions: Critical Essays.* Lanham: Rowan & Littlefield, 2006.

Mann, William. "Augustine on Evil and Original Sin." In William Mann, Ed. *Augustine's Confessions: Critical Essays.* Lanham: Rowan & Littlefield, 2006.

Marshall Tucker Band, The. "Am I the Kind of Man." (1976). http://www.azlyrics.com/lyrics/marshalltuckerband/amithekindofman.html (accessed, 3/26/2016).

Martin, Bernice. "The Sacralization of Disorder: Symbolism in Rock Music." *Sociological Analysis.* Vol. 40, No. 2 (1979) 87–124.

Maskell, Shayna. "Performing Punk: Bad Brains and the Construction of Identity." *Journal of Popular Music*, Vol. 21, No. 4 (2009) 411–426.

Mazullo, Mark. "The Man Whom the World Sold: Kurt Cobain, Rock's Progressive Aesthetic, and the Challenges of Authenticity." *The Musical Quarterly*, Vol. 8, No. 4 (2000) 713–749.

McMillan, John Mark. "How He Loves." (2010). http://www.azlyrics.com/lyrics/anthonyevans/howheloves.html (accessed 7/3/15).

McNeil, Legs and Gillian McCain. *Please Kill Me: The Uncensored Oral History of Punk.* New York: Grove, 1996.

Miller, Donald and Tetsunao Yamamori, *Global Pentecostalism: The New Face of Christian Social Engagement.* Berkeley: University of California Press, 2007.

Minor Threat. "Straight Edge." (1981). http://www.darklyrics.com/lyrics/minorthreat/minorthreat.html#4 (accessed 2/13/2016).

Moberg, Marcus. "The 'Double Controversy' of Christian Metal." *Popular Music History*, Vol. 6, No. 2 (2011) 85–99.

Moltmann, Jürgen. *The Coming of God: Christian Eschatology,* Trans. by Margaret Kohl. Minneapolis: Fortress, 1996.

———. *Theology of Hope: On the Ground and the Implications of a Christian Eschatology,* Trans. by James Leitch. New York: Harper & Row, 1967.

Mudhoney. "Touch Me I'm Sick." (1988). http://www.metrolyrics.com/touch-me-im-sick-lyrics-mudhoney.html (accessed, 4/30/16).

MxPx. "PxPx." (1994). http://www.azlyrics.com/lyrics/mxpx/pxpx.html (accessed, 2/6/2016).

Naylor, Ben, Chris Mugan, Colin Brown, and Charlotte Cripps, "Rock Against Racism: Remembering That Gig That Started it All," Independent (2008), http://www.

independent.co.uk/arts-entertainment/music/features/rock-against-racism-remembering-that-gig-that-started-it-all-815054.html (accessed 6/27/2016).

Nantais, David. *Rock-A My Soul: An Invitation to Rock Your Religion*. Collegeville: Liturgical, 2011.

Nazworth, Napp. "After 29 Years, Cornerstone Festival Comes to a Close." *The Christian Post*. (2012). http://www.christianpost.com/news/after-28-years-cornerstone-festival-comes-to-a-close-75316/ (accessed 8/7/15).

Newfield, Jack. "Who Really Invented Rock 'n' Roll." *The New York Sun*. (2004). http://www.nysun.com/arts/who-really-invented-rock-n-roll/2037/ (accessed, 3/25/16).

Nickoloff, James. "Gustavo Gutiérrez Meets Giuseppe Verdi: The Beauty of Liberation and the Liberation of Beauty." *Religion and the Arts*, Vol. 17 (2013) 203–221.

Niebuhr, H. Richard. *Christ & Culture*. 1951 repr. New York: HarperCollins, 2001.

Niebuhr, Reinhold. *The Irony of American History*. Chicago: The University of Chicago Press, 1952.

Nietzsche, Friedrich. *The Birth of Tragedy: Out of the Spirit of Music*. Trans. by Shaun Whiteside. 1872 repr. London: Penguin, 2003.

Nirvana. "Even In His Youth." (1989). http://www.azlyrics.com/lyrics/nirvana/eveninhisyouth.html (accessed, 5/14/2016).

———. "Lithium." (1991). http://www.azlyrics.com/lyrics/nirvana/lithium.html (accessed, 4/30/16).

Norman, Larry. "Why Should the Devil Have All the Good Music?" (1972). http://www.azlyrics.com/lyrics/cliffrichard/whyshouldthedevilhaveallthegoodmusic.html (accessed 8/6/15).

Novara, Vincent and Stephen Henry. "A Guide to Essential American Indie Rock (1980–2005)." *Notes*. Vol. 65, No. 4 (2009) 816–833.

Oh, Sleeper. "The Finisher." (2009). http://www.jesusfreakhideout.com/lyrics/new/track.asp?track_id=12789 (accessed 1/4/15)

Osborne, Grant. *The Hermeneutical Spiral: A Comprehensive Introduction to Biblical Interpretation*. Downers Grove: IVP Academic, 2006.

Penchansky, David. *Understanding Wisdom Literature: Conflict and Dissonance in the Hebrew Text*. Grand Rapids: Eerdmans, 2012.

Pendelty, Mark. *Ecomusicology: Rock, Folk, and the Environment*. Philadelphia: Temple University Press, 2012.

Peterson, David. *The Prophetic Literature: An Introduction*. Louisville: WestminsterJohn Knox, 2002.

Pinn, Anthony, Ed. *Noise and Spirit: The Religious and Spiritual Sensibilies of Rap Music*. New York: New York University Press, 2003.

Powell, Mark. *Encyclopedia of Contemporary Christian Music*. Peabody: Hendrickson,2002.

Prato, Greg. *Grunge is Dead: The Oral History of Seattle Rock Music*. Toronto: ECW,2009.

Priest, John. "Humanism, Skepticism, and Pessimism in Israel." *Journal of the American Academy of Religion*, Vol. 36, No. 4 (1968) 311–326.

Proudfoot, Wayne. "Immediacy and Intentionality in the Feeling of Absolute Dependence." In Brent Sockness and Wilhelm Grab, Eds. *Schleiermacher, the."Study of Religion, and the Future of Theology: A Transatlantic Dialogue*. Berlin:Walter de Gruyter GmbH & Co., 2010.

"Quotes by Barth," Princeton Theological Seminary Library, http://www.ptsem.edu/Library/index.aspx?menu1_id=6907&menu2_id=6904&id=8450 (accessed 6/13/16).

Radiohead. "Creep" (1993). http://www.azlyrics.com/lyrics/radiohead/creep.html (accessed 6/13/2016).

Rasmussen, Larry, Ed. *Reinhold Niebuhr: Theologian of Public Life*. Minneapolis: Fortress, 1991.

Ramone, Marky and Rich Herschlag, *Punk Rock Blitzkrieg*. New York: Touchstone, 2015.

Ramones. "Blitzkrieg Bop." (1976). http://www.azlyrics.com/lyrics/ramones/blitzkriegbop. html (accessed, 2/6/2016).

Regev, Motti. "Producing Artistic Value: The Case of Rock Music." *The Sociological Quarterly*. Vol. 35, No. 1 (1994) 85–102.

Relient K. "Balloon Ride." (2000). http://www.azlyrics.com/lyrics/relientk/balloonride. html (accessed, 2/6/2016).

"Repentagram." (2012). http://saintsinarmor.blogspot.com/2012/03/repentagram_26.html (accessed 1/4/15).

Ribowsky, Mark. *Whiskey Bottles and Brand-New Cars: The Fast Life and Sudden Death of Lynyrd Skynyrd*. Chicago: Chicago Review, 2015.

Riches, Gabrielle. "Embracing the Chaos: Mosh Pits, Extreme Metal Music and Liminality." *Journal for Cultural Research*, Vol. 15, No. 3 (2011) 315–332.

Roberts, Jeremy. *Bob Dylan: Voice of a Generation*. Minneapolis: Lerner, 2005.

Rocheleau, Jordan. "'Far Between Sundown's Finish An' Midnight's Broken Toll': Enlightenment and Postmodernism in Dylan's Social Criticism." In Peter Vernezze and Carl Porter, Eds. *Bob Dylan and Philosophy*. Chicago: Open Court, 2006.

Sackllah, David. "Arctic Monkeys' Whatever People Say I Am, That's What I'm Not Turns 10." Consequence of Sound (2016). http://consequenceofsound.net/2016/01/dusting-em-off-arctic-monkeys-whatever-people-say-i-am-thats-what-im-not-turns-10-sg/ (accessed 6/4/16).

Sarachik, Justin. "Sleeping Giants Frontman Tommy Green Finds Jesus Through Affair; Woman's Husband Commits Suicide and Tells Singer to 'Stick Around.'" Breathecast. (2014). http://www.breathecast.com/articles/sleeping-giants-frontman-tommy-green-finds-jesus-through-affair-woman-s-husband-commits-suicide-and-tells-singer-to-stick-around-18514/ (accessed 6/4/15).

———. "'The Christianity I see is Rated R' Says Sleeping Giant Lead Singer; Tommy Green Feels Church Struggles with 'Loving the Unlovable.'" Breathecast. (2014). http://www.breathecast.com/articles/the-christianity-i-see-is-rated-r-sleeping-giants-lead-singer-tommy-green-feels-church-struggles-loving-the-unlovable-18525/ (accessed 6/4/15).

Savage, Jon. *England's Dreaming: Anarchy, Sex Pistols, Punk Rock, and Beyond*. New York: St. Martin's, 2001.

Scharen, Christian. *Broken Hallelujahs: Why Popular Music Matters to Those Seeking God*. Grand Rapids: Brazos, 2011.

———. *One Step Closer: Why U2 Matters to Those Seeking God*. Grand Rapids: Brazos, 2006.

Schleiermacher, Friedrich. *The Christian Faith*. H.R. MacKintosh and J.S. Stewart, Eds. 1830 repr. Edinburgh: T&T Clark, 1989.

Selders, Kevin. "The Heart of John Mark McMillan." *Relevant Magazine*. http://www.relevantmagazine.com/culture/music/features/22158-the-heart-of-john-mark-mcmilan, (accessed 5/12/15).

Sex Pistols. "God Save the Queen." (1977). http://www.azlyrics.com/lyrics/sexpistols/godsavethequeen.html (accessed, 2/6/2016).

Shaefer, Jake. "Sleeping Giant: An Interview with Tommy Green." *Theology* 21. (2011). http://www.theology21.com/2011/08/29/sleeping-giant-an-interview-with-tommy-green/ (accessed 6/4/15).

Skancke, Jennifer. *The History of Indie Rock*. Farmington Hills: Lucent, 2007.

Skillet. "Salvation." (2013). http://www.azlyrics.com/lyrics/skillet/salvation.html (accessed 5/15/2016).

————. "Sick of It." (2013). http://www.azlyrics.com/lyrics/skillet/sickofit.html (accessed, 5/15/2016).

Sleeping Giant. "Descending Into Hell." (2009). http://www.songlyrics.com/sleeping-giant/descending-into-hell-lyrics/ (accessed 7/4/15).

Smith, Michael. *Rebel Yell: An Oral History of Southern Rock*. Macon: Mercer University Press, 2014.

Sorabji, Richard. "Time, Mysticism, and Creation." In William Mann, Ed. *Augustine's Confessions: Critical Essays*. Lanham: Rowan & Littlefield, 2006.

Spargo, R. Clifton and Anne Raem. "Bob Dylan and Religion." In Kevin Dettmar, Ed. *The Cambridge Companion to Bob Dylan*. Cambridge: Cambridge University Press, 2009.

Stassen, Glen, D.M. Yeager, and John Howard Yoder. *Authentic Transformation: A New Vision of Christ and Culture*. Nashville: Abingdon, 1995.

Stimeling, Travis. "'To Be Polished More than Extended': Musicianship, Masculinity, and the Critical Reception of Southern Rock." *Journal of Popular Music Studies*, Vol. 26, No. 1 (2014) 121–136.

Stowe, David. *No Sympathy for the Devil: Christian Pop Music and the Transformation of American Evangelicalism*. Chapel Hill: University of North Carolina Press, 2011.

Strother, Eric. "Unlocking the Paradox of Christian Metal Music." PhD diss., University of Kentucky, 2013.

Sweet, Leonard. Ed. *The Church in Emerging Culture: Five Perspectives*. Grand Rapids: Zondervan, 2003.

Sweet, Michael. "Interview: Michael Sweet of Sweet & Lynch and Stryper." (2015). http://crypticrock.com/interview-michael-sweet-of-sweet-lynch-and-stryper/ (accessed 8/14/15).

Thompson, John. *Raised by Wolves: The Story of Christian Rock & Roll*. Toronto: ECW, 2000.

Thurman, Howard. *Deep River and the Negro Spiritual Speaks of Life and Death*. Richmond: Friends United, 1975.

Tisdale, Leonora Tubbs. *Prophetic Preaching: A Pastoral Approach*. Louisville: Westminster John Know, 2010.

Tillich, Paul. *Systematic Theology: Three Volumes in One*. Chicago: The University of Chicago Press, 1967.

————. *The Courage to Be*. Third Edition. Repr. 1952. New Haven: Yale University Press, 2014.

Tow, Stephen. *The Strangest Tribe: How a Group of Seattle Rock Bans Invented Grunge*. Seattle: Sasquatch, 2011.

Train, Dane. "Jesus Christ and the Headbanger." (2009). http://www.metalstorm.net/pub/article.php?article_id=611 (accessed 9/17/14).

Unterberger, Richie. *Turn! Turn! Turn!: The '60s Folk-rock Revolution*. San Francisco: Backbeat, 2002.

Velvet Underground, The. "Heroin" (1967). http://www.azlyrics.com/lyrics/velvet underground/heroin.html (accessed 6/11/16).

Villafañe, Eldin. *The Liberating Spirit: Toward an Hispanic American Pentecostal Social Ethic.* Grand Rapids: Eerdmans, 1993.

Wallace, George. "Inaugural Speech." (1963). http://www.pbs.org/wgbh/amex/wallace/sfeature/quotes.html (accessed, 4/2/2016).

Walser, Robert. *Running with the Devil: Power, Gender, and Madness in Heavy Metal Music.* Hanover: Wesleyan University Press, 1993.

Watkins, Ralph. *Hip Hop Redemption: Finding God in the Rhythm and the Rhyme.* Grand Rapids: Baker Academic, 2011.

Weinstein, Deena. *Heavy Metal: The Music and Its Culture*, Revised Edition. Jackson: Da Capo, 2000.

Westphal, Merold. *Whose Community? Which Interpretation?: Philosophical Hermeneutics for the Church.* Grand Rapids: Baker Academic, 2009.

Wilentz, Sean. *Bob Dylan in America.* New York: Doubleday, 2010.

Wilsey, John. *American Exceptionalism and Civil Religion: Reassessing the History of an Idea.* Downers Grove: IVP Academic, 2015.

Wolterstorff, Nicholas. "Suffering Love." In William Mann, Ed. *Augustine's Confessions: Critical Essays.* Lanham: Rowan & Littlefield, 2006.

Wood, Jessica. "Pained Expression: Metaphors of Sickness and Signs of 'Authenticity' in Kurt Cobain's *Journals.*" *Popular Music*, Vol. 30, No. 3 (2011) 331–349.

Wood, Robert. *Straightedge Youth: Complexity and Contradictions of a Subculture.* Syracuse: Syracuse University Press, 2006.

Young, Neil. "Alabama." (1972). http://www.azlyrics.com/lyrics/neilyoung/alabama.html (accessed, 4/2/2016).

———. "Southern Man." (1970). http://www.azlyrics.com/lyrics/neilyoung/southernman.html (accessed, 4/2/2016).